THE OBEDIENT BANKER

Jeremy Tait

AuthorHouse™ UK Ltd.
500 Avebury Boulevard
Central Milton Keynes, MK9 2BE
www.authorhouse.co.uk
Phone: 08001974150

© 2011. Jeremy Tait. Alll rights reserved.

No part of this book may be reproduced, stored in a retrieval system, or transmitted by any means without the written permission of the author.

First published by AuthorHouse   3/09/2011

ISBN: 978-1-4567-7139-3 (sc)
ISBN: 978-1-4567-7140-9 (e)

Any people depicted in stock imagery provided by Thinkstock are models, and such images are being used for illustrative purposes only. Certain stock imagery © Thinkstock.

This book is printed on acid-free paper.

Because of the dynamic nature of the Internet, any Web addresses or links contained in this book may have changed since publication and may no longer be valid. The views expressed in this work are solely those of the author and do not necessarily reflect the views of the publisher, and the publisher hereby disclaims any responsibility for them.

ABOUT THE AUTHOR

The author in Beverly Hills in 1972

Jeremy William Tait, also known as Jerry, was born in London on 7 June 1931 and was educated at St. Edwards Oxford where he obtained a Distinction in English Literature and a Credit in English Grammar. Although he passed the Civil Services Entry Examination he decided to join the London City branch of The Hongkong and Shanghai Banking Corporation in 1951 as a trainee Foreign Staff Officer and he was transferred to the Bank's Head Office in Hong Kong in 1952.

For the next thirty years Jerry served with the HSBC Group in eighteen branches in ten countries in four continents and his book of Memoirs *The Obedient Banker* covers this exciting period. After twenty three years of front line banking in cities including Tokyo, Calcutta and Beverly Hills, where he was the bank's Executive Vice President and served on the World Trade Committee of the Los Angeles Area Chamber of Commerce, he transferred to Internal Audit in 1974 and this involved him in thirty four audits and investigations in places such as Saigon, Hamburg, Mauritius and Bangkok. He was elected a Member of the Institute of Internal Auditors in 1978.

In 1979 Jerry was appointed as the Group's first Internal Auditor in Dubai and he supervised over twenty audits in the U.A.E. before being promoted as Manager Corporate Services in his bank's Head Office in Hong Kong, taking charge of the Group's Economic Intelligence Unit, the Library and Data Bank and the Editorial and Publications sections, producing monthly economic reports, the popular Country Business Profiles, and with an Editorial Coordinator and several journalists, the writing of speeches and articles for senior management.

An imprint of Jerry's personal Chinese Chop (Seal) *Tai Jer Lee*, implying intelligence, knowledge and ritual is reproduced here and the seal itself is carved from a piece of polished Sau King Mountain Stone from the Temple of Heaven in Beijing. This seal was presented to Jerry in 1982 as a retirement present by the Bank's then Chief Economist Vincent Cheng, and it remains a treasured possession of the author.

When Jerry retired from the Bank he came to Spain from where he has written numerous articles for local magazines on a wide range of subjects both humorous and serious. He is married and has a twenty two year old son in university.

Contents

PREFACE		ix
Chapter 1.	TRAINING IN LONDON	1
Chapter 2.	INITIATION IN HONG KONG	7
Chapter 3.	JAPAN	26
Chapter 4.	BOMBAY AND SINGAPORE	62
Chapter 5.	COLOMBO AND CALCUTTA	90
Chapter 6.	HONG KONG, AND PROMOTION TO MANAGER	112
Chapter 7.	CALCUTTA AGAIN, THEN CALIFORNIA	130
Chapter 8.	INTERNAL AUDIT, WORLDWIDE	154
Chapter 9.	DUBAI, HEAD OFFICE AND RETIREMENT	192

PREFACE

This story is neither an autobiography nor is it a history; although it may read like a novel it is actually a selection of my experiences while working overseas as a young bank officer in an environment which saw the closing days of a colonial system which prevailed at the end of the Second World War, particularly in the Far East. This environment continued to exist for many years in several countries and territories in Asia after they gained independence, and India is a classic example. Many of the personal experiences and anecdotes in this book are amusing, but one should realise that at the time they took place most of them were quite normal and therefore accepted without question by the elder generation, although many post war officers, myself included, began to question the wisdom of old systems in the face of increasing technology and emerging nationalism. Since my retirement I have frequently recounted my experiences to friends and acquaintances who invariably suggest that I should write a book, and this is exactly what I have now done.

It was quite by chance that I became a colonial banker, and we must remember that bank officers were highly respected members of society in the 20th century, which sadly is not always the case at present. In fact it was decided from an early age that I should join the Royal Navy in the footsteps of my grandfather, my father and my two uncles, but this was not to be. I was educated at St. Edwards, Oxford and when I left "Teddies" in 1948 at the age of 17 I tried to enter the Royal Naval College Dartmouth but the Navy was still disbanding after WWII and the last thing they wanted was an influx of new cadets. Out of some 3000 applicants 300 were called for interview and only 30 boys were selected, and I came 57th! Although I had passed the Civil Services exam and was eligible for entry into either Sandhurst or Cranwell, my father refused to consider either the Army or the Air Force as suitable careers and he arranged for me to be articled to a firm of solicitors for four years in Salisbury, Southern Rhodesia where his elder brother Admiral Sir Campbell Tait had been Governor. I still had my National Service obligation to fulfil and the thought of studying law for four years filled me with horror. Fortunately I had an aunt in Dover who played golf with the Chief Inspector of the Hong Kong Bank (now HSBC) and as the bank was at that time expanding in Asia, unlike the Navy which was contracting, I attended an interview in London and was accepted as a trainee Foreign Staff officer, and this enabled me to decline the Rhodesian offer.

HSBC is now well known as a leading multinational bank headquartered in London but few people are aware of its origins in 1865 when it was first established by a group of colonial traders as The Hongkong and Shanghai Banking Corporation, with branches in Hong Kong, Shanghai and London to which Yokohama, Calcutta, Saigon and Manila were added a few years later. The primary objective was to create a local bank headquartered in Hong Kong to finance the Pacific Rim coastal trade and to compete with banks operating locally, but with head offices in London. By the time I joined the bank it had already become a leading colonial bank throughout Asia, highly regarded in the City of London as being in a class of its own, although still suffering from the closure of most of its branches during the war. The "Honkers and Shankers" was to other overseas banks what the East India Company had been to other overseas trading companies, and we operated somewhat independently under a colonial Banking Ordinance, and our competitors regarded us in much the same light as regular army regiments would view the Ghurkhas. Probably the worst that could be said about the bank was that it was snobbish, but we were in fact a family bank inasmuch as our officers worked together as a family, we adhered to a very strict code of ethics, and above all we were completely loyal to the bank and we accepted its regulations as if we were in the army, and this applied particularly to inter-branch "postings" which were arbitrary and unquestioned. Many of us junior officers had similar backgrounds and upbringings and this helped us to adapt to our new lifestyle which required our complete obedience to the bank's rules and regulations. Hence the title of this book.

Acknowledgements are due to Stephen Green and Richard Lindsay of HSBC for their encouragement and for permission to include a quotation on the 1955 bank strike in Japan from Volume IV of Frank King's History of the Bank.

The final acknowledgement is to our close friend Annabel Weaver for her patience in proofreading the book prior to its submission to the publishers.

Dedications these days are considered somewhat old fashioned but nevertheless I would like to dedicate this book to those of my contemporaries in the bank who survived the indignities of the Chopping Desk and the used notes Cash Cage in Hong Kong, and who, like myself, deserve the title of Obedient Banker.

Care has been taken while writing the book to avoid any possible embarrassment to members of the Bank's staff and their families and to other people who are mentioned in the book and in many cases their surnames have been omitted for this reason. However, the author would welcome any comments or corrections regarding the book that readers may care to make.

Jeremy Tait, Marbella 2010.

CHAPTER ONE
TRAINING IN LONDON

In December 1951, at the age of 20, I joined the London City office of The Hongkong and Shanghai Bank which was situated in Gracechurch Street opposite Leadenhall Market, and I then began my training for what would turn out to be almost 31 continuous years of service with the same banking group. My father initially put me into the YMCA hostel in Tottenham Court Road but I soon found two other trainees willing to share digs with me and the three of us then moved into Mrs. Rogers' house in New Beckenham, which was close to the bank's sports ground, where we spent our weekends.

Jerry on his 1927 AJS motor cycle, with friend from the OBC Documents Desk, at the Bank's Sports Ground

My pay at that time was five pounds ten shillings a week lunch included and Mrs. Rogers charged us each three pounds ten shillings a week with breakfast and supper included, so we only had two pounds a week left for our personal expenses which were mainly drinks and transport, although my father continued to give me the fairly generous allowance which had supplemented my army pay, and I continued to receive this allowance until I was transferred to our Head Office in Hong Kong.

I remember that I used to drink mild ale mainly because it was only 5½d a half pint, but we had a beer kitty at the Sports Club to which the senior bankers would contribute quite generously after the Saturday rugger game was over. These senior bankers were mainly members of the "Home Staff" but they always treated us trainees with respect because they knew that once our training was over we would become "Foreign Staff" and thus senior to them! Home Staff were constantly trying to transfer to Foreign Staff, but very few made the grade. Traditionally the bank selected its Foreign Staff trainees from university graduates supplemented by applicants already employed by U.K. banks and also from personal recommendations from senior serving officers and other reliable sources, and trainees were seldom sent overseas until they had passed Part One of the Bankers Institute exam. At the time I joined however the demand exceeded the supply, so I was lucky to be accepted as a trainee based upon my credentials. In fact I well remember my initial interview by the Senior Accountant of our London office, who was the most important member of the Home Staff, all our London managers being members of the Foreign Staff. After slowly reading through my qualifications and references the Senior Accountant looked me straight in the eye and surprisingly asked me if I played rugger. When I told him that I had been a wing three quarter at school he replied that this was exactly what they wanted in Hong Kong, he then rose to his feet, shook my hand, and said "Welcome to the bank; when can you start work?"

My so-called training in London was not exactly onerous. I had been assigned to a back room department, well away from the main banking hall, known as OBCs which was an abbreviation of Outward Bills for Collection, being part of the Exports section of the branch. The important part of Outward Bills was the Bills Receivable section because the BRs were purchased by the bank from its customers upon presentation either because they were drawn under Letters of Credit or because of the good credit rating of the exporter. The proceeds of BCs however were not paid to the exporter until the bank had been advised by the Imports department of the branch to whom the documents had been sent that the importer had paid for or accepted the documents. These documents were very important because they were documents of title to the goods which they covered so all the documents had to be presented to the bank in duplicate, in case the originals became lost or destroyed in transit. My desk in OBCs was the Documents Desk which was a huge metal framed structure with overhead racks for storing documents and we all sat on high stools at this desk while performing our duties. I was the only trainee officer in the department and most of my colleagues on the Documents Desk were young girls who had great difficulty in climbing up onto their high stools because of the long tight skirts that they wore in those days, so one of my unofficial tasks was to assist the girls in getting on and off their stools, and this used to annoy the head of our department intensely, as he had no time for trainee officers having worked his way up through the branch from the time he had joined the bank as a messenger. His desk faced us and he spent a lot of his time simply looking at the girls' legs, but I cannot blame him for this as he was due to retire from the bank in a few months anyway.

Our duties on the Documents Desk were first to split the documents into two, and we would then process the originals by checking their accuracy while retaining the duplicate documents separately. When the original documents had been found to be in order it was then our job to schedule them and this we did by inserting sheets of carbon paper between the schedules which were pinned together in triplicate and we then had to enter full details of the drafts and all the documents, which consisted of invoices, bills of lading, certificates of origin, inspection certificates, etc and have the schedules with the attached documents signed by the head of our department and one of the Foreign Staff managers. We were each responsible for our own schedules until such time as they were ready for dispatch so after having my schedules checked and signed by the Head of the Department I then had to take them to one of the managers for final signature.

I was advised by my colleagues on the Documents Desk that the best time to get the managers to sign our schedules was mid afternoon when they were less busy with customers and were generally in a mellow mood, having consumed several gin and tonics before their lunch. These men had all served extensively in the Far East and were enjoying their last jobs with the bank before retirement, so at this stage of the day they were far less likely to ask awkward questions such as "Don't Christmas crackers need import licenses in India?" or "What sort of company is this exporter?"

However I soon discovered that once a manager had identified me as a Foreign Staff trainee he would invariably recount stories or give me some advice on life in the colonies, and I well remember one such story relating to sedan chairs in Hong Kong. I was told that in Hong Kong there were four types of sedan chairs, the 2-coolie, the 4-coolie, the 6-coolie and the 8-coolie chairs. "Always use the 2-coolie chair and never be tempted to use an 8-coolie chair" I was told. I then asked the expected question "Why not use the 8-coolie chair sir?" "Ah" replied the manager "the Governor uses a 4-coolie sedan chair, the bank's Chief Manager uses a 6-coolie sedan chair but the 8-coolie sedan chairs are used by the White Russian ladies of leisure from Pedder Street to practice the oldest profession of the world behind the sedan's silk curtains". When I first arrived in Hong Kong some months later I discovered that sedan chairs had been totally replaced by rickshaws, but at the time I listened to the manager's friendly advice, little did I know that some 25 years later in 1976 I myself would be occupying his leather chair and sitting at his mahogany desk! After obtaining a manager's signature on my schedules all that then remained was to bundle the drafts, documents and schedules into brown envelopes known as mail packets for dispatch to the importing branches by listing all the sealed packets on a mailing schedule which we then had an officer in Correspondence department check and sign for.

On 6 February 1952 King George VI died and the new Queen Elizabeth flew back from Kenya to assume her father's throne. Then in May, some five months after I had started my training, I was summoned to the desk of the head of our department who showed me two letters from our Calcutta and Colombo branches respectively each of them stating that they had received the other branch's duplicate BCs, which we had sent to them by sea mail some five weeks earlier, and that they had therefore exchanged these documents with each other. The department head then showed me a signed roster indicating that I had been the person responsible for mailing Calcutta's duplicate documents to Colombo, and vice versa, on the day in question, and did I have any explanation for my error. I replied that I must have mistakenly stamped the Calcutta envelope with the rubber chop containing Colombo's address and vice versa, but that as the original documents had been sent to the correct branches by airmail and the Bills had long since been paid, surely it was not that much of a problem. I well remember the pause before the department head replied that the fact that the misdirected documents were duplicates rather than originals did not affect the gravity of my mistake and that this would make no difference to his report on my conduct in his department. I returned to the Documents Desk in a state of despondency and it was while I was being consoled by my lady colleagues that a messenger came up from the banking hall and told me that the Senior Accountant wished to see me immediately. This is it, I thought, as I was ushered into the Senior Accountant's glass cage, now I will never get confirmed and my father will be furious. The Senior Accountant however was smiling when I entered his cage, and he came to the point immediately. "Congratulations Tait, your training is complete and you have now been selected for overseas service and you will be transferred to Hong Kong as an executive officer on the Foreign Staff provided your parents agree, because you are under the age of 21". I could hardly restrain myself when I returned to my department and I immediately went to the desk of the department head and I gave him the news and told him that he was the first person I would invite to my farewell party, and the man replied that I had been one of the best trainee officers that he had ever had in his department, but that he always gave trainees a hard time to prepare them for their forthcoming responsibilities!

I well remember my last two days in London. I had been given the relatively large kit allowance of two hundred pounds, from which I had to buy tropical gear, but part of which we all used to pay off our debts and to throw a farewell party in a City pub on our last evening in the country to which the managers, all trainees and those friends we had on the Home Staff were invited. These parties were either held at the Jamaica Wine House or at the Half Moon which was more or less opposite the bank, and I chose the latter venue not only because it was more convenient but also because I was a regular customer. As a final gesture, I had intended to drive my 1927 AJS motorbike over the edge of London Bridge, jumping off at the last moment, but common sense prevailed and I sold it to a friend for the same price that I had originally paid for it. My father had arranged for me to spend the night with an aunt in her Notting Hill Gate house, and I was then to catch the 12 noon boat train from Victoria station to Southampton where I would board the P & O s.s. "Canton" for the first class passage to Hong Kong, which would take about one month.

The farewell party in the Half Moon lasted longer than expected and when the pub closed we carried on at another pub on Villiers Street in Charing Cross which had extended hours so long as one ordered food. I remember that the girl sitting next to me at the bar spilled her drink so I helped her dry her clothes, one thing led to another, and the next thing I remember was waking up at 6 o'clock in the morning in a strange house in

Jeremy Tait

Stepney. I then beat a hasty retreat and immediately phoned my aunt who was remarkably calm although she said that my parents had not got much sleep during the night. When I arrived at Kensington Park Road, my aunt then gave me coffee and a boiled egg for breakfast, before putting me and my steamer trunk and suitcase into a taxi to get to Victoria, and my bed in her house was never slept in! When I set sail from Southampton later that day little did I know that I was destined to serve in eighteen different branches of the Hong Kong Bank Group in ten separate countries in four continents during the next thirty one years. However, before describing my arrival in Hong Kong it would perhaps be appropriate to make mention of the outward voyage which helped to prepare me for the new lifestyle that I was about to experience in the colonies.

CHAPTER TWO

INITIATION IN HONG KONG

The bank generally sent its new junior officers out east in pairs and my companion Harry, who was from Dundee and whose uncle Willie Stewart was the *taipan* of Davie Boag in Hong Kong, had been recruited from a Scottish bank and we shared a first class cabin on E deck. We had been warned by the Senior Accountant in London to behave ourselves on the voyage because also sailing on the "Canton" would be the bank's new Chief Manager Mike Turner (later to become Sir Michael) and his wife Wendy, and Mike was returning to Hong Kong after home leave to take charge of the bank from the retiring Chief Manager Sir Arthur Morse. Harry and I would therefore be invited to large welcome parties in honour of the new Chief Manager designate at each port of call where we maintained a branch. As a prelude to this, our first shore excursion after Gibraltar was at Port Said where the bank did not have a branch and we did what most tourists have always done in Egypt which was to be enticed into emporiums and perfume outlets and Harry and I were absolutely thrilled by our first encounter with Arabs, although we were able to resist making any unnecessary purchases in Simon Artz or getting involved with the girls who were offered to us. However, after a very liquid lunch we were quite easily persuaded to follow a man into the depths of the souk where we were promised an erotic floor show which was a far cry from what we had ever seen before in Soho. I think that we had expected to see belly dancers but it would not be appropriate to describe what we actually witnessed so suffice it to say I remember telling Harry after we left the premises that I had never thought that the Egyptians would use both humans and animals in their floorshows! This was indeed an initial experience long to be remembered.

Canton post card. Reproduced by kind permission of P&O Heritage

No Egyptian hawkers were allowed on board but there were crowds of them on the quay alongside the ship and we haggled with them from the deck railings. When a bargain had been reached the merchandise was hauled up in a basket attached to a rope which the hawkers flung up to us and the money was then put in the basket and returned to the hawker below. The critical banter between the British passengers and the Egyptian hawkers was pure music hall, but without being offensive. The ship did however allow several Egyptian magicians called Gully-Gully men to come on board in Port Said with their gunny sacks before the ship sailed and they entertained us on deck by performing incredible acts with snakes and chickens appearing out of empty silk handkerchiefs and fezzes, and by swallowing eggs which they then discovered in our pockets and purses. These men were then put ashore at Suez with the tips we had given them and they returned to Port Said on other ships going in the opposite direction, and they were called Gully-Gully men because when they were about to start their act they shouted out in Arabic in order to attract a crowd, and what they shouted sounded like "Gully Gully"!

After leaving Port Said it was time to celebrate my 21st birthday on board while we were passing through the Suez Canal, and this was done

The Obedient Banker

in style with a private Cocktail Party in the starboard lounge followed by a special Dinner Party in the Dining Room.

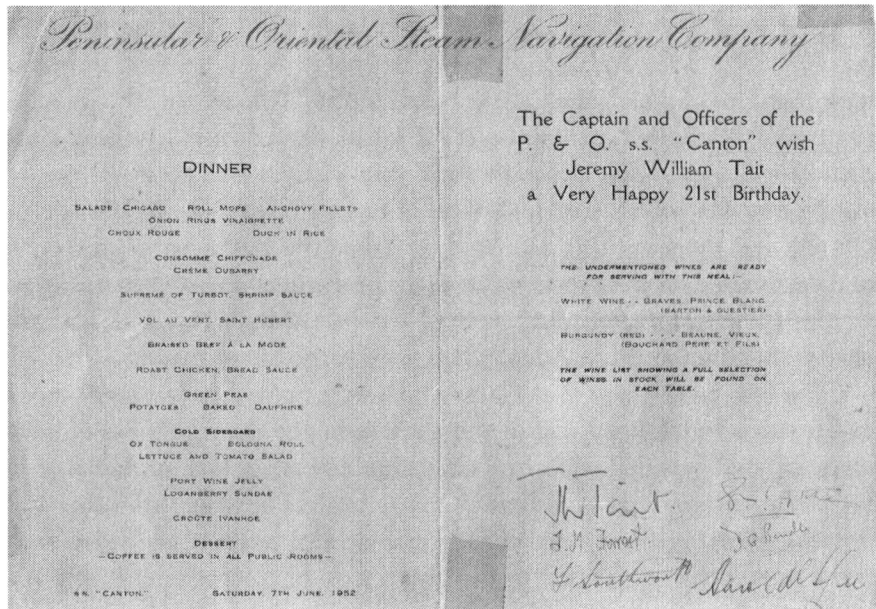

Canton menu. Reproduced by kind permission of P&O Heritage

Evening entertainment on board was generally provided by a four piece orchestra who were crew members and somewhat reminiscent of the orchestra in the film *Titanic*. They accepted requests for favourite tunes and these dance evenings were interspersed with competitions and fancy dress parades.

On my birthday we were fortunate to have a surprise Belly Dance performance in the ship's Ballroom after dinner as the Captain had allowed a troupe of Belly Dancers to come on board with the Gully-Gully men, and this was an unexpected addition to our celebrations.

Although conduct onboard was extremely formal and the dress code was strict, the comfort in no way matched what we are now used to on modern day cruises.

Our two bunk cabin was minute, it had no balcony and without air-conditioning it was stifling at night with only a metal scoop resembling a bottomless coal scuttle which our steward screwed into our open porthole in order to give us a breath of fresh air. Harry and I therefore obtained permission from the Purser to sleep on the boat deck and we were provided with hammocks which were slung between the lifeboats and this gave us some relief from the heat. However the lascars hosed down the boat deck each morning at dawn and they took great delight in tipping us out of our hammocks, which they had to do in order to clean the deck properly. On the first morning this occurred we asked the bosun to tell the crew to turn their hoses onto us to wake us up properly and this then occurred regularly each morning until we had passed through the Red Sea and reached Steamer Point in Aden, when we returned to our cabin.

The first bank party that Harry and I were invited to was in Bombay and it was a lavish luncheon in the gardens of the manager's house with scores of small wooden tables and chairs underneath garden umbrellas and my main memory was of almost as many bearers in white uniforms and turbans, carrying silver trays of food and drinks, as there were guests. It was a revealing introduction to the grand style of entertaining that was a tradition within the bank, although it did not prepare me for the somewhat rough and ready living conditions that could also exist alongside this extravagant lifestyle.

Our next entertainment ashore took place in Colombo, and it was here that I was treated to a double whammy. During the latter stages of WWII my father had been Deputy Superintendent and King's Harbourmaster at Sheerness Dockyard and his Number Two Commander Harper, who I had known as a child, had later obtained the Harbourmaster job in Colombo, and he had invited me to lunch on the day our ship arrived there. A Navy car was waiting for me when the ship berthed and after breakfast I was driven directly to the Colombo Club where Commander Harper, now a Captain, and a group of his planter friends were seated in huge wicker chairs in the Verandah Bar. Harper introduced me to his friends, and he then asked me the all important question: "Do you still drink ginger beer, Jeremy? If not, they have some excellent mango juice here". "No thanks" I replied "I think I'd prefer a pink gin". Captain Harper's response was immediate: "I don't know what else your father taught you, but he certainly steered you in the right direction". We had several rounds of drinks before our curry tiffin and I remember forcing myself to keep up with the planters. Eventually it was time to leave, and a Navy car then took me back to the ship where a Bank car was waiting to take Harry and myself to a Cocktail Party at the Manager's house. It is not surprising that I am unable to remember very much about this party!

The Penang celebration was a luncheon with Mike and Wendy Turner as the guests of honour but it was not quite as formal as the Bombay and Colombo affairs and after we left the party Harry and I were invited to the bachelors' Mess for more drinks before being driven back to the ship. The bank Mess overlooked Guthries' bachelors' Mess and we teed up some golf balls and took it in turns to drive them between the chimneys of Guthries' Mess, but this exciting diversion came to an abrupt end when Guthries sent a messenger to tell us that one of our golf balls had broken an upstairs window and that a bill for the repairs would be sent to the bank. It was at a pre-dinner Cocktail Party some days later in the Singapore manager's house Mount Echo that I somehow or other managed to drop and break two crystal glasses and I remember Wendy Turner taking me out onto the verandah where there were only a smattering of guests and advising me to stay there until we all sat down for dinner.

Upon arrival at our main office in Hong Kong in June 1952 I underwent the usual treatment given to new junior officers by starting off in Cash department and gradually working my way upwards into Current Accounts, such movements being made as and when fresh trainees arrived from the U.K. We were a huge bank in Hong Kong not only because we were the largest commercial bank there but we also performed the duties of a Central Bank by issuing 90 percent of the Colony's bank notes, and we were also the Lenders in the Last Resort. The Chinese name for the bank was *Wayfoong*, literally meaning Abundance of Remittances, and the junior officers all lived in a large bachelors' Mess on Plantation Road towards the top of The Peak, which was aptly called "Cloudlands", and which we reached by taking the famous Peak Tram, which was actually a funicular railway dating back to 1888. The lower terminal of the tramway in Central district had a large clock face and was situated on Garden Road just above the Helena May Institute, which was a hostel for single ladies several of whom were bank employees. Although the upper terminal was not far from Cloudlands it was a steep climb, so sometimes when the heat was really oppressive we would take a rickshaw, and our cold *San Migs* would be waiting for us when we arrived at the Mess. Cloudlands was always damp and it was not unusual to discover centipedes in our beds and all our wardrobes were fitted with primitive dehumidifiers which would destroy any clothes that came in contact with them.

It might seem strange that a twenty year old could be appointed a junior officer after only five months cursory banking experience, but the system was in fact quite logical because upon arrival in Hong Kong we started at the absolute bottom of the ladder. However, in the three tier staff system which existed in Hong Kong in the 50s we as the Foreign Staff were at the top, next came the Portuguese Staff who operated in a supervisory capacity and the main workforce of the bank consisted of the Local Staff who were Chinese and were selected by the bank's Compradore who guaranteed them on a commission basis. This three tier structure however was to be gradually phased out over the next few years, with the abolishment of the Compradore system and the appointment of Regional Officers.

The customers' area of our huge Cash department was divided into two sections, the first being where the coolies paid in their cash and the second section was where individual merchants and customers were attended to, although the paying-in system was basically the same in both areas. All cash deposited in the bank was accompanied by Pay-In booklets and each leaf in these booklets had two identical sections separated by a perforation. The Chinese shroffs at the pay-in counters would count the cash, which they placed in their tills, check that the details were correct and identical on both slips which they would then initial. A messenger would then bring the pay-in books to a large square table around which there were up to six of us junior foreign staff officers and sometimes even eight, and we sat facing each other. Our job was then to double check the initialled entries on the pay-in slips, sign the top half with our signatures, initial the bottom half and then chop the perforation with a large rubber stamp bearing the name and crest of the bank. We then tore off the counterfoil which we placed in a large locked wooden box in the centre of the table. Occasionally instead of waiting for the messengers to collect the pay-in books to give to the shroffs for return to the coolies we stood up and threw the books over the top of the glass and bronze counter barriers, much to the delight of the coolies who tried to catch them. The large square table we sat at was known as the Chopping Desk and by the time the bank was closed to the public our heads were spinning with all the checking we had done and our hands were covered with purple ink from all the chopping we had performed throughout the day. The head of the department would then unlock the wooden box and our next job was to number each counterfoil and enter its details into our ledgers which we later added up and agreed the totals with the shroffs' cash balances.

Our final job of the day was to enter a large Cash Cage where all the soiled and frayed bank notes that were to be taken out of circulation had been stamped with a large Cancelled chop and placed in bundles of 100. It was our task to manually count these smelly notes to make sure that there were exactly 100 in each bundle, and we then placed our initials alongside the initials of the shroff who had prepared the bundle. This was before note counting machines had been invented and it was thirsty work, but drinking alcohol in the banking hall was strictly forbidden so when we placed our afternoon tea orders with the 7th Floor Mess the whiskies came in tea pots and the brandies came in coffee pots, and we solemnly drank our preferred drink in the Wedgwood tea cups and saucers provided, much to the amusement of the Chinese staff. This lasted for several months until one day the bank's Chief Inspector Os Skinner, who was a teetotaller, smelled the liquor on the tea tray when coming down in the same lift as the Mess Boy, and we then had to revert to Earl Grey.

The junior foreign staff in Cash department were always on very friendly terms with the Compradore and his staff who helped us in many different ways. Although we were *gwailos* we were all given official Chinese names, the characters for which we used on our business cards and my Chinese name Tai Jer Lee had an auspicious meaning connected with intelligence, knowledge and ritual. In those days I was known as Jerry Tait and this became Tait Jerry or Tai Jer Lee because the Chinese invariably pronounce their "r"s as "l"s. We were also given nicknames by the shroffs when we first arrived at the Chopping Desk and these nicknames remained with us throughout our entire careers with the bank. I remember being particularly friendly with a shroff called Tang and one day I asked Ah Tang about my nickname. At first Ah Tang refused to disclose it as this information was only for the Chinese staff but under pressure he eventually told me that it was Peter Pan, the Boy who Never Grew Up and I took this as a compliment. It was certainly a better nickname than that given to the head of our department which was Itchy Pants, the Man on the Run. Sadly the department head had never fully recovered from a bout of amoebic dysentery he had contracted while he was interned in a P.O.W. camp during the Pacific war! Another example of the friendliness extended to us by the Chinese staff was a procedure which we called Borrowing from the Compradore. All our expenses in the bank Messes were signed for with chits and our chit accounts had to be settled at the end of each month. Our pay at that time was not significant and we often had difficulty in making ends meet, so on the last day of the month the Compradore would allow us to draw cash from his Fund to help us meet our obligations, and we would then pay him back on the first working day of the following month, or as soon as possible thereafter. This procedure was not specifically authorised by the bank but because all of our senior management had served time on the Chopping Desk and most of them had borrowed from the Compradore at one time or another, the procedure was allowed to continue.

Not all of our initial experiences in Hong Kong were pleasant experiences, but they all helped to mould us and prepare us for what was to lie ahead. I had a 350 cc Royal Enfield motor bike for the year I was in Hong Kong, and I was allowed to park it in the senior management's garage in the bank building alongside the Rolls and the Bentleys because it did not take up much space. Most of the junior officers tended to use the same repair shop in Wanchai for our vehicles, and I remember one evening when putting my bike into Chu's Garage for repair, Ah Chu showed me a cancelled bank note that he had found in the car of one of my fellow Cash Cage colleagues. I was appalled at this, and I immediately realised that I had three basic options. One was to refuse to become involved in the matter, the second option was to take the note and give it back to my colleague and the third option was to take the note and give it to the head of our department the following morning. I knew that in fact I really had no choice but to take the latter course of action, and the next morning I was taken by my department head into the inner sanctum occupied by the bank's Chief Accountant to whom I related my story. The bank took swift action. We were one short in the Cash Cage next day, and one more London office trainee was about to be confirmed and sent out East!

In due course sufficient new junior officers had arrived from London to enable me to move up into Current Accounts and I was given my own Section with three ledgers N – R, a Portuguese Supervisor and several clerks. I had survived the Chopping Desk and the Cash Cage, my signature had become more streamlined and I had learned how to speed count banknotes, a skill that I still possess! I quite enjoyed my time in Current Accounts. I was still signing pay-in slips but these were for cheques and drafts and not for cash, and I soon became familiar with the names of all the different Chinese banks and their clearing code numbers, and shortly afterwards I started to memorise the signatures of most of the account holders in my Section, thus obviating the need to refer to the specimen signature cards, when authorising payment of their cheques. In those days we operated with a standard double-entry bookkeeping system as single-shot posting had not yet been introduced. Although our journals were mechanised with the use of new NCR machines which were constantly breaking down, all the cheques and credit vouchers had to be hand posted to the ledgers and it was my duty to "call" my ledgers with another foreign staff officer and to initial all the entries in the ledgers, in fact we did almost everything except the actual posting. Once a week we "balanced the books" and all errors had to be corrected before we were allowed to leave the banking hall, but the no alcohol rule was lifted on balance nights. This routine was interspersed with brief meetings with customers who had questions about their accounts or who wanted cheque books and we were also responsible for checking the documentation for all new accounts opened such as signature cards, joint account mandates, standing instructions etc. Now I was really beginning to learn something about basic banking procedure.

Strangely enough there was not that much variety in the entertainment available to us in Hong Kong apart from bank cocktail parties, the somewhat seedy Suzy Wong type bars in Wanchai, and club activities where on special occasions we often had quite lavish balls.

A Christmas Ball at the Royal Hong Kong Yacht Club in Causeway Bay. L to R: Edwina, John Jekyll, Unknown, Ernest Charles, Zoë, John Dilworth, Fay, Mark Taylor, Jerry's partner and Jerry

To begin with in Hong Kong I started to go to early evening Chinese Tea Dances with a couple of friends and apart from the *dim sum* which we ordered the main attraction was dancing to Chinese music in semi darkness and this dancing involved holding your partner close to you and moving your body from side to side on a very crowded dance floor and I can still remember the fierce aroma of the cheap jasmine scent that the girls used as well as the coconut oil which they put on their hair. Pleasant as this activity was – and it certainly helped me forget the Chopping Desk – we had to pay the girls by the minute, so this activity soon died a natural death. There were several massage parlours and bath houses available to us but the best of these were illegal and the bank took exception whenever we got involved with the police, so we tended to spend quite a lot of our leisure time in the Peak Mess. On occasions we would make weekend visits to Macau, which was a four hour journey on the *Fatsan* ferry which departed at midnight, and this was before the hydrofoils became popular. Macau was then a Portuguese colony with an entirely different atmosphere from Hong Kong, and the Lisboa Casino there was one of the enclave's main attractions. Launch picnics to Cheung Chau and other outlying islands on the bank's boat "Wayfoong" were also immensely enjoyable and it was almost obligatory on these occasions to sit back in our wicker chairs on the return journey sipping Singapore Gin Slings. On some evenings we would go swimming at either Big Wave Bay or Repulse Bay, where we rented beach tents, and we would invariably stop off at a Wanchai bar on our way back to the Peak Mess. The original name Hong Kong means Fragrant Harbour but the Chinese habit of dumping their rubbish into the sea meant that it was not unusual to encounter numerous plastic bags when swimming, and by 1952 the harbour was anything but fragrant. Sometimes on Sundays we would drive out to the New Territories to climb up Tai Mo Shan, Hong Kong's highest mountain, and this would help to clear our hangovers, although we took our bottles of San Miguel with us.

When driving to Big Wave Bay we often used Mark's new black Vauxhall which I used to help him drive because he had never driven a car before. I only realised this when he stalled his car on the tramlines in Causeway Bay in front of an oncoming tram and he was unable to restart the engine because it was still in gear! I took over and we escaped before the police arrived but when they later discovered that Mark had no driving license he was forced to sell his car and we then used David's huge but ancient maroon Pontiac which could seat at least seven of us. Whenever

The Obedient Banker

we arrived at Big Wave Bay in David's car the look-see boys would greet us with shouts of "Fioline, fioline" and David asked me why the boys who looked after his car called him Fioline and I was unable to answer his question until I noticed that the number plate of his car was 309. This original Hong Kong number plate was probably worth more than David's car on the resale market. Sometimes Ernie would allow us to go to the beach in his classic Buick but he was very proud of his car and would spend hours polishing it. Ernie's Buick was one of many vintage cars that he would own during his career with the bank, and to my knowledge he still has amongst others a 1968 Bristol Prototype which he exhibits at car rallies in the U.K.

On occasions we would visit a somewhat run-down establishment on the Wanchai waterfront called the Luk Kwok hotel which overlooked the *praya* where small fish were laid out to dry in the sun and the smell from these fish mingled with the opium fumes which came from the surrounding tenements. Although there was a massage parlour in the Luk Kwok the main attraction there was a Night Club and on one occasion we found ourselves in the midst of an argument on the dance floor, and one of our group who was with the Hong Kong Police, but was in plain clothes, drew a revolver and fired several shots into the dance floor between the legs of the girl with whom I had been dancing. My friend Donald, who was an insurance man with Gilmans, immediately grabbed the pistol while the rest of us dragged the policeman, who had consumed a lot of liquor, out of the Night Club and we were all allowed to leave the Luk Kwok after the police officer had identified himself to the management. Most of our group wanted to forget the matter but Donald persuaded me to make a formal complaint with him to the Superintendent of Police, as a result of which I had to appear as a witness to testify before a secret enquiry at Police Headquarters, and not only was the rookie police officer dismissed from the force but I received a personal commendation from the Commissioner for my participation.

At the time I arrived in Hong Kong the Peak Mess was in a bad state of repair and had not yet been rebuilt, as a result of which our evening parties there often got out of control and it was not unusual to wake up in the morning with flowerpots in your bed and surrounded by broken furniture, and often water hoses were used on the chaps who preferred not to participate in these activities. Our bedrooms were sparsely furnished with only the bare necessities but each room had a small wooden bedside loudspeaker which was connected to Hong Kong's Rediffusion which was mainly piped music interspersed with newscasts with a choice of two channels either English or Cantonese. Before going to sleep I would switch my Rediffusion speaker onto the Chinese channel and regularly at 7 am each morning I would be woken up by a blast of Cantonese opera music which was far more effective than any alarm clock would have been. Our behaviour in the Mess was somewhat akin to that of overgrown schoolboys, and in retrospect we certainly overdid things from time to time.

When the servants went off duty at 11 pm a Night Boy called Ah Fung took over, and Ah Fung was not particularly good looking because he only had one eye, not that this worried us very much. Strangely enough we seldom kept liquor in our rooms and whenever we wanted a drink we simply pressed our room bells. Ah Fung knew exactly what drink each officer preferred, so when you pressed your bell once this meant you were ready for another drink but if you pressed your bell twice this meant that you required female company. Thursday evenings were Mess nights, we all dressed in dinner jackets and the Mess President presided at the long dining room table, and a general discussion took place after the meal was finished and the liqueurs were served. I well recall that at one of these meetings a member of the Mess asked the President why there was so much delay in obtaining service when he pressed his room bell twice and the President replied that he would ask the Mess Secretary to look into the matter. The following week the President announced that he had investigated the matter and that Ah Fung had been told that any participation that he himself wished to engage in should take place after and not before the demands of the officer who pressed the bell had been satisfied!

There were regular cocktail parties to which the junior foreign staff were invited on a selective basis and I remember being introduced to the Chief Manager's wife at one of them. Lady Morse was sitting in an upholstered chair in a corner of the 7th Floor Mess which was frequently used for bank cocktail parties. She was knitting a jersey at the time, possibly for Sir Arthur's use during his forthcoming retirement, and as she extended her hand to me without interrupting her knitting she murmured "Welcome to my husband's bank, we hope you will be very happy here… one plain, two pearl one plain".

The Morses lived in the bank building where they occupied the 9th floor while the Chief Manager's new official residence "Sky High" on the top of the Peak was being built. Access to the 9th floor was by means of the Chief Manager's lift which could only be used for access to other floors in the building at certain times of the day, and the lift was constructed in such a way that when it arrived on the 9th floor it opened directly into Sir Arthur's living room. One evening, after a particularly enjoyable cocktail party, a group of us decided to round up an assortment of stray cats and dogs from the streets of Hong Kong which we placed in the Chief Manager's lift before pressing the button for the 9th floor. Both Sir Arthur and Lady Morse were in their living room and no doubt Lady Morse was knitting at the time the deluge of animals swarmed out of the lift.

The matter was investigated the next morning and although we were all severely reprimanded by the Chief Accountant no further action was taken against us because a very senior banker, who was a bachelor and who often joined in with the junior officers, had participated in the prank and he took full responsibility for the incident. We were indeed very fortunate on this occasion, but the senior banker himself was beginning to get into trouble as this was by no means the first incident of this nature that he had been involved in. He already had a reputation in the colony, and not long before this incident he had entered the "Gripps" while seated in a rickshaw which he had the rickshaw boys carry up the steps of the old Hong Kong Hotel before entering the bar, much to the astonishment of its occupants. In a similar manner I myself had followed in his footsteps when I drove my motor bike along the top of the bar of the Hong Kong Football Club in Happy Valley a few weeks later without breaking anything. The Club Secretary advised the bank of the incident, stating that his committee had decided not to take any disciplinary action against me as I had done it as a bet in order to obtain free drinks, and even the Secretary himself had bet against me as he considered that it would be an impossible feat. However the Club asked the bank to ensure that there would be no repetition of the incident.

Sir Arthur Morse was a formidable character of the old school who had done much to put the bank back on an even keel after the end of the Pacific war, and the stories surrounding his actions and exploits are legion but in 1953 it was time for him to retire and hand over to a younger man. Before this occurred however I was to be a frontline witness to Sir Arthur in action, and at his most forceful, inside his own banking hall. One of my colleagues was in charge of a section of Current Accounts which catered to foreigners, rather than to Chinese customers. A senior naval officer from H.M.S. Tamar, which was the R.N. shore establishment in Hong Kong's dockyard, had complained about waiting for his deposit receipt and although my colleague had gone to the counter to explain that the receipt was being processed as quickly as possible, the naval officer took his complaint right the way up to the Chief Manager.

Some of the senior management had their offices on the mezzanine floor and the Chief Manager's office was in the centre of these offices and it had a small balcony where Sir Arthur could stand and observe all the activities taking place below him in the banking hall. On this occasion he brought the naval officer out of his office and onto his little balcony and his booming voice could be heard throughout the bank: "I have heard your complaint sir and I have to remind you that you are not on your quarterdeck, you are in my bank, and I require you to leave it now". My colleague's joy at hearing this was however short lived. As soon as the naval officer had left the bank, Sir Arthur sent for my colleague and then brought him out onto his balcony, and we once again heard Sir Arthur's booming voice: "I will not tolerate any further customer complaints involving junior officers in my bank, under any circumstances".

After Sir Arthur's retirement, the bank entered a new phase under the leadership of Sir Michael Turner, whose wife Wendy was the exact opposite of Lady Morse. When the Turners moved into their newly renovated residence "The Cliffs", which was next door to the Peak Mess "Cloudlands", Lady Turner inspected our living quarters and was appalled at the conditions she encountered. I remember my mess boy Ah Chang telling me that Lady Turner asked him where he slept because there was no sign of his *kang* in the servants' quarters, and he replied that he normally slept in a wardrobe drawer which became available after one of our rowdy parties had destroyed an officer's wardrobe. On another occasion she asked the Mess Secretary why the walls of one of the officer's rooms were covered with soot and his fireplace cracked, and the Secretary replied that as the officer was not very popular some of his colleagues had put a bunch of Chinese fire crackers down his chimney as a joke, but the crackers had turned out to be more powerful than anticipated. However this officer was to suffer a far more degrading experience than this mainly because he never ever participated in any Mess activities, preferring to keep to himself, and besides this he never drank alcohol, his favourite drinks on Ah Fung's list being Watson's orange juice or Green Spots. One evening we decided to lace his drink with vodka and after he fell asleep we carried his bed, with him inside it, and deposited it amongst the rose bushes in the Chief Manager's garden next door. Reportedly Lady Turner spotted the bed next morning while having breakfast and she told her amah to have the gardener remove it, only to be told that not only was there was a naked man inside the bed, but that he was "one of ours". Sir Michael was not amused but once again no disciplinary action was taken against us, as the innocent victim of our prank had had enough and he left the bank.

I had not been in Hong Kong for very long when several of the junior foreign staff were invited to a Chinese *Chow* by the Hang Seng Bank which at that time was the largest Chinese bank in Hong Kong, and this was several years before it became part of our group. The banquet was served in a private dining room in their own premises and the highlight of the meal was *shéh* which consisted of snake in a seasoned sauce on top of which we sprinkled dried chrysanthemum petals, and our hosts told us that this delicacy was a potent aphrodisiac. We were plied with drinks and there were a variety of girls present and after the banquet we needed no encouragement to take the girls onto the dance floor.

It was shortly after this dinner that Hang Seng Bank introduced a new application form that their customers needed to complete when opening Letters of Credit, and this form bore a remarkable similarity to our own customers application forms, and we were later advised by our Chief Accountant that Hang Seng Bank were copying many of our procedures, and that we should be very careful in future when socialising with them, in case we inadvertently disclosed privileged information. I much enjoyed my initiation to snake, and I have since then participated in such delicacies as birds nest soup and hundred year old duck eggs, but so far as I know I have never eaten monkey brains or roasted dog, both of which were illegal in Hong Kong. My favourite meal however was a species of fresh water Shanghai Crab and we were told that these mutants only bred in a particularly deep section of the Pearl River and they had to be brought into Hong Kong in wooden buckets of Pearl River water on the Kowloon Canton Railway trains, and it was in October that they were served in a few Hong Kong restaurants. After we had inspected the crabs to make certain that they were still alive, they were cooked and served with steamed white rice and a special Chinese wine that tasted like sherry.

During the time I was in Hong Kong I continued to use my motor bike for transport and I had no less than three accidents. The first accident occurred on Easter Sunday in the precincts of St. John's Cathedral on Garden Road just before the morning service was about to start. While looking for a suitable place to park, I was driving my motor bike very slowly past a Jaguar which had stopped in front of the main entrance doors to the Cathedral. Without any warning the back seat passenger door of the Jaguar suddenly opened sending me and my bike crashing into a row of ornamental flower pots, and geraniums were scattered all over the cathedral entrance to the amazement of the congregation who were waiting for the arrival of the Bishop. The Jaguar belonged to Jock Macgregor who was the taipan in charge of Caldbeck Macgregor, a long established importer and retailer of liquor in the colony, and it was Macgregor himself who had opened his car door onto my bike, and he was absolutely furious. As Macgregor picked his way over the broken geranium pots a nearby Chinese policeman with red tabs on his uniform, which meant that he spoke English, helped me pick up my bike and told me not to worry as he had witnessed the incident and he would file a report to the effect that it was not my fault, and he wrote down the registration numbers of both the Jaguar and my bike in his notebook.

I remember writing to my father and telling him about the incident, and he replied that he knew Jock Macgregor very well and that he had played rugger with him in Hong Kong, but on no account was I to tell him this, so I appeared to be on my own. In the event I was summoned to appear before a Senior Inspector of the Hong Kong Police and when I had sat down at his desk in Police Headquarters he closed the door and told me confidentially that Macgregor "was out to get me", but this I already knew. He then told me the good news which was that Macgregor had been persuaded to drop the case against me because the area where the accident had occurred was private property as it belonged to the Cathedral and an ancient Hong Kong law required all vehicles using the Cathedral precinct to have a closed road permit, which Macgregor did not have! I was however advised in future not to take my motor bike into the Cathedral precincts. Somehow or other an old colonial regulation had turned out to be in my favour.

My worst traffic accident however was a few months later when I was driving down the Peak Road one morning on my way to the office in blinding monsoon rain, my bike skidded and I lost control, careering across the road and I hit my head on a roadside rock. We did not wear crash helmets in those days but fortunately I was spotted by a taipan shortly after the accident walking down the road with severe concussion, with blood pouring down my face and my Saigon linen suit in tatters. The taipan had his chauffeur stop the car and pick me up and although I insisted that I should get to my office desk this was due to my concussion and fortunately the taipan's driver took me straight into the Peak's Matilda hospital. Once there my head was stitched up and I was given a tetanus injection but instead of being discharged I was kept on as an in patient for almost two weeks until my concussion had been cured.

It was during my sojourn in the Matilda hospital that I became very fond of my nurse Amy who was a Chinese girl from a prominent Shanghai family, and this liaison, which was to continue after I was discharged from hospital, was frowned upon by both the bank and her family. It was young love however and we both knew that we were in forbidden territory and that we should be discreet if we were to continue our relationship. This we were not, and I remember taking Amy out for dinner one evening to the Parisian Grill, only to discover that Sir Michael and Lady Turner were dining at a adjoining table. We would have been better off eating at a *dai pai dong* in Causeway Bay, and I should not have taken Amy to the P.G. which was one of the most exclusive restaurants in Hong Kong, and to make matters worse I noticed in my mirror while driving Amy up the Peak on the pillion of my motor bike after the dinner that we were being followed Sir Michael and Lady Turner in their Rolls. The next morning the head of my department told me that Wendy had asked him to compliment me on the legs of my girlfriend which she had admired, because when wearing a cheongsam Amy had no option but to ride side-saddle. I was naive enough at that time not to realise that the remark was intended as a warning of wrong doing rather than a compliment, and I continued with my relationship with Amy.

Jerry's Chinese girl friend, Amy Chu

Although Queen Elizabeth had assumed her royal duties in February 1952 it was not until 2 June 1953 that she was crowned, and Coronation Day in Hong Kong was declared a public holiday and was celebrated in style, with all the important buildings heavily decorated and lion dances and processions taking place all over the colony. The picture of Hong Kong's Statue Square, which appears on the front cover of this book, was taken at this time and a replica of the Queen's crown on the top of the Bank is clearly visible as are all the old model cars which at that time were allowed to park in the square. The Coronation celebrations took place not long after a series of parties which were held to mark Sir Arthur Morse's retirement, and there was no lack of entertainment during my last few months in Hong Kong.

I had at this time been in the colony for about one year, which was our unofficial probation period there, and because I was not in the first rugger XV I was eligible for transfer. This transfer was in all likelihood accelerated by my friendship with Amy and it was not long after receiving Lady Turner's message that I was told that I was to be transferred to Japan, which was one of our better postings. The precise method used at that time to determine where each junior was to be posted after his first year in Hong Kong is uncertain. The Staff Controller (as he was then known) had a dart board in his office and rumour had it that each time there was a clear-out of juniors he would place the names of the branches where there were vacancies on his dart board and the names of the officers who were to be posted were then placed on the darts. Although I doubt that there was any truth in this I do believe that not too much attention was given to these early postings and that insofar as we were concerned it was pretty much the luck of the draw. The Staff Controller naturally had the confidential reports of each officer in front of him but he would also be influenced by any suggestions made to him by his colleagues in the senior management team, and I myself had been recruited upon the recommendation of the bank's Chief Inspector, although the first time I met him was upon arrival in Hong Kong. Some branches were considered as hardship posts, and the smaller remote branches would not be suitable for all of us. This somewhat casual approach was however to undergo a radical change in the not too distant future.

I remember that a colleague of mine had been posted to Kuala Belait shortly before I was transferred to Japan and Kuala Belait was at that time a "one man office" meaning that there was only one foreign staff officer in the branch, and the normal tour of duty there was one year. My colleague told me later that after serving there for about a year and a half he had written to the Staff Controller asking when he could expect to be relieved. The story has it that he had been forgotten because his name had been omitted from the Staff Controller's Planning Chart, and when the letter arrived the Staff Controller asked his secretary "Are you sure we still have a branch in Kuala Belait?" Like the dart board story, one cannot help but feel that this episode was exaggerated.

Anyway, I had been given Japan and although I was excited at the prospect of moving on, this excitement was tempered by the realisation that the posting would effectively end my relationship with my Chinese girlfriend. Nevertheless I resigned from my clubs, sold my motor bike to Ah Chu and packed my belongings in my steamer trunk, supplemented with two tin lined wooden crates used for storing bank notes which I had acquired from the Compradore. I then threw a traditional farewell cocktail party in the 7th Floor Mess and underwent a painful parting with a tearful Amy. Once again I was to fulfil my role as an Obedient Banker.

CHAPTER THREE

JAPAN

There is a fundamental aspect of Japan that sets it aside from most of the other countries and territories in the Far East where the Hong Kong Bank operated. Whereas most Asian nations were either colonies or had at one time or another been colonised by the Portuguese, Dutch, French, British or Spanish, Japan had remained isolated from the rest of the world for many centuries. Indeed it was not until the middle of the 19th century, when Commodore Perry's gunboat expedition of 1853 partially opened up Japan to foreign trade that this isolation began to show signs of changing. The evolution of Japan was thus almost unique in the region and the suppression of Christianity, the expulsion of Portuguese settlers in the 1600's, and the fact that Japan did not share her borders with any other country enabled her to maintain her national secularism until the enactment of the Meiji constitution in 1889. Although Japan imported considerable art from China and reached out into Korea and Russia to extend its empire, the country's development was virtually untouched by the West. In fact when Japan surrendered to the Allies in September 1945 it was the first time in its history that the country had been occupied by a foreign power, and it was not until 1952 that Japan regained full sovereignty with the signing of the San Francisco Peace Treaty. This was the year before I arrived in the country, where I was to discover and enjoy a heritage that countless generations of shoguns, samurai and scholars had created over the centuries. Alongside this heritage was a defeated Emperor who had been stripped of his divinity as a direct descendent of the Shinto sun-goddess, and a population who were experimenting with a new Constitution that had been written for them by General MacArthur's

S.C.A.P. staff. Sadly much of Japan's traditional culture was soon to be eradicated by the adoption of western procedures, but if there was ever a time for a young 22 year old Englishman to visit Japan, this was it, and I was in fact destined to stay on in the country for the next three years, serving six months in Tokyo, followed by two years in Osaka with a final six months back in Tokyo, and during this time I resided in Yokohama, Kobe and Tokyo respectively.

As I was the junior foreign staff officer in Tokyo I was given the junior job which was Number Two Outward Bills, and the Head of the department was a foreign staff officer who was several years senior to me and he was also President of the bachelors' Mess, which was on the first floor of our office building in Yokohama. Mess procedure in Yokohama was very different from what I had become used to in Hong Kong and although we had occasional cocktail parties in Yokohama, the entertaining of single women in the Mess was not permitted. There were only three of us in the Mess at the time I arrived and the cost of the meals we ate and the drinks we consumed were divided equally between the three of us at the end of each month, so there was a definite incentive to make full use of the Mess facilities. I remember the Mess President telling me that I could make any recommendations for changes that I wished but that I should bear in mind that as President of the Mess he had the casting vote! I recall that at one stage I asked for more variety in our meals and for nuts to be available during our prolonged drinking sessions before dinner was served, and as a result I was allowed to have sardines on toast for breakfast once or twice a week and bowls of peanuts were placed on the drawing room table each evening.

My main job in Outward Bills was to negotiate export documents drawn under Letters of Credit, which meant ensuring that all the terms of the Credit were fulfilled, that the documents provided were exactly as specified in the LC and that there was no conflict between them. Although my London office training was helpful, the job was somewhat specialised so I was given a copy of the 1951 revised edition of The Uniform Customs and Practice for Documentary Credits published by the International Chamber of Commerce, and this was to be my bible which I studied and memorised over the next few months. I had great respect for the department head and he was very helpful to me in many ways. I recall that on one occasion I told him that I had noticed that some export documents were being presented regularly by one of our more important customers every couple of weeks covering the same shipment of walnuts, and that the value of the walnuts appeared to me to be greatly inflated, since the invoice value was much more than the retail cost of the walnuts I used to buy in Japan for my own consumption. Ron looked at me for a while before replying: "Jerry, your job is to check the accuracy of the documents and not to question the integrity of the exporter. You must always remember that the bank deals with documents, not with goods". Ron's reply did not completely satisfy me but he was the head of the department and several years my senior, so once again I decided that my best course of action was to continue to be an obedient banker. I later discovered that the walnuts were being shipped regularly each month under a Ministry of Trade and Industry export incentive scheme, whereby a percentage of the value of the exports was retained as an import quota, as import licenses were in short supply due to Japan's adverse balance of payments at that time, and these quotas could be sold profitably on the open market. This part of the procedure was handled personally by the head of the department, and my inadvertent intrusion was another example of finding things out the hard way.

My obedience and my continued negotiation of the walnut documents were soon to be rewarded, as I was invited to join a small group for a long holiday weekend in a forest resort on the outskirts of Tokyo and the invitation came from none other than the exporter of the walnuts, who we called S.K. The resort, which was previously one of Emperor Hirohito's hunting lodges, turned out to be an exclusive Geisha House and it resembled a miniature castle. As I recall there were at least four of us invited and we were overwhelmed by the services provided. The geishas would enter the room where we sat cross legged on floor cushions with small side tables, and they would then commence a Nihon Buyo performance.

For those people who have never witnessed Kabuki, the Nihon Buyo can best be described as being somewhat reminiscent of a cross between a western Congo dance where the participants follow each other in unison, and a procession of models on a catwalk, but in the Madame Butterfly style. A gesture to any one of the ladies was all that was needed, and she would then join us on the cushions and her initial task was to refill our drink glasses and engage us in conversation.

The Obedient Banker

The Geisha House near Tokyo. L to R: S.K. Lai, Jerry, Geisha and Ron Wyatt

My geisha told me in fluent although somewhat stilted English that this was the very first time she had ever refilled a customer's glass with brandy and soda, instead of the traditional sake, and that I should please show her the exact proportions that I liked in my glass. She had a remarkable knowledge of textbook western culture, and when she asked me which I preferred, the music of Brahms or Beethoven, and I said that I liked Neill Diamond, she replied that she considered Neill Diamond a trifle brash and that she found Frank Sinatra more to her taste. This was my first experience with geishas and I was fascinated not only by their knowledge but also by their desire to please. As the evening wore on our activities became more mundane and we allowed ourselves the luxury of plunging into the hot spring baths with massages to follow, before falling asleep in our *futons* on the *tatami*.

I had discarded my pillow during the night because it was made of straw so when I woke up in the morning I had acquired a splitting headache and I asked my geisha for some aspirin tablets, which revived me sufficiently to order fried eggs for breakfast. It is strange what one remembers and what one forgets after the passage of time, but I still have a vivid recollection of the tray containing my breakfast plate which had been carried down the lodge's corridors from a distant kitchen. Firmly fixed to the centre of the plate were two stone cold fried eggs on the top of which the cook had sprinkled some chopped parsley, and next to the eggs was a mound of cold boiled rice with a pair of chopsticks and a bottle of soy sauce. By this time my companions were already enjoying their second round of gin tonics so I declined to take any breakfast and I showed my geisha how to mix me a pink gin instead! Another thing that I clearly remember about the weekend was looking out of my bedroom window in the morning and watching a gardener re-arranging the stones and the plants in a rock garden below my room. My geisha joined me and I told her what a beautiful rock garden it was and that we did not have such ornate gardens in England. "Ah so, Jerry-san" replied my geisha "you tried to walk out of the window last night and you fell onto the rock garden. Now a gardener is repairing it, but fortunately you did not fall on any of the rocks". In the middle of the night I had obviously mistaken the large sliding bamboo windows for the bathroom door, but this was a mistake that I would be unlikely to repeat in the future.

Life in Japan was not always as pleasant as my long weekend in the Geisha House had been. As I lived in Yokohama this entailed travelling to and from Tokyo each day and although we sometimes commuted by train and metro this mode of travel was very uncomfortable due to the overcrowded trains, so Ron and I usually took it in turns to drive our cars into Tokyo. The roads in Japan at that time were still patrolled by American Marines in their Military Police jeeps and if one of them caught us speeding then an exciting chase often took place. If we noticed that there were no Japanese police inside the jeep then we allowed ourselves to be caught, and we took great delight in telling the MPs that as we were foreign civilians they had no jurisdiction over us. However if we noticed the presence of a Japanese policeman in the jeep we then had two alternative courses of action. We could either slow down and plead ignorance of the speed limit because this was the first time we had ever driven on this stretch of road, and we would also apologise profusely for our mistake and promise never to exceed the speed limit again, and this invariably saved us from a fine. Alternatively if we were close to the boundary separating Yokohama from Tokyo then we would accelerate and try to cross the border before the jeep could reach us, because the Yokohama police had no authority outside their own prefecture, and they had to turn back when they reached the Tokyo boundary.

It was not always that we returned immediately to Yokohama after a hard day's work because Tokyo offered a far more tempting variety of night life than Yokohama. The Ginza nightclubs had started to open up and some of them had special *arubeito* sections for *gaijins* (foreigners). There

The Obedient Banker

was also plenty of excitement in the fringe bars surrounding Shimbashi railway station which was not only a notorious red light district but it was also where the black market stalls operated and which we frequently visited not only to purchase things but also to sell our own personal imported items that we no longer needed, at inflated prices. I also used to visit the pachinko parlours where I became quite adept at operating the machines there. The old fashioned pachinko machines were simply glorified spring-loaded pin ball machines and the noise that the metal balls made was deafening. The system was to exchange your accumulated winning balls for prizes, since cash payments were not allowed, and you then went to the back door of the parlour where you sold your gifts back to the parlour's supplier for cash at a discounted rate.

The bank's office in Tokyo at Naka 9th was in the centre of the financial district and the Maranuchi Hotel was nearby. This hotel had been used extensively by the Commonwealth troops during the occupation and by arrangement with the surviving regulars the Marble Bar remained as a favourite meeting place for the British and the Australians and to my recollection I never ever saw an American there. The main attraction of the Marble Bar was their ridiculously low prices but this was to some extent compensated by the vast amount of liquor that was consumed there. Several Australians had stayed on in Japan in civilian capacities after their regiments had departed and one of my Australian friends was in fact the Editor of Japan News, a local daily newspaper which had started life as the official Newsletter for the Commonwealth forces in Japan. We helped Alan to proof-read first print run copies of the paper regularly at 5.30 pm each evening in the Marble Bar and if we could find more than a dozen errors on the first page then Alan would stop the press and buy us all a drink. On one particular evening I was having difficulty in finding any errors when I noticed that the captions of the two photographs on the front page had been switched so that "Crown Prince Akihito opens new Sports Stadium" and "Sir Winston Churchill visits Paris" had been printed beneath the wrong pictures. All my drinks that evening were given to me with the compliments of Japan News.

I had not been in Japan very long before I had my first experience of an earthquake. It occurred in the middle of the afternoon while I was seated at my office desk negotiating export documents, and the first indication I had was when the suspended ceiling lights started to swing from side to side. I then noticed that a street lamppost that I could see through an office window also appeared to be moving from side to side, but this of course was an illusion because it was actually our building that was moving, and not the lamppost. I later learned that the earthquake measured four and a half on the Richter magnitude scale, which was fairly normal for earthquakes in Japan. The second earthquake that I experienced was far more exciting. A small group of us were in a dimly lit bar in an area of Yokohama known as the Tunnel which was not only a popular haunt of foreigners but was also a favourite gathering place for the local girls. It was almost 2 am and the bar was about to close when the earthquake occurred. Immediately the wooden walls of the bar began to shake with gaps appearing between the thin strips of wood, and all the bottles of liquor on the shelf above the bar began to move from side to side. Everyone in the bar then took cover except the four of us, and we instinctively put our arms across the shelf and thus prevented the bottles from breaking. When the earthquake had subsided the Japanese bartender was beside himself with gratitude and in addition to filling up our glasses with more *Suntory* he told us that all our drinks would be "on the house" for the next week. A week later when we thanked the bartender for his hospitality he replied "My only wish is that you English gentlemen had taken cover with my other customers, as I would have been better off with the broken bottles".

The third earthquake that I remember took place at about 4 am in the morning while we were asleep in our beds in the bachelors' Mess in the bank's Yokohama office building. The banks' original building had been completely destroyed by the 1923 earthquake that had taken 140,000 lives in the Kanto area and the new building had been built on rollers embedded in the foundations and these rollers enabled the building to move six feet in both directions, and my bed skidded repeatedly from one wall in my bedroom to the other and back again, and I was absolutely petrified and I thought that my end had come. After the building settled I remember that the three of us sat together in our pyjamas at the dining room table and Ron poured us glasses of whisky which we drank without saying a word to each other. All three of us were in a state of shock, and I shall never forget the experience.

There was no Borrowing from the Compradore in Tokyo but we did have a similar arrangement which we called Borrowing from St. George. The Royal Society of St. George was quite active in the Kanto area and our annual Balls rivalled those of St. Patrick and St. Andrew. One of our second tour foreign staff officers was the Treasurer of the Society and he operated its current account which was kept with the bank. At the end of each month the Treasurer would go round the office asking each of us if we wanted to borrow from St. George. For some reason I never liked the idea of borrowing from St. George and this instinct later turned out to be a wise decision. The Accountant Neill, whose nickname was Fuji, performed the duties of an Operations officer and one of his tasks was to scrutinize the previous day's current account entries by checking the bound bundles of debit and credit slips which were "in house" transfers. At the end of one particular month his suspicions were aroused when he spotted some matching debit and credit entries to the St. George's account which were similar to separate credits and debits to the individual accounts of several foreign staff officers. When questioned the Treasurer explained the situation and pointed out that the operation was a form of window dressing, that no permanent diversion of funds was involved, and that by using value dates and "ringing" the compensating entries the transactions did not appear on St. George's current account statements.

In retrospect this practice was certainly irregular and it had to be stopped, and although the Accountant had sufficient seniority and authority to do this, he decided instead to refer the matter to the Manager, George Stacey. As some senior members of the foreign staff were involved they asked Stacey to be lenient but the Manager was a strict disciplinarian and instead of dealing with the matter himself he reported it to the Chief Inspector in Hong Kong. The next thing we knew was that the Treasurer was recalled to Hong Kong, leaving his wife and children in their married quarters in Yokohama, and when his family left shortly afterwards we learned that not only had he had been forced to resign but all the officers who had borrowed from St. George were placed on three months probation, and I was asked to take over the job of Treasurer. I mention this episode in my career in some detail because it sheds considerable light not only on the conditions under which we worked, but more importantly the attitudes that were adopted when dealing with these situations. I know that if I had been either the Accountant or the Manager I would have dealt with the matter myself, rightly or wrongly, without passing it upwards, but often the earlier training of many of our pre-war staff did not include any degree of delegation of responsibility.

Shortly after this episode a vacancy occurred in Osaka and Stacey, who was also the Senior Manager Japan, chose me to fill the position. This selection was not a promotion as such because it was more of a progression upwards as my job in Tokyo was then filled by another junior from Hong Kong who had completed his spell on the Chopping Desk. This system broadened our knowledge because the new postings brought us into contact with different aspects of banking procedure all of which had to be learned and absorbed if the Obedient Banker was ever to become an Experienced Banker.

When I left Tokyo I had my car to take with me and although Neill supported my request for reimbursement of the cost of shipping the car by rail the Manager refused to agree to this, and as a result I was exceptionally allowed to drive it down to the Kansai by myself. The bank had a system of "wiring on" their foreign staff when posted and the telegram simply had the code name of the operation followed by the name of the officer and the date of his arrival at his new post, and this date was recorded by Head Office in their records and by the destination branch who then assumed responsibility for the payment of the officer's salary from the date mentioned. In my case the Tokyo Accountant had inserted the code word for "anticipated" in the telegram before my arrival date and Head Office queried this unusual insertion. Neill had not been in favour of my driving down to the Kansai, so in his reply he said that the date of my arrival in Osaka could only be anticipated due to the remote mountain passes that I had to drive through, the bad state of the roads I would have to navigate, and the unreliability of my car which had a history of breakdowns. Osaka then responded that I had indeed arrived safely three days after leaving Tokyo with my car intact, and the incident was forgotten.

When I arrived in our Osaka office I discovered that it was a modern and spacious branch on the ground floor of our own building on Midosuji and one of our tenants was the British Consulate General. We had five foreign staff officers including myself, a Japanese Liaison Officer called Fundo, and the Manager's Private Secretary Miss Dann, who was American. The Manager handled the Exchange, the Accountant was in charge of Operations and the two other foreign staff officers were in charge of the two largest departments in the branch Imports and Exports which we continued to refer to as Inward Bills and Outward Bills. Once again I was the junior officer but this time I was in charge of all the remaining departments in the branch which consisted of Cash, Current Accounts, Remittances, Correspondence, Books and Telegrams and I much preferred being a big fish in a small pond as compared to Tokyo office where I had been very much a small fish in a big pond. I had no problems in handling the Cash and Current Accounts as I knew the procedures, but it took me quite a while to learn how the other departments operated and I was very fortunate because the Accountant Derek took me under his wing, so to speak, and I learned a lot from him in the forthcoming months. I was fascinated with the somewhat complicated practices that the bank used in its Telegrams department. This was partly due to the enormous amount of business that was conducted by cable including the receipt and dispatch of documentary credits and the handling of inward and outward payments, known as telegraphic transfers. All important cables had to be authenticated by the use of ciphers and many of them were also encoded for the sake of privacy, and the Telegrams safe contained a huge assortment of code books, cipher charts and phrase books and each book had its own instruction manual. By the time I left Osaka I was somewhat of an expert insofar as codes and ciphers were concerned, and this was to stand me in good stead in future assignments. In fact the bank's Telegrams system as a whole became so complex that many of our larger branches hired outside experts as regional officers to run their Telegrams departments.

Although Fundo-san's main duty was to assist the Manager in his dealings with the Japanese authorities, he also acted as a bridge between us and our staff and our customers, and this was particularly helpful in resolving problems which often arose due to the differences and misunderstandings between us. Many of our local staff were quite young and inexperienced and some of them had been personally recruited by our manager, who had been brought up in Japan as a child. The help and intervention of the Liaison Officer was therefore very important and it contributed greatly towards maintaining a friendly atmosphere in the office. Sadly this situation was to undergo a radical change a year later, but in the meantime I learned as much as I could about my new job and I enjoyed every minute of it.

Living in Kobe and working in Osaka was far more relaxing than my Yokohama/Tokyo experience had been. Not only was the pace slower but the opportunities for making friends and participating in local activities were much greater. Driving to Osaka was difficult so we practically always commuted on the local Hankyu train which ran from Kobe to Umeda station in Osaka. Although crowded, the trains were fast and efficient and there was ample parking for our cars at Kobe's Sannomiya railway station. None of us lived in Osaka, and although the Manager and Accountant had bank houses in between Kobe and Osaka the rest of us lived in the Nagata-ku area of Kobe which had a large foreign community and it was where the Consulates and foreign companies had their Messes and their houses. The bachelors' Mess itself was situated in a Bank Compound and two of us from Osaka shared it with the Kobe office bachelors. Also in the Compound was the house of the Kobe Manager and the houses of several of the married staff in both offices, and the Compound had a beautifully landscaped garden with its own pond over which a typical Japanese bridge had been built, and the bachelors were allowed to use the garden provided our activities did not get out of hand and we did not disturb the other occupants of the Compound.

We had numerous parties in Kobe and many of these took place in our own Mess as well as the adjoining Dunlop Mess, but one of our favourite watering holes was the American Consulate's Ladies Mess which was also nearby. This Mess was particularly popular not only because of its charming occupants but also because of the profusion and variety of diplomatic liquor that was always available there. One of our favourite cocktails was the Straphanger, which I myself had invented. The ingredients were equal parts of Gordon's gin, Hennessey Brandy, Cherry Heering, Dom Benedictine, and sweetened lemon juice and although a few people drank it neat or on the rocks, most of us added soda water as a mix. To popularise this drink I threw a Cocktail Party in our Mess and I still have a copy of the copperplate invitation which reads as follows. "Jerry Tait at Home 8 p.m. Tuesday 7th June 1955 Special, Mambo, Straphangers, R.S.V.P." The drink had already been introduced by me before my party, which was to celebrate my 24th birthday, and it had been given the name Straphanger by the British Vice-Consul in Osaka who had experienced great difficulty in hanging on to the train's strap while commuting to Osaka after drinking several of my concoctions the night before. When Sydney had arrived in Osaka he considered it inadvisable to go to the Consulate so he had gone to one of the bars we used to frequent on the top floor of the Gas Building in Osaka, and he phoned me in the bank from the bar saying that he was on his second beer and could I join him for lunch. Shortly after this I received another phone call from Sydney's wife asking me if I knew where her husband was because she had just received a phone call from the Consul General Harry Oldham saying that Sydney had failed to turn up at the Consulate. I then told Sydney's wife that her husband was in the *Gasu Biru* having a beer because he had lost his voice and was unable to talk properly, and all this was of course blamed on me. After this unfortunate episode Sydney told me that he had underestimated the potency of my cocktail and that in future he would dilute it with soda water.

There is a sequel to the above story. Not long after Sydney had lost his voice I was with a friend of mine from the Chartered Bank in the Kings Arms in downtown Kobe, and Pete asked me if I would care to join him in a drink that a bartender had introduced him to recently which was called a Straphanger. I told Peter that I preferred not to switch from the pink gins which I was presently drinking, but that as a matter of interest it was me who had originally invented the Straphanger, but Pete refused to believe me because he had assumed that Straphangers like Sidecars were a product of the twenties. The King Arms was very popular with foreigners and Japanese alike because it was a replica of a British pub and it was owned by a chap called Courtney Browne who was the epitome of an English squire and he invariably wore a tweed jacket and corduroy trousers. Courtney presided over his bevy of attractive barmaids but the main difference between the Kings Arms and other Japanese bars was that Courtney's bargirls poured drinks and cracked jokes with their customers, but nothing else, and we all respected this arrangement. Interestingly there was often a Japanese gentleman in the Kings Arms who used to dress in the same manner as Courtney, and he would buy us drinks and engage us in conversation. There was something about the chap that made me suspicious of him and my instinct was proved correct when one day Courtney advised me confidentially that the man was a plain clothes policeman whose job it was to mix with foreigners in an attempt to penetrate the active black market which flourished at that time. This would also explain why he was often dressed like a cowboy in the Texas Tavern which was further down the street and where you could get the best chilli con carne in town. Sometimes even the Japanese overdid things.

The Kings Arms was also the venue where the Triangle Club met every Saturday, and although the majority of the club's members were Australians, both Peter and I had been granted membership after we had demonstrated our ability to comply with the club's rules. Pete worked in Kobe so he always joined the Saturday group earlier than I did because I had to commute from Osaka. This was to my advantage, because although the rules of the club were relatively simple they were also somewhat deceptive. Everyone had the choice of what they drank but each person must have at least three drinks in front of them at any time and the glasses containing these drinks had to form the shape of a triangle. When you started drinking you initially ordered three drinks, but as soon as anyone went down to two drinks then another drink was added to his two glasses to preserve the triangle, and everyone else automatically got another drink no matter how many triangles they had in front of them. Everyone paid for their own drinks, and if you shouted out "Triangle" then no more drinks were added but you had to finish your drinks before you left. Every time someone shouted "Triangle" he was greeted with boos and hisses and shouts of "Chicken", so everyone tried to stay in for as long as they could.

On one particular Saturday afternoon I arrived in the Kings Arms at about 2 pm and Pete already had five pints of beer in front of him, so when I finished my first pink gin his beers were increased to six which I knew would be about his limit and I was proved correct when shortly after he shouted "Triangle" and we all flapped our arms and made suitable clucking noises to signify our disapproval, in keeping with the club's procedure. Although I was careful to order single pink gins instead of doubles and had joined the group much later than most of the participants, I too decided to quit shortly after Pete mainly because I wanted to get back to the Mess for lunch and an afternoon siesta before going out again in the evening, and when I left I said goodbye to Pete who was still on six pints in two perfect triangles. Later that evening, after waking up in the Mess, I took a refreshing shower and once downtown I decided to look in again at the Kings Arms for my first brandy soda mainly because the more exciting bars did not come to life until much later on. Poor old Pete was still there and he was obviously having great difficulty in finishing off his final pint so I advised him to leave it as all the other members of the Triangle Club had long since departed, but to his credit he ignored me and I watched him with considerable admiration as he slowly drained his glass. Before he left I asked Pete why he didn't make it easier for himself by ordering half pints of beer, and he simply looked at me and said that he never drank halves.

Although there were several good restaurants in the *Chuo-ku* area of downtown Kobe we seldom ate there and if we had not already had dinner in the Mess then we would often visit the numerous food stalls which were scattered around the bars. One of our favourite dishes was *economiyaki*, which was basically fried noodles and bean sprouts spread on a hotplate to which a batter of beaten eggs with anything from chopped meat to prawns or oysters was added, and the mixture was then cooked in front of us, and served on wooden plates with chopsticks, to which we added as much soy sauce as we needed. Another favourite was Nagasaki champon, and this was more like a stew containing all sorts of exciting things such as Japanese radish and bits of liver and sometimes even a chicken claw, and this we ate with a flat bottomed ceramic spoon. Even the tempura we ate at these roadside stalls was delicious.

It was about a year after I arrived in the Kansai that I became unwell and initially the bank's doctor was unable to determine the nature of my illness. Eventually it was diagnosed as a mild case of paratyphoid fever probably caused by drinking contaminated water as there was a minor epidemic in Kobe at the time. I had foolishly allowed my vaccination to lapse and I was admitted to a hospital run by the Catholic Church until my cure was complete. Each evening I would entertain visitors in my hospital room and my friends brought their own bottles of liquor as well as a supply of glasses. The nuns who ran the hospital were very tolerant, and my stay there was more of a holiday than an imposition.

Not all our activities were confined to Kobe because there was a wealth of culture to be discovered in Kyoto which was not far away and we made several visits to temples and castles there as well as watching Kabuki in numerous theatres. Although we were able to capture the atmosphere of these performances many of them were beyond our comprehension but there was a westernised version of Kabuki at Takarazuka and this we visited quite often because it was closer to Kobe than Kyoto, and the Hankyu line had a train station there which was an intermediate stop between Kobe and Osaka. In fact the terminus of the Hankyu Railway was at the Kawaramachi station in Kyoto and this was also relatively easy to reach by a direct train from Sannomiya. We also took weekend trips to the nearby island of Awaji by car ferry where we explored the unspoiled island and one of the main attractions there were the squid fishermen and their families most of whom had never seen foreigners before.

On occasions we were invited to weddings or other family functions by members of our staff and we soon learned to take off our shoes whenever we entered a Japanese house, and we also pretended to eat and swallow the welcome cakes we were given each time we visited a new home. This was achieved by holding the heavy dumpling in your hand, putting you hand across your mouth and then placing your hand in your trouser pocket where you deposited the cake. There was nothing worse however than discovering an abandoned welcome cake in your trouser pocket some hours later. Springtime in Japan was cherry blossom time and we were sometimes invited to join happy groups of picnickers who were ceremoniously drinking sake underneath the boughs of the cherry trees and this was a pastime that I was always happy to participate in.

The 1955 St. George's Society Ball at the K.R.A.C. was a particularly successful event. Shortly after I had assumed the position of Hon. Treasurer of the Society I was asked by our new president Reg Iberson of Dunlops if I would additionally assume the duties of Hon. Secretary with a view to increasing our membership, and this I agreed to. Initially I sent membership application forms with covering letters explaining the functions of the

Royal Society of St. George to all British subjects who were customers of the bank. However, this distribution was subsequently increased when Sydney allowed me to use his list of British subjects who had registered with the Consulate, which at that time was an annual requirement, but Sydney had asked me not to reveal this disclosure. Within a month our membership had more than doubled and I was asked at a subsequent committee meeting not only to explain the remarkable increase in our membership but also why so many missionaries who were not renowned for their social activities had joined our ranks, and I replied that apart from the Kansai bars and clubs I also visited the local Anglican church, which had several missionaries in their congregation.

Being on the committee of St. George's Society automatically put me on the VIP list of all the other national societies in the area and it was normal to start our Ball with a private cocktail party for our VIPs which included local dignitaries and government officials. Then, after the main guests had been greeted and the speeches and renditions of the UK and Japan's national anthems had been made, the Ball was officially opened with the playing of one of my gramophone records of Elgar's "Land of Hope and Glory" performed by the Royal Philharmonic which with the aid of an amplifier and four loud speakers reverberated from one end of the hall to the other, and this recording set the seal for a party which was to extend into the early hours of the morning. Indeed, it was not until after 2 a.m. that Reg told me that as all the VIPs had departed apart from the American Consul General and his wife, I would be left in charge and that I should close the bar as soon as the American contingent had departed.

At 2:30 am the American Consul General shook my hand and thanked the Brits for their hospitality but his wife refused to leave with him and she expressed herself in no uncertain terms: "Do yourself a favour Wilmer, and drop dead twice" she shouted. This was the first time that I had ever heard this expression and I could not prevent from smiling and this prompted the Consul General's wife to lead me onto the dance floor whereupon her husband told his driver to take him home, leaving his wife with me on the dance floor. Fortunately one of my American guests Homer L. Newhouse Jr. who was a Yale graduate and a junior officer with the Chase Manhattan Bank in Osaka was still at the party so I asked Hal to help me take care of the American Consul's wife as I was at that time in dire need of some sort of chaperon. Hal and I eventually persuaded the lady to leave and having driven her back to her residence she then insisted on inviting us inside where she poured us drinks, put on a gramophone record and once again insisted on dancing with me.

St. George's Society Ball, L to R: Hal Newhouse, Sakamoto-san (Governor of Osaka), Selwyn Lloyd (St. David's Society), Harague-san (Mayor of Kobe), Jerry, Reg Iberson (President, St. George's Society)

The commotion had aroused the Consul General who came downstairs in his pyjamas and once again I was to hear a much expanded version of the "DDT" expression. After Hal and I had managed to extricate ourselves, Hal confided in me: "You certainly scored a hit with the Consul General's wife Jerry but don't worry about it because she wont remember much about it when she wakes up and the Consul himself is pretty much used to this sort of thing by now and he won't hold it against you". In fact, at our next committee meeting I was complemented on the part I had played in making the Ball such a success, and Reg announced that although the roast beef and Yorkshire pudding had been well within the budget, the huge bar bill would cost the missionaries a bit more money next year if they decided to renew their annual memberships!

Not all of our experiences in the Kansai were pleasant. I remember driving back to Kobe one Sunday evening after a weekend at a nearby hot spring resort and being stopped by the police who told us that our Mess had been burgled, and that we were needed there immediately. How were the police to know that it was us in the car that they had stopped and how were they to know that it was our Mess that had been burgled? The answer is simple. The movements of all foreigners were at that time secretly monitored by the police and the registration number of my car had been routinely recorded when we left the Hyōgo prefecture, so it was relatively easy for the police to contact me regarding the burglary on my way home, and they even knew the name of the hotel where I had spent the night. Anyway, when I entered my bedroom I noticed that a number of my bottles of black market liquor had been left on the floor by the thief who had abandoned them when he was surprised by one of the maids who had come upstairs to investigate the disturbance. I was scared that I would be in trouble with the police when they discovered that my liquor bottles had no tax paid labels but they were only interested in spraying the bottles and then taking fingerprints.

We all made claims on our insurance companies for the items we had lost in the burglary and the matter was forgotten until some months later when in the midst of a Mess party one of the maids told us that there was a policeman at the door who wanted to see us. This man had been given the waistcoat belonging to a suit that the thief had stolen from the Mess President's wardrobe and the policeman's job had been to search all the second hand cloths shops in the area until he found a jacket and trousers that matched the waistcoat. He had achieved this in a small shop in the suburbs of Osaka and this led to the arrest of a man whose fingerprints matched the prints on my bottles of black market liquor. Surprisingly the policeman had brought the thief with him and he asked us what action we wished to take because the fate of the thief now appeared to be in our hands. Dick, who was the owner of the suit, was no longer in Japan and in fact I was the only person in the Mess that remembered the burglary, so I told the policeman that I did not wish to take any further action in the matter, and I duly signed the release paper that he gave me. The policeman then thanked us profusely and told us that as honour had been restored to his sub-station he looked forward to resuming his normal duties now that his task had been completed. Once again I was reminded of the differences between the East and the West when it came to such matters as investigating a run-of-the-mill burglary. I could not imagine the same thing happening anywhere in the U.K., but I preferred not to contemplate what fate lay in store for the thief who had put the Nagata-ku police to so much trouble when he decided to rob *gaijins*.

As the junior officer in Osaka it was my job to bring the Mail Packet for Kobe back to the Mess every evening and this packet contained the day's correspondence with Kobe including the schedules of mail transfers and drafts purchased etc. My Kobe office counterpart and I then exchanged mail packets in the Mess and I would bring Kobe's packet into Osaka the following morning. This task was a constant source of concern to me because we would often take advantage of the Osaka bars' Happy Hours before catching the train to Kobe, and I had to take my briefcase containing the Mail Packet with me on these bar crawls.

Eventually the inevitable occurred when I inadvertently left my briefcase on the Hankyu train and although I realised this as soon as I was on the Sannomiya platform, the train was already pulling out of the station and a railway attendant prevented me from re-boarding the train. What then ensued was a typical example of the methodical efficiency of the Japanese railway system as a whole, and the privately owned Hankyu Railway in particular. Having failed to get back onto the train to retrieve my briefcase I rushed to the Station Master's office at the end of the platform and told the official behind the counter that I had left a briefcase containing important documents on the train. Amazingly, the official had direct communication with the guard on the train which was at that time without passengers and was about to turn around and commence its return journey to Kyoto via Kobe and Osaka. Within two minutes the guard phoned the Station Master to confirm that he had recovered a briefcase which he would hand over to him in five minutes time when the train pulled into a different platform.

I immediately recognised my briefcase, but the official refused to return it to me until I had signed a receipt for the itemised contents which I had described as important documents. The briefcase was then opened in the presence of the Station Master and the English speaking official solemnly read out the contents which were recorded onto a duplicated receipt form. In fact my important documents were conspicuous by their absence and I can still remember the listed contents that were read out aloud by the official without any expression on his face. "One paperback novel *It's Safer with Your Shoes On* by William Falconer, one flask of whisky, one apple, one half-eaten ham sandwich, one penknife, one packet containing three Durex contraceptives, one bottle of aspirin tablets and one sealed envelope". The sealed envelope was of course the Kobe mail packet, and when I bowed to the Station Master while telling him *"Gomen nasai, domo arigato gosaimasu"* he actually managed a smile, but I think that this smile was one of pity for a *gaijin* rather than one of amusement.

There was a Shinto shrine at Sanbun Matsu close to our Mess and it was almost directly opposite the police sub-station that had become involved in our burglary. Unlike most religions Shintoism has no organised teaching, no known founder and no moral code. On occasions when returning home late at night we would join the circle of people who were walking or running around the shrine beating drums and ringing the bells that hung from the branches of the trees. This activity was in general a form of worship to nature and more specifically it was to honour one's ancestors and certain sacred spirits and although we participated for another reason this made no difference to the worshipers there who welcomed both our presence and our participation.

Another art which we learned was how to perform the Tankō Bushi which was a Japanese Coal Miners Dance which had its origins in the Miiki Mine in Kyushu and which was performed each year as a Bon Odori event during the July festival. The movements in this dance included digging, cart pushing and lantern hanging, in fact all the movements that the miners would make during their work underground, and these movements were interspersed with hand clapping. We performed the dance regularly at our parties and the American Consulate girls were very proficient at it so if one did not know the precise movements you simply followed the actions of the girl in front of you. It was all great fun, and sometimes we invented movements that were not part of the original dance, but this frivolity was to come to an abrupt halt with the outbreak in 1955 of a full scale bank strike in our office which was to entirely change not only our lives but also our attitudes.

In reality the underlying reason for the strike had little to do with improving the pay and working conditions of our staff although this was the declared purpose of our union when they went on strike. The real reason for the strike was political and it was in fact instigated by the main parliamentary opposition party in an effort to overthrow the existing Hatoyama government, although the actual organising of the strike was left to Sohyo, the General Council of Trade Unions of Japan which was founded in 1950. Sohyo was potentially a very powerful body because it had evolved as a result of the liberal labour laws which MacArthur's staff had introduced into the Japanese constitution. The abolishment of the Zaibatsu, which owned 40 percent of Japan's equity, was probably a good thing, but the creation of new liberal labour laws which were based on American law relating to industrial disputes, collective bargaining and strikes and lockouts in the U.S., were of doubtful benefit to the country, but the new laws were about to be tested for the first time since Japan regained its sovereignty.

Sohyo used its bank employees' union to spearhead the demonstrations and the plan was firstly to paralyse a foreign bank after which a Japanese B class bank would go on strike and once this had succeeded then the strike would spread to the A class banks, which was considered sufficient to overthrow the government. The Hong Kong Bank was chosen to start the process, because not only were we the largest foreign bank in Japan but we also had branches in all four of the main financial centres, Tokyo, Osaka, Kobe and Yokohama. At first our union, which was called Zenringen or something similar, was slow to respond but as the strike dragged on they were forced to resort to more positive action and Sohyo sent in groups from the Students Union Zengakuren to help them in their struggle. The planned deadline for the bank's capitulation had passed, our staff were without pay and were borrowing money, and their wives and children were being threatened because no other bank union would declare a strike until our union's strike had been successful. The position was precarious.

In Volume IV page 437 of The History of The Hongkong and Shanghai Banking Corporation, Frank King makes mention of the strike in Kobe and how the foreign staff managed to keep the office open, four or five doing the work of forty-five, and he records that the strikers permitted the foreign staff and Japanese Manager (Liaison Officer) access to the office and that there was no violence. Professor King then continues his narrative as follows:

"The story was different in the larger Tokyo and Osaka offices, where the Managers were not particularly popular, and the Board of Directors in Hong Kong were kept in touch with the developments at every meeting. The senior Manager in Japan, H.V. Parker, was told to hold firm and advised not to argue; representations were made through the Embassy to the Japanese Government and eventually a settlement, on September 27, 1955, was reached which fell far short of the Union's demands. There was no victimization; at least one of the strike leaders was hired by the Bank and became the Chief Personnel Officer. Many striking Bank staff were embarrassed by the affair and apologized privately to members of the junior staff; the latter had been offered an opportunity to transfer if they considered that the event had caused them to lose face, but only one

Jeremy Tait

Foreign staff member asked to be transferred. At the same time the Board voted them and the Japanese Manager, S. Hayashi, bonuses.

The success in keeping open during the strike was used as an argument in support of the then system of Foreign staff training. All such staff could, as a result of having started on routine tasks, actually perform the work done by the clerks. They had not moved in at the top. As it happened, it was fortunate the officers had received such training, but it was hardly a sound argument for the continuation of the system.

In fact, it is an exaggeration to suggest that the Foreign staff as then constituted in Japan kept the operation going. The Bank had to fly in additional staff; they entered the country on tourist visas. They did not go to the Bank itself but remained in their Tokyo hotels; work was smuggled out from the Bank office; the officer had to shake off his Union tail, reach the hotel undetected, deliver the work to be done, and return later to collect it.

The ramifications of the Bank's Japan business were world-wide and were particularly significant to London Office".

As one of the few surviving foreign staff officers of the bank who were in Japan at the time of the strike I have no hesitation in confirming the accuracy of Professor King's résumé of the events that took place, and the personal experiences that follow will fully support and complement his brief but composite description of the situation. There are however one or two things that Professor King fails to mention. It is true that the Tokyo and Osaka Managers were not particularly popular with the local staff who went on strike, but this was due to entirely different reasons. Because the Tokyo Manager was strong and resisted the Union, the strikers respected him, but conversely as the Osaka Manager was weak and often pleaded with the strikers, he was universally despised. This became very evident on the first working day after the strike was called off. When the Tokyo manager entered his office all the staff greeted him in silence with bowed heads, whereas when the Osaka manager first re-entered his office, and I was with him at the time, he was greeted with jeers and hisses. Although it is true that only one of us opted to leave Japan after the strike I told the Tokyo manager that I thought it would be in the bank's best interests to remove me from Osaka because of the antagonism that had arisen between myself and some of my staff during the confrontations, but that I would have no objection to returning to Tokyo as I only had another six months of my tour to complete, and I therefore swapped places with a junior officer in Tokyo who was sent to Osaka. I had survived the strike by

The Obedient Banker

facing the strikers head-on and my unflinching attitude was derived from my contempt for the strikers because to challenge the bank with organized disobedience was entirely against my principles.

With regard to the bonuses it is true that I was given an ex-gratia payment of one hundred pounds along with a letter signed personally by the Chief Manager thanking me for my loyalty, although I remember thinking at the time that this recognition fell somewhat short of what I deserved in return for what I had undergone. This disappointment was tempered by the fact that the Tokyo Manager agreed that the bank should pay the huge bill that we had accumulated while carrying out the bank's business in the bars of numerous Osaka hotels and restaurants during the strike, and my relief on hearing this decision strengthened my resolve to continue to be an obedient banker.

When the strike started not all of our staff participated and a small section remained loyal to the bank with the Union allowing them to continue to perform their duties. This was not to last long and after about a week my Head Cashier Kawata advised me that he along with several of the other loyal staff were joining the strike due to mounting pressure from the Union which included threats to their families. In fact most of the loyal staff did not participate actively in the strike, preferring to stay in their homes, so they became passive rather than active members of the union. The first stage of the strike was now over.

The second stage was also to last about a week during which time the five of us assisted by the Liaison Officer and the Manager's Secretary managed to keep the branch open to a dwindling number of customers and also to maintain a rough record of the business we conducted, despite the taunts and threats of the strikers who surrounded our desks while we were working.

We had access to the banking hall on the ground floor, but the basement where the vaults and record room were situated had been taken over by the Union and it became their headquarters where they ate their meals and some of them even slept there at night. At the top of the stairs leading down into the basement the Union had placed a loudspeaker and we were subjected to a continuous playing of recordings of militant chanting and marching music while we worked.

Members of the union demonstrating inside the bank

    My Current Accounts ledger keeper Suzuki was one of the most active of the Union's demonstrators and I remember when I was posting entries into one of his ledgers he was screaming obscenities at me and I think he would have attacked me if his companions had not restrained him. With the help of a Sohyo manual based on MacArthur's new Labour Laws the Union were very resourceful and while our Manager and the Liaison Officer were kept occupied in collective bargaining the rest of

The Obedient Banker

us were subjected to a form of persuasion that was extremely unpleasant. In fact I was beginning to wonder just how long I could continue under these conditions when the strike entered its third phase when the Union declared a Lock-Out and we were prevented by picket lines from entering the office.

This lock-out was illegal because we owned the building, but the main danger to us was that we might lose our banking license because the bank was effectively closed to its customers. Our Japanese lawyer advised us however that the Bank of Japan would not revoke our license provided we made an effort to enter the banking hall each morning, and this meant attempting to break through the picket line which was a solid wall of our staff, all holding hands. The first time we did this the Union took it as a physical assault against them and when they retaliated I emerged from the fray with several bruises and our Liaison Officer was kicked in the groin and had to be taken to hospital. Discussions took place immediately between our lawyer and the Union leaders and in an effort to avoid any repetition of the unfortunate incident it was agreed that we would in future be allowed to penetrate the picket line one at a time, provided we agreed to passive persuasion. We mistakenly thought that this might gain us entry to the bank, but this never happened. To be entirely isolated and surrounded by a crowd of hostile strikers chanting "foreign devil" and "unfair labour practice" was a harrowing experience, and once we had managed to extract ourselves from the picket line the next thing we had to do was to disperse and then meet together again in a secret place. This was difficult because we were followed by strikers wherever we went, so we often used the metro jumping into trains going in different directions just as the doors were closing. If this did not work, we then caught taxis and this was practically always successful in shaking off our followers, and this was why we later referred to ourselves as The Taxi Bankers Club, because so much of our working time was spent in taxis.

When we had all arrived at our secret meeting place the day's activities were planned and agreed and we then got down to conducting the bank's business as best we could in almost impossible circumstances. The two officers in charge of Imports and Exports used their homes to process their documents and unknown to the Union several loyal staff helped them in their work along with some bank wives and their friends. My job was very different. I had already collected the bank's mail from the Post Office where I had the key to our P.O. Box and the authority to sign for registered mail. This mail was sorted and distributed amongst us as necessary, and I then posted all the cheques and deposits to a shadow register simulating our current account ledgers which I had created with names and believed balances from memory. I had a cheque book for our account with the Bank of Japan and the Manager had signed several of these blank cheques. We were a sub-clearing bank and our clearing bank was The Sanwa Bank and at midday I went to a private room in their Head Office where a group of their senior officers were there to help me in every way they could because they were fearful that if we gave in to the strikers then their bank might also have a strike on its hands. I handed them all the cheques and drafts drawn on other banks that I had in my possession and this comprised our outward clearing which they themselves listed and calculated for me. Sanwa had already sorted and listed all the cheques and drafts they had drawn on us, and this comprised our inward clearing. If the difference in the totals of our inward and outward clearings was in their favour then I would simply fill in the amount on one of my blank Bank of Japan cheques which I then signed and gave to them, but if the difference was in our favour they would pay the amount into our account with the Bank of Japan. If we were short on our daily liquidity ratio, which was a Central Bank requirement, Sanwa would simply arrange a Short Loan to Banks and Brokers in our favour at a discretionary rate, and if our liquidity was excessive, then they would conversely take a Short Loan from Banks and Brokers from us, and this was achieved by an exchange of Promissory Notes, and our Manager had previously given me a few of these pre-signed blank Notes to carry with me which I could then countersign. This was banking in the raw, and we could never have survived the strike if The Sanwa Bank had not given me the help and support that they did, and I gained an enormous amount of knowledge of basic banking procedure as a result of my dealings with Sanwa.

Not all the other banks in Osaka were as kind to us as Sanwa. I remember in the early days of the strike taking the British Vice-Consul into the Mercantile Bank, which was on the opposite side of the street to our office, to enable the Consulate General to open an account because we were unable to handle their business properly, only to be asked by Mercantile's Accountant to leave the bank because their Union had recognised me and this was causing the bank some embarrassment. At that stage Mercantile Bank was a competitor of ours and not yet a partner, and I was furious at the treatment I had received from them, so I later submitted a report on what had occurred, although I believe it was ignored. We also lost one of our more important customers to the Bank of America, mainly because we were unable to continue to handle the large volume of import and export business they gave us. However, when the strike was over the company returned to us in spite of the efforts of Bank of America to keep their business, and my successor in Osaka later told me that the company's Treasurer had told him that the main reason they returned to us was because of the personal attention they received from our foreign staff, and my successor promised a continuance of this relationship. Of considerable help to us was the fact that much of our Bills business came from the smaller Japanese B class banks that sent us their own customers' documents for re-negotiation and dispatch because of our experience and our superior correspondent banking relationships, and this business was conducted on a split commission basis. When the strike broke out this business was diverted to other foreign banks, but after the strike ended the business was returned to us.

It is very probable that our Union were unaware of my secret meetings with Sanwa, but they knew exactly where I lived and I was often followed when I arrived back in Kobe after an exhausting day of taxi-banking, and on these occasions I had probably consumed several drinks in order to keep my sanity, and I was in no mood for further contact with our Union. On one such occasion I remember collecting my parked car at Sannomiya only to find it surrounded by strikers wearing their familiar red and white headbands and waving banners. I tried to ignore them by jumping into my car and driving away as fast as I could but at the last minute one of the demonstrators jumped onto the bonnet of my car and refused to let go. I remember accelerating in an effort to get rid of him but although he kept sliding down the sloping bonnet he somehow or other managed to pull himself back again each time he was about to fall to the ground, and I did not feel inclined to either slow down or stop for fear of a confrontation. By this time we were approaching the Mess and instead of driving past our friendly police station in Nagata-ku I drove my car directly through the open front doors of the sub-station and by suddenly braking I catapulted my unwelcome passenger literally into the arms of the astonished policemen who were seated behind the counter. I then reversed my car and drove on to the Mess and I heard nothing further from either the police or the Union regarding my action, which I later jokingly referred to as a citizen's arrest.

On another occasion I was walking up the hill returning to our Mess after an evening in the Sannomiya bars when I noticed that my path was blocked by three strikers who insisted in passive persuasion but I reckoned that this was neither the time nor the place for collective bargaining, so I pushed my way past the trio. I am not exactly certain what happened next but one of the strikers punched me in the face and I immediately responded by hitting him over the head with my umbrella. At this stage two of the strikers ran away but the man who had punched me stood firm and it was evident that he was going to hit me again if I tried to pass. My umbrella was broken so I threw it away and I picked up a small rock instead which I held in my clenched hand. As I tried to pass the man he lunged out at me and in return I hit him fairly and squarely with the fist containing the small rock and this ended the confrontation. I am not particularly proud of what I did and nor am I sorry because it was in self defence, but I still have a crooked little finger, which was broken at the time, and this is a permanent reminder of an unpleasant incident. When I reached the Mess I discovered the reason why the trio of strikers had been in the area, as the outside walls of the Mess had been covered with painted messages in both Japanese and English, and these messages were unnecessarily unpleasant because they were intended to incite our local neighbours. One message read as follows: "These foreign devils are desecrating our women". Surely it was normal for us to have Japanese girl friends! Although there was no violence in our Kobe office, the Osaka staff were more belligerent but as far as I can recall this occurrence and our picket line experiences were the only two incidents involving physical violence during the entire strike.

At one stage we thought that we had a breakthrough when a senior Government official, who was a respected member of Japan's Diet, had agreed to arbitrate in our lock-out dispute with the Union and we all entered the bank for collective bargaining. I was carrying a large leather briefcase and the first thing I did was to unlock my safe in the Cash Cage and to put several Promissory Notes, some cheque books and a number of important rubber chops into my briefcase. There was also a pile of hand delivered mail which the Union had not disturbed and I put it all into my briefcase. My next act was to copy down some of the current account balances into my shadow register and I had almost completed this when the negotiations broke down in the Manager's office and the Union forced us all to leave the bank. When I reached the door the Union asked me to open my briefcase because they suspected that I might be taking some important documents out of the bank, but I firmly refused to either unlock it or to hand it over to them. The Union was adamant and so was I and we appeared to have reached a stalemate. I recall that the Manager, who had no idea of what was going on, suggested that I open up my briefcase for

The Obedient Banker

inspection as requested so that we could all leave the building, but I told him that it was my briefcase and that the Union had no justification in demanding to see the contents. A long discussion in Japanese then ensued and it was finally agreed that if I would give the politician my solemn promise that there was nothing in the briefcase that I had not brought into the bank, then the politician would give the same assurance to the Union, and we would be allowed to leave, and this I did.

When I later opened my briefcase in our hotel the Manager was appalled at my breach of promise, but I told him that if he had asked me about the contents I would have told him the truth, but as the politician had sided with the Union and as the Union's occupation of our bank was illegal and the items I had removed belonged more properly to us than to the Union, I considered my actions to be fully justified in the circumstances. Not only was I able to return Sanwa Bank's Promissory Notes to them the next day and obtain release of our guarantees, but we were also able to sign our cheques with the proper rubber chops. How obedient can a banker get?

Eventually our union were obliged to negotiate a settlement with terms which were a far cry from what they had hoped for, and we were able to celebrate the occasion with parties in each office which our Tokyo manager attended.

Party to celebrate the end of the strike. L to R: Arthur Fryers (Inward Bills), Fundo-san (Liaison Officer), Verne Parker (Manager Tokyo and Senior Manager Japan), Miss Dann (Manager's Secretary), Gordon Waller (Manager Osaka), John Boyer (Outward Bills), Derek Self (Accountant Osaka – partially hidden) and Jerry in the foreground

It was a great relief for me to leave Osaka and to be sent back to our Tokyo office and my new job was Correspondence and Telegrams and traditionally the Telegrams Officer was given his own little house in Tokyo, much to the envy of all the other bachelors who were housed in the Yokohama Mess and had to commute back and forth each day. I loved my little Japanese house in Kojimachi which was close to the Emperor's Palace and gardens and not far from the Diet building. I was provided with a live-in housemaid cum cook and the ground floor consisted of a toilet, a dining room, and a kitchen with an adjoining room for my a*masan*. There was no bathroom as such in the house, but there was an *ofuro* (wooden tub) in an alcove on raised wooden floorboards halfway up the stairs and Nakana-san taught me the traditional Japanese way of taking a bath which was scrubbing yourself with soap and water and then rinsing before entering the tub which she kept full of hot water. There were two rooms upstairs, the bedroom and the living room, and the walls were so thin that when I was hanging a picture in my bedroom, the nail protruded through the wall of the living room so I simply hung a separate picture in the other room using the same nail for both pictures.

My supervisor in Correspondence department was the Head of the Union but we were very polite to each other and we had no trouble whatever in getting along together, and I found him to be both efficient and intelligent although much of his time was taken up with Union matters specifically helping to heal the wounds that the strike had produced. In fact I got on better with my supervisor than I did with my new Manager as Verne was one of the strictest men I had ever worked for. I had no difficulty in coping with my Telegrams duties in which I had considerable experience, and the correspondence job was relatively easy once one had got the hang of things. The early morning was a difficult time for me as I had to decode and decipher all the telegrams, type them onto the telegram sheets, and distribute these sheets to the Manager, the Sub-Manager and the Accountant as well as to all heads of departments, and the Manager expected to have his copies of the telegram sheets waiting for him on his desk when he arrived in the office. My next job was to sort and distribute all the inward mail to the respective departments and it was while I was doing this that I was also required to enter Verne's office, and place his telegram sheets into his loose leaf telegram folder and when I inserted the new sheets I was supposed to remove the oldest sheets so that the folder contained exactly one month's telegrams. The Manager's secretary Joanna would alert me when Verne was free so that I could enter his office to perform this ridiculous task and I remember on one occasion that each time I tried to enter his room he was either on the telephone or a customer had got in to see him first, so I devoted my attention to what I considered was a more important task, and that was to get the day's mail out to our department heads as soon as possible.

Inevitably my phone rang shortly afterwards, and it was the Manager who demanded to know why his telegram sheets were still on his desk and I was instructed to attend to this matter immediately. When I entered Verne's office I apologised for the delay explaining that each time I had tried to enter his office he was busy, and that I also had to get the mail out to department heads. Instead of accepting my apology the Manager told me to ensure that that this dereliction of duty would never happen again, and at the time he said this I was in the process of placing his new telegram sheets into his open folder. Instead of doing this however I took all the sheets out of the folder and I then threw them up into the air and walked out of his office. The Manager had pushed me too far and he knew this because he never mentioned the incident to me, but Joanna told me later that when asking her to tidy up the sheets which were scattered all over the floor of his office he also told her that he had upset me unnecessarily, and that in future she would be the person responsible for maintaining his telegram folder, and when he told her this he knew that she would pass the information on to me. I had put my role as an obedient banker in jeopardy, but I had got away with it. I doubt that I got a very good report from Verne when I went on leave six months later but our Head Office knew that he was a tough man and I was reasonably confident that my Osaka reports had been favourable.

One reason why it was important for the Telegrams officer to live in Tokyo was because it was his duty to check all the telegrams on public holidays to see if there was anything urgent, so if I was away I would have to find another officer to do the job for me. Christmas Day was no exception, and after I had gone to the bank and checked the telegrams on that day I noticed a single telegram in a sealed cover addressed personally to the Manager by name. It was about 10 am on Christmas morning so I telephoned Verne in his house, told him that I had a telegram for him, and would he like me to open it up and read it to him. "No thanks, Tait" he replied "you had better bring it to me at the house, but hurry up because we are going to church at 11". The Manager's house was some distance away but I managed to get there about half an hour later and I rang the front door bell. A maid came to the door but I told her that I wished to give the telegram to the Manager personally, which I did as soon as he appeared. He opened the envelope in front of me, and then read out the telegram. "Merry Christmas and Happy New Year from Aunt Susan" he said "but now its time for church", and he closed his front door without even thanking me for bringing him his telegram. Merry Christmas to you too, I thought, as I prepared to drive back to my Kojimachi house. On this occasion I felt that I was being treated more like a delivery boy than an obedient banker.

Living in my own house in Tokyo however gave me considerably more freedom than the bachelors Mess and I gradually built up an entirely new circle of friends, many of whom were unconnected with the bank. Some Swiss friends who worked for a pharmaceutical company had given me some medicine for headaches and I was taking these tablets regularly without realising that I had an allergy to them. Fortunately my doctor discovered this in time and in January 1956 I was admitted into Tokyo's International Catholic Hospital for two weeks with a blood disorder known as agranulocytosis and upon discharge I was advised to convalesce for a further two weeks before returning to work. For the first week I stayed in the Yokohama house of a senior bank couple and I shall be forever grateful to Neville and Eileen for taking such good care of me at that time.

It was then agreed that I could spend the last week of my convalescence in a *ryokan* (Japanese Inn) in the hot spring resort of Atami in Shizuaka prefecture. This week in Atami was reminiscent of the long weekend I had spent in a Geisha House some two years earlier, the main difference being that instead of a geisha I had arranged for a companion to join me on the holiday. A few days earlier Neville and Eileen had left their house to go to a Cocktail Party and I took the opportunity to visit a friend and to ask her if she would like to come with me to Atami, and she readily accepted the invitation, but since I was supposed to be convalescing this arrangement had to be kept secret. Accordingly Midori-san met me at the railway station where we boarded the Tokaido train for Atami, and we had a glorious week together mainly in the hotel spa enjoying the hot springs, but also with side trips to Mount Fuji and Hatsushima and some sailing on Lake Ashi. It was on this holiday that I finally shook off the residual effects of the strike, but when I reported back to my Tokyo Manager the only thing Verne said to me was "I cant say that you look any better after your convalescence than you did before it", and I cannot help but wonder if there might have been some truth in his somewhat unkind remark.

The Obedient Banker

One of the bank's British customers lived almost next door to me in Kojimachi and we soon became friends, spending many enjoyable evenings together, and he spoke fluent Japanese and our respective girl friends got on well together. Geoff had been a Squadron Leader in the RAF in Japan at the end of the war and he avoided repatriation by obtaining a job as an attaché with the British Embassy, before setting up his own company in Japan. At the time we first met his company was quite small and I once asked him why he called himself Adams & Co and he told me that he had chosen the name because it was always top of the list in any alphabetical directory. Geoff was the sole agent in Japan for several well known brands and these included Christy's hats, Church's shoes and Morgan cars, and he told me that Church's had sent him two dozen shoes as samples but as they were all left-footed shoes he had a Japanese shoemaker make him two dozen right-footed copies, and he was now waiting for a free sample from Morgans!

At one stage Geoff needed a small loan from the bank and he naturally asked me if I could help him. I had a distinct feeling that the Manager would turn him down, so I told him to come into the bank on a Saturday morning when the Manager's job was being done by the Sub-Manager, as they took alternative Saturday mornings off. I also told Geoff that the Sub-Manager was a keen golfer and that he always brought his golf clubs into the office on Saturdays. I introduced Geoff to the Sub-Manager and left them together to discuss the loan request. Shortly afterwards Geoff came out of the Sub-Manager's office smiling and he told me he had got the loan he wanted. When he had gone, the Sub-Manager called me into his office and told me that he had approved the loan. "What a nice chap your friend is" Roy said to me "Just look at what he took out of his pocket and gave me", whereupon the Sub-Manager showed me half a dozen new Dunlop 65 golf balls, which were virtually impossible to get in Japan, except on the black market. Geoff subsequently offered me a job with his company, and this would not be the only time I was to be tempted to leave the bank. I gave the matter some thought and then told him that I preferred to continue to pursue my career with the bank, and although Geoff's company went from strength to strength, I still believe that I made the right decision.

Shortly before I left Japan I was told that the Manager wanted to inspect my house as the rental agreement was coming up for renewal with the owner, who was a retired officer of the bank, and the Manager wished to satisfy himself that the house was suitable for his Telegrams officer. Verne was an hour late but eventually the front door bell rang and I opened the door. He then walked into the house ignoring the slippers that Nakana-san offered him and without taking off his shoes he strode through the house inspecting each room. When he came to my living room he asked where the chairs were and I replied that we normally sat on the floor with cushions to support us because the side tables were too low for arm chairs. When we then came to my minute bedroom he noticed that virtually all of the floor space, apart from a narrow pathway in front of my dressing table, was taken up by a double mattress that I had managed to acquire from a bank house that no longer needed it. "Where is your bed?" asked the Manager, and I replied that I preferred to sleep with the mattress on the floor, because it was far more comfortable than the original *futong* and *tatami* that were in the house when I moved in. "Definitely substandard" Verne muttered before he left, and I later learned that I was the last Telegrams officer to live in the little Kojimachi house.

My first four year overseas tour of duty with the bank was now coming to an end, and it was time to say *sayonara* to the land of the cherry blossom. I was due eight months home leave and the next P & O liner to leave Japan was their flagship the s.s. "Chusan" and I joined the ship in Yokohama and stayed onboard for its entire 5 week voyage to Tilbury. Although my time in Japan had been exciting it had also been tiring and I had not seen my parents since I was twenty years old, so I was not sorry to board the ship and on this occasion I had a first class cabin to myself. The ship set sail from Yokohama on Sunday 22 April 1956, which was the day after I had attended the Kanto St. George's Ball where I was the outgoing Treasurer and Secretary, and the event had been held at the YCAC, the Yokohama Country and Athletic Club. On arrival in Kobe on the 23rd I was invited to my second St. George's Ball by the Kansai members at the KRAC, the Kobe Recreation and Athletic Club, and I recall barely managing to get back onboard just before the ship sailed at midnight. One of the main differences between passenger ships in the 50's and modern day cruising is that in the old days passengers were embarking and disembarking at each port of call so you were constantly meeting new people, whereas nowadays it is normally the same group of passengers that join and leave a cruise ship together, and you therefore seldom get any variety at your dining room table.

I thoroughly enjoyed my voyage on the "Chusan" and I was able to meet up with several of my bank contemporaries when I went ashore in the various ports where we had branches. There were a number of people of my own age on board several of whom joined the ship in Bombay and I remember that when we complained to the maître d' that the ship's curries were not hot enough he arranged for a group of us to have a special seating twice a week in the dining room for curry *tiffins*. We called ourselves the Curry Club and we decided that our last *tiffin* of the voyage should be a curry eating contest. I remember that after four plates only two of us were left in the contest and my opponent was a huge Scotsman with an enormous appetite. He managed to eat half of his fifth plate before becoming unconscious and slipping under the table, so although I was only a quarter of the way through my fifth plate I was declared the winner by default!

In Singapore we had a large influx of new passengers, many of whom were planters from up-country Malaya, and two of these planters with their wives joined my table in the dining room, and we became very friendly and I often joined them in after dinner drinks. On one occasion I thought I noticed one of the husbands going into his cabin with his friend's wife but when I saw the other chap enter his cabin with the other wife, I realised that I must have muddled them up and I told them so at our next dinner together. There was a long pause before one of the planters responded: "The thing is Jerry that one day I found Bill in bed with my wife on the plantation so I started to go to bed with his wife, but after a while we went back to our own wives. However, it was such fun that we decided to switch wives again on this voyage, but we will stop this once we get back to the U.K.". This was real life Somerset Maugham.

On one occasion when returning to my cabin after a late session in one of the bars I heard piano music coming from the Music Room and when I entered the room I found it empty apart from a Japanese girl who was seated at a grand piano in a corner of the room. When she had finished playing I introduced myself and asked her to play another tune. She told me that she only played classical music, I continued the conversation, and it transpired that she was on her way to England to study in the Royal College of Music, she came from a very wealthy Japanese family and she had all her meals served to her in her suite as she preferred not to mix with the other first class passengers, which is why I had not noticed her before. Takana-san and I met on several different occasions after this but it was always in her suite and never in the ship's public rooms, and we became good friends. Before the ship docked in Tilbury we agreed to meet each other in London, and in many ways it was a classic shipboard romance.

In spite of escalating problems with Egypt over the Suez Canal our ship encountered no difficulty in either entering or leaving the canal and in fact I joined a group who were allowed to leave the ship and travel overland by jeep to visit the Pyramids and we rejoined the "Chusan" in Port Said where we did encounter some difficulty with the port authorities, and we had to leave without refuelling. As a result of this we made an unscheduled visit to Djibouti to refuel and although P & O had no agency arrangements in Djibouti a small group of us were allowed to go ashore on our own initiative provided we retuned to the ship by 6 pm. We found the town to be practically deserted with most of the shops closed, and the main square had the appearance of a ghost town in a Western movie, so we started to walk down a side street in the hope of finding a café where we could get a beer. At the end of the street we noticed a pile of sandbags and as we approached them a group of legionnaires suddenly stood up from behind the sandbags and we found ourselves facing a line of rifles pointed directly at our heads. We showed the troop captain our passports and told him that we were passengers on a British ship and he replied: "Don't you know there's an uprising here and you are breaking the curfew. Get back to your ship immediately." Djibouti was of course a French territory at that time and we had unconsciously walked into the middle of a dispute over a recently created Territorial Assembly, and we were to read all about it in the ship's Newsletter next morning.

There was a chap from Harrisons & Crossfield on board called Leslie Eaglestone who had joined the ship in Singapore and who had been stationed in Labuan for several years and I remember going ashore with him in Marseilles, which was our last port of call before Tilbury. Leslie had managed to find a French girl and shortly before it was time to return to the ship he asked me to do him a big favour. "Jerry" he said "I have decided to stay on in Marseilles with this girl; she is the first white girl I have been with for three years. Please ask my cabin steward to pack my suitcase and have the Purser send my luggage to the Overseas League to await my arrival, and send the bill to H & C". I remember thinking how fortunate I had been to be sent to Japan instead of to British North Borneo.

We were late in leaving Marseilles and I soon discovered the reason when an Assistant Purser came up to me and asked me if I had any idea of the whereabouts of Prince Christian of Denmark because he had not yet returned to the ship. I told the officer that I had last seen Christian in a Bistro in Marseilles where we had lunched together with Leslie, but we had left him there because he had insisted on finishing off the bottle of

Drambui that he had ordered. In fact Prince Christian's official reason for being on the ship in the first place was to promote Carlsberg, but this made no difference to the Captain and a few minutes later we started to steam out of the harbour accompanied by the pilot's tug which was alongside our starboard bow. Shortly after we set sail another tugboat drew up alongside and I watched with fascination as a double line was slung from the tug to our ship and as soon as it was secured a bundle containing Prince Christian was hauled on board. When the tarpaulin was opened out stepped Prince Christian and he promptly joined me and ordered a double Drambui.

My final shipboard reminiscence concerns my cabin steward. Before we reached Marseilles Fred had told me that he was a bit strapped for cash so would I mind giving him his tip in advance, and this I did without giving it a second thought. I was very surprised therefore to find that on returning to my cabin to dress for dinner after Christian's unceremonious return a new steward was turning down the sheets on my bunk. "What happened to Fred?" I asked my new steward. "Oh, you mean Cynthia" was the lisped reply. "Cynthia is so silly; he tried to rape a waiter in the galley, so now he's in the clink". This would cost me another tip of at least five pounds.

CHAPTER FOUR

BOMBAY AND SINGAPORE

Before recounting my experiences in Bombay and Singapore, which were to be my next two postings, some mention should be made of the time spent between my first and second tours which was accumulated "home leave" on full pay, and which was designed not only as a period of rest but also to give bachelors an opportunity to get married, in which case the prior permission of the bank was required. In addition to this all foreign staff officers on leave were warned not to spend more than six months in any tax year in the U.K. as this could make us U.K. residents and would affect our tax-free salaries.

My companion on the "Canton" in 1952 was on leave at the same time as me, so Harry and I along with Laurie, another junior officer, decided to take a short holiday together on the Continent. Laurie's car was an ancient Triumph Roadster convertible and the three of us sat on the front bench seat where we took turns in driving, and we had a large dickey-seat at the rear of the car which we could unfold and use for additional passengers. However, it was not until we were in Barcelona that Harry told us that he had decided to marry his girl friend in Dundee, so we drove the car back to Marseilles where we put him on a train and Laurie and I continued the holiday together, and when we returned to the U.K. we found Harry's wedding invitation waiting for us.

Our exploits and experiences in Spain and France were both exciting and varied and can best be described as recreational rather than cultural. We spent a lot of time in Barcelona and its outskirts and we discovered that the Catalans were quite liberal when it came to enforcing Franco's restrictive programmes particularly in the back street bars and night clubs on either side of Las Ramblas. In France we liked the beaches and the bars of the Côte d'Azur and to save money Laurie and I would often sleep in our car in a Camping site in the hills overlooking Nice. I think that I drank more wine in six weeks than I had in the preceding four years!

We had planned to spend about a month on the continent but on the way home Laurie's car broke down when passing through St. Pierre le Moûtier and we had little option but stay there for an extra ten days while the car was being repaired with a new part which had to be ordered from the U.K. The town itself was more of a mediaeval village than a town and it had been captured by Joan of Arc in 1429, and her statue stood in the centre of the town square where we spent most of our time in a sidewalk café consuming countless jugs of Montbazilac, which was a regional wine. The local girls used to join us in the evenings, by which time we were quite mellow, and although the townsfolk who were mainly farmers thought we were completely crazy they were very friendly and when the car was finally repaired and it was time to go, they gave us a farewell party.

I spent most of my home leave at my parents' home in Selsey, Sussex and I remember my father telling me that he was glad that I had not joined the Navy because "the Service is not what it used to be" but in fact I think he was pleased with my job in the bank, about which he had previously had some doubts, and he must have known that I would never have been happy with Navy discipline. Another thing I remember about this holiday was that my father did not like me chatting up the local girls in our Selsey pubs, one of whom was our gardener's daughter, so I was forced to drive my rented car to more distant pubs where our family was not known, because village life in Selsey was still very insular in those days. The owner of the local hardware shop even refused to repair my radio because it was Japanese.

I made frequent visits to London while in the U.K. and when there I used to stay at either the Overseas League off the Haymarket or the Victory Club in Marble Arch. On one such occasion I invited my shipboard pianist friend Takana-san to a ballet at Sadler's Wells and I had purchased two centre seats on the fifth row of the Orchestra Stalls, but the entire evening turned out to be a total disaster. When I collected Takana-san in a taxi I was surprised to discover that she was dressed in full Japanese traditional dress, and I stupidly took her into the Overseas League for a pre-theatre drink. Not only did everyone stare at us, but after a while a footman came up to me in the Lounge Bar and asked me to leave the club as my guest was not welcome there. I had totally forgotten that the main membership of the Overseas League in those days was drawn from the colonies and ex-colonies, and that the war with Japan was still very much remembered. It was no better when we entered the theatre to see Swan Lake, and I think that we attracted almost as much attention as the ballet dancers. During the interval I took Takana-san back to her Kensington home, and she was in floods of tears because she had dressed up like Madame Butterfly not only to please me but also because she thought it the correct thing to do. I never saw her again.

After returning from our continental holiday I remember going into the bank in London and asking the Senior Accountant if he had any news of my next posting. "Ah yes, Tait" he replied "your posting to Singapore has been changed and you are now going to Bombay instead and your friend's posting to Bombay has been changed to Singapore". What the Senior Accountant did not tell me however was that Laurie had been placed on six months probation and that this probation could be better monitored in the large Singapore branch rather than the smaller Bombay office, and in those days Bombay was considered as a "hardship post". Sadly my friend did not survive his probation and I had been given Bombay instead of Singapore through no fault of my own but simply because I was in the wrong place at the wrong time, but unknown to me subsequent events were to correct this situation.

Although Egypt had nationalised the Suez Canal on 26 July, P & O were still using it until the joint British and French attack on Cairo airport on 3 November, and I was about to book a passage to Bombay on a suitable P & O vessel when Nasser responded by sinking the 40 ships that were passing through the Canal at that time thus effectively closing it to all shipping until early 1957. The bank then advised me that it was my responsibility to start work in Bombay not later than 23rd December and that they would pay for my passage round the Cape if I wanted but any delay in arrival would not be tolerated. I gave the matter some thought and finally decided to take my chance with BOAC and I obtained a first class ticket on an Arganaught flight whose departure from London was first delayed by fog and which was subsequently diverted to Karachi, where we were all put up in a hotel and taken for a sightseeing tour of the city. In the event I did not arrive at Bombay's Santa Cruz airport until 22 December, which was my allotted deadline.

My first impressions of Bombay were not favourable and initially I found it difficult to adjust to my new lifestyle and surroundings. My father had taken me to Veeraswamy's restaurant in Regent Street, where the waiters wore starched white uniforms and turbans with fake rubies, but until now this had been my only contact with the Indian sub-continent. I was appalled at the squalor and poverty I saw everywhere I went and I found it difficult to accept the huge gap that separated the rich from the poor. I did not understand the caste system which placed all Indians in a hierarchy, and which was still very much in evidence, nor did I particularly care for the *Raj* system which automatically gave us *sahib* status. In due course it was inevitable that I would adapt to these conditions, but I was never ever able to accept them.

I was given the job of Number Three in Inward Bills and my specific task was to handle the "snag" bills. I had never worked in an Imports department before and the snags were the problem bills which had gone wrong for one reason or another, and half of the cases were under litigation. The job was complex, and in my opinion it should not have been given to a junior officer without Inward Bills experience, but I was still very much an obedient banker so I buckled down and made the best of it. The officer who was handing over his job to me, and who was four years my senior, tried to teach me as much as he could about the job in the short space of time that he had before he went on leave, and the Number Two of the department subsequently gave me a lot of help. I was to learn the complexities of Imports before the fundamentals, but this was to stand me in good stead in the future.

It was standard practice in the bank to take care of the chap who replaced you and in my case Roger did all he could to help me settle in. Three days after I arrived it was Christmas Day and I had nowhere to go, so Roger included me in his rugger club group but this was not my scene and I knew that I would have to find a different leisure activity if I were to survive my time in Bombay.

Unlike Japan public transport in Bombay, apart from taxis, was not an option for us and to import a car was beyond my means and new cars were expensive, so initially I spent much of my spare time in garages looking for a suitable second hand car that I could afford. One evening I discovered a low mileage 4/4 Morgan Sports in B.R.G. (British Racing Green) which appeared to be in perfect condition, and I asked the owner of the garage if it was for sale. I was told that the car had been impounded by the police after an incident when the British owner was negotiating a roundabout the passenger door had opened throwing out an American sailor who was killed instantly. Eventually, after the owner had left the country, he entered a monastery in Cornwall, the car was still registered in his name and there were unpaid storage fees and police costs pending. To cut a long story short with the help of a lawyer I managed to get the owner to execute a limited power of attorney in my favour, we paid the fees, the embargo was lifted, and the car was transferred into my name, and it was to be my pride and joy for the next two years.

Jerry in his 4/4 Morgan in Bombay

Although the car had a folding hood I seldom used it except in the Monsoon season, but I soon discovered that whenever I parked in the street the seats soon became covered with the butts of *bidis* and stained with the bright red juice from the betel nuts that the Indians chewed and then spat out from the windows above my car. I therefore had a cover made for the car with zip fasteners and the interior of the car could be completely covered when unoccupied or I could unzip a quarter of it when I was driving by myself or half of it when I had a passenger. This gave me a much needed protection.

Our branch was in an area of Bombay known as Churchgate, although this name was later changed to Veer Nariman Marg, and I generally parked my Morgan in a side street underneath a window which was behind my desk. Thursday mornings were leper days as this was the day in the week when the police allowed the lepers to come out of their colony and pass through the streets of Bombay begging for money. The lepers' route took them past my window and the first time I saw this disgusting procession I could hardly believe that what I was seeing was real. All the lepers were dressed in filthy rags which made them look like ghosts, and very few of them had hands or feet, their arms and legs simply being short stumps. Those who could walk or crawl on their stumps did so but those who couldn't were pushed or dragged with ropes in makeshift wooden orange boxes. When the lepers reached my Morgan they would stop and announce their presence with a series of screams and they did not move on until we had thrown them sufficient coins from our upstairs windows. Not only was the sight and sound of these creatures enough to turn my stomach but some of the staff used to heat their coins with lighted candles used for sealing wax before throwing the coins out of the windows. When I objected to this I was politely told that the heated coins did not affect the lepers and in fact it made it easier for them to pick up the coins with their stumps.

The majority of the foreign staff officers in Bombay were bachelors and we lived in separate flats in two large buildings in a Compound on the top of Malabar Hill, which was one of Bombay's better residential areas. On one side we had a view of Marine Drive which was also known as the Queen's Necklace because its lights at night took the shape of a semi-circle, and on the other side we had a view of the Hanging Gardens and The Towers of Silence, which was a Parsee burial ground. The five Towers or *Dakhmas* were black granite structures covered with white chunam dating back to 1672 and they were situated in a secluded overgrown garden which was occupied by a colony of vultures and only the Parsee priests were allowed to enter the gardens. When there was a burial it was the job of the priests to lay the body on a grille on the top of one of the towers, the vultures did their work, and the bones then dropped through the grille into the hollow tower below. This we would watch with binoculars from the flat roof on top of our building but we ourselves were often attacked by huge black crows who would swoop down and take any food they could find, and on one occasion I even had a cigarette snatched from my mouth when I was about to light it. I had a .22 rifle at that time and as I was a crack shot I used to pick off the crows one by one with high velocity bullets as they swooped down on their scavenger missions. Crows are not stupid and after a while they realised what was going on, and we were never again bothered by crows when we went up on the roof.

This was not the case in the nearby Breach Candy Club which had India's largest swimming pool built in the shape of the sub-continent, and a baby in a pram was attacked there by a crow who was after its milk, and the baby had to be taken to hospital. The crows were a constant problem at Breach Candy and the bearers always covered the tea time sandwiches with wire mesh covers to prevent the crows from emptying the plates but whenever you took a sandwich off a plate you had to eat it fast! There was not much else the Club could do about this problem.

It was partially the fun that I had with my .22 rifle and the Malabar Hill crows that prompted me to buy a double barrelled 12 bore shotgun and go in search of something better than crows over the weekends. Game was not that plentiful in the immediate area of Bombay but there were snipe and duck to be taken if one had the patience and there were plenty of wood pigeon available on the way to the airport. Several of us used to go on pigeon shoots and although the pigeon were easier to bag in the late afternoon after they had fed we preferred to shoot them in the mornings because they had less grain in them at that time. We shot for the pot and although most of us were bachelors one of the foreign staff was married, so Ian's German wife Kathi used to have her cook boy make us delicious pigeon stews, and we all contributed with drinks at these communal meals. Although the pigeon were cooked together in the stew it was my pigeon that were the most popular because they were the only pigeon that had no lead shot in them because I had used my rifle to bring them down. This I could achieve on occasions when the pigeon were on the wing, but I found it easier when they were stationary. My pigeon were easily recognisable in the stew because they were the only pigeon without any heads!

One of my "snag" bills customers was a Sikh called Hercurat Singh and we naturally called him Hercules. Hercules imported spare parts for automobiles and in the case of his snag bill the documents we had received from the negotiating bank agreed with the terms of our Letter of Credit. However when Hercules took delivery of the goods he discovered that the motor vehicle parts had no boxes, they were partially used, and they had all been placed together and wrapped in oily newspaper. To quote the exact phrase used by Hercules in his letter of complaint: "There were all my oily parts lying together, naked and unashamed, in a newspaper". This is a classic example of the type of snag bill I had to deal with. Hercules had paid us in good faith for his documents of title, and we could not claim the money back from the negotiating bank because the terms of the Credit had been complied with and no Packing Lists had been called for in the Letter of Credit. As far as I can remember a compromise solution was reached when the exporter agree to send Hercules some empty printed cartons so that he could package his motor vehicle parts and then sell them to local garages.

The Obedient Banker

Hercules, like many Sikhs, was a heavy drinker but as he could not drink at his home he often visited me in my flat where he was a welcome guest because he always brought several bottles of liquor with him, and I would generally ask some other bachelors to join us. On one such occasion he offered to take us out in his car for a meal at his expense and imagine our surprise when instead of going to a restaurant he drew up behind a horse and cart alongside a row of food stalls and we selected our meal from trays which the stall owners passed through the car windows. One of the back doors of Hercules' car was missing as it was under repair, and this attracted several dogs and beggars who tried to participate in our meal. Fortunately I was sitting in the front seat with Hercules, but for me the evening was yet another example of a new lifestyle that I would have to adjust to. I had experienced my very first drive-in Indian Take-Away!

The State of Bombay had introduced prohibition in 1949 and the month before I arrived these restrictions were extended to neighbouring parts of Hyderabad and Madhya Pradesh and it was not until 1960 that Bombay State was partitioned to form the new States of Maharashtra and Gujarat. One of the first things I therefore had to do in Bombay was to visit the bank's doctor who after a cursory examination gave me a certificate stating that I was alcohol dependent. I then took this certificate to the Prohibition Police who duly gave me a foreigners' Liquor Permit. The maximum quota obtainable with a permit was four units per month and each unit could get you one bottle of spirits, three bottles of wine or twelve large bottles of beer. Wine was seldom drunk in those days but we did buy the occasional bottle of dry vermouth for our martinis, although I preferred to drink pink gins. We generally used our units to purchase beer, although we always left enough in our permits to order drinks in the hotel bars who then marked off fractions of a unit for each drink that we consumed, depending upon whether we ordered *chotapegs* or *burrapegs*, and there was always a prohibition policeman in the bar. Every so often it was one's turn to buy the policeman a drink, and sometimes we had to wake him up to do this, but it ensured that our units were not used up too quickly!

We generally obtained our bottles of spirits from bootleggers who smuggled the liquor into Bombay by boat at night, often burying the bottles in the sand at Juhu beach. I was given the unofficial task of acquiring a sufficient quantity of bootleg liquor for the foreign staff and then storing it in the vaults of the bank, and it was distributed on a daily basis as and when needed. This arrangement worked well enough until we received a circular from our legal adviser in Calcutta stating that any violation of the Bombay Prohibition Act was considered as a criminal offence which would render us liable for dismissal from the bank if convicted. The Accountant then told me that my job as i/c Liquor had now ceased to exist and that I should remove all the bottles from the bank's vaults. He also told me off the record that I should store the liquor in a safe place and that he would continue to require at least a dozen bottles of gin each month for his own personal consumption. I always asked a couple of bachelors help me test every new batch of bootleg liquor before purchase, and we seldom had any problems. This was necessary because even if the seals of a bottle were unbroken it was possible to withdraw a portion of the contents by inserting a syringe with a red hot needle and to dilute the contents with surgical spirit, so we insisted on random tasting.

On one occasion we had taken a trial case of bootleg Navy rum which appeared to be genuine and the price was much lower than we were being charged for whisky and gin. One of our bachelors was going to a weekend Yacht Club party and needed a couple of bottles of liquor so he decided to give the new Navy rum a try. On Monday morning his bearer told us that his sahib was ill so we went to his flat where he was still in bed and unable to speak, because he had lost his voice. He wrote us a note telling us that he thought he had been poisoned and we immediately wrote him a note back saying that it was probably the Navy rum that was the cause. The poor man then wrote us another note, which read as follows: "Don't be stupid. Stop writing me silly notes. I can't talk, but I can hear every word you say". We took him to hospital and he was placed on a diet of milk and scrambled eggs until his stomach lining was repaired, and the remaining bottles of Navy rum were returned to an apologetic bootlegger.

There was an alterative to the smuggled liquor and that was the toddy which we called Jungle Juice and which was produced from the sap obtained by tapping palm trees. The prohibition police were constantly discovering and closing illicit stills which were often concealed in attics or underneath floorboards. So successful were the police that the toddy was often distilled in the countryside and then brought into Bombay, and a favourite method was to pump the toddy into the tyres of bicycles which were then ridden into town. We were often invited to toddy parties and we tried to mix it with pineapple juice or even ginger beer, but the taste was so vile that we eventually decided that if you had to drink it then the best way was to swallow it neat in one gulp, in the same way as the Russians drink their vodka. I well remember that towards the end of a Cocktail Party in one of the bachelor's flats we were raided by the Prohibition Police. A few guests without liquor permits locked themselves in the bathroom toilets and the rest of us stood firm while the police checked our permits and the remaining liquor. Fortunately the quantity of unconsumed liquor was less that the total of the units in our permits so no bribes were necessary, although we gave the officer in charge a twenty rupee note as a matter of course.

I had in my possession a Women's Institute booklet on home made wine and a group of us decided to ferment some apples and to produce a quantity of cider to supplement our meagre supply of liquor. I asked my cook boy to buy the apples in the market which we had the servants crush and mix with an equal quantity of sugar, and after simmering the mixture for several hours we poured it into several large glass carboys, the yeast was added, the corks were hammered into place, and the carboys were placed in our wardrobes, everything being in accordance with my W.I. recipe. It was important to involve our servants in this operation and they were promised a portion of the product when it had matured, as otherwise they could have reported us to the prohibition police with dire consequences. All went according to plan and after ten days or so the mixture started to bubble so in anticipation we invited all the foreign staff officers and their wives to a celebration party in a week's time.

At this stage we encountered a problem when my bearer phoned me in the office to tell me that the carboys had blown their corks and that a foaming mixture was coming out of the tops of the carboys. I rushed back to my flat, consulted the troubleshooting section of the W.I. booklet, and asked the cook boy to collect as much sugar as he could lay his hands on. This I added to the mixture, the foaming subsided and we hammered the corks back into the carboys. What we had achieved was a method of double-fermentation which increased the alcohol content, and by Friday night the mixture had settled and although it was still a little cloudy it had a great taste so we poured it into several dozen empty gin bottles, and the party started promptly at noon the next day. When the party was over and as we still had two more untouched carboys we invited everyone back the following morning by which time we had refilled the empty gin bottles, and we started all over again. The party lasted all day until someone suggested we play bowls using the empty gin bottles as skittles. This was an unfortunate suggestion because an unusually fast bowl from one of the bachelors broke several of the bottles and a piece of flying glass struck one of the bank wives who was standing nearby. Fortunately the injury was superficial, but the senior staff decided it was time to leave and it was later agreed that the bachelors had more than repaid the past hospitality that they had received from the married staff.

As a junior bachelor I was allocated three servants a Bearer, a Cook Boy and a Hamal who was also known as a Sweeper. The bearer was the senior position but the cook was in many ways just as important as the bearer because it was the cook who was in charge of the kitchen, he was given the money to buy supplies and the other servants relied upon him for their meals. As my cook was a Muslim he would not cook my breakfast bacon so this became the job of the bearer. All servants in India helped themselves to any supplies of food they could lay their hands on and all purchases were overcharged as this was an established way of life. For this reason all liquor and reserve supplies had to be kept locked up and current supplies had to be checked regularly to keep petty thieving to a minimum. I remember on one occasion I noticed that the contents of my after shave lotion on my dressing table were disappearing so I told my bearer to stop using it and he was most indignant and said the culprit must be the hamal. The hamal was not allowed into my bedroom but he had to pass through it to get to my bathroom as it was his job to clean the toilet. The bearer later told me that he hid behind a bedroom curtain and when the hamal had finished cleaning the toilet he unscrewed the top of my bottle of after shave lotion but instead of rubbing it on his face he raised it to his lips and took a huge gulp before leaving the room, and this was his daily fix. The episode may be difficult to comprehend these days but when my bearer told me about it I accepted it as an entirely normal occurrence.

My snag bills supervisor in the office was a low-caste Hindu called Tawde and although he was not well regarded I liked him because he worked hard, he was straightforward and he had a sense of humour. In those days like many of us I was a heavy smoker and I remember that I kept a cigarette box on my desk which I would refill every so often. As I was smoking far too much I inserted a piece of paper in my cigarette box on which I had written "Do Not Smoke!" and each time I opened the box I saw my message and this helped me to cut down on my consumption. It was the duty of my office hamal to clear my desk top each evening and lock away all my pens, inks, chops, etc and these bits and pieces included my cigarette box. One morning Tawde came up to me and said "Sahib, your hamal has told me how sorry he is and he promises never to do it again if you will not punish him". "Tawde" I replied "what on earth are you talking about?" and Tawde responded: "Every evening when your hamal clears your desk top he helps himself to three or four of your cigarettes from the box before he locks it up, but last night he noticed the little note you had written for him; what a kind-hearted sahib you are, and we all love to work for you".

The longer I stayed in Bombay the more I realised that I was not very popular with the branch manager. Francis, like my last manager in Tokyo, was a member of the old school and although both of them in all likelihood were very able bankers neither of them spared much time or thought on such mundane matters as staff welfare. A Chief Manager of the bank was once asked by a junior officer which was more important to him, his wife or his job, and the reply was "The Bank must always come first", and that is how it was in those days.

The Manager quite rightly expected all his officers to be at their desks when he arrived in the office, and I had evolved a simple procedure which enabled me to comply with this requirement. At some stage during my breakfast my bearer would announce "Sahib, burrah-sahib's car leaving now" so I would finish off what I could of my meal before jumping into my Morgan and charging off down the hill. Both the Manager and the Accountant had bank cars and drivers but even the Manager's new model Hindustan Ambassador was no match for my Morgan and I normally had no difficulty in overtaking him on the way to the office. On one such occasion the Manager's car started to accelerate in an obvious attempt to stop me overtaking, but this idea was beyond the capability of the Manager's driver. It is inconceivable that the driver would have accelerated on his own initiative so I can but presume that it was Francis himself who had told his driver to accelerate in an effort to prevent me reaching the office before him, and these incidents were unlikely to have scored me any Brownie points.

Confidential reports on all officers were sent to Head Office regularly and these reports were secret and were never discussed with the officer concerned. In those days the reports had sections for Punctuality, Attitude to Customers and Attitude to Fellow Officers but it was the Overall Performance which was probably the most important part of the report. It was fortunate that the Accountant supported me on many occasions and I suspect that he advised the Manager that my performance in the office was quite satisfactory even though I sometimes failed to conform to accepted procedures. However there were times when even the Accountant had to reprimand me. An example of this occurred on a Saturday morning when I was summoned to the Accountant's office: "What do you think this is

Jerry, a fancy dress party?" "But I thought you said we could wear shorts on Saturdays" I replied. "White drill shorts with white stockings and shoes, yes" said the Accountant "but not blue shorts with socks and sandals. Get back to your flat and dress properly before the Manager sees you in a pair of blue shorts". Once again I was learning the hard way, but little did I know that some ten years later in 1968 I myself was destined to become the bank's Accountant in Calcutta.

Club life in Bombay was somewhat restrictive because no liquor could be served and although we used Breach Candy for swimming it was the Gymkhana Club that we generally frequented for our social gatherings.

A party at the Gymkhana Club Bombay with the bank's officers and their wives. Note the profusion of Coca Cola bottles

Although it was only soft drinks that could be ordered and consumed openly we all carried hip flasks and the "Gym" had a huge men's changing room with a long line of toilets. We would often sit on these toilets while the bearers topped up our glasses with either soda water or tonic depending whether our flasks contained whisky or gin, and the mixes were served to us on silver trays with ice cubes, swizzle sticks and peanuts, and after a while we would rejoin the ladies and our coca colas. This was an unusual extension of the *Raj* system but we took it very seriously and on these occasions we broke the club's rules by tipping the bearers with a few rupees for obvious reasons.

On weekends however we would try to get away from Bombay and the bank had a beach bungalow at Juhu which was used by the foreign staff and their families on a roster basis. When we were not at Juhu we would explore further afield and there was a hill station in the Western Ghats at Marbleshwar where we used to spend our weekends, and we took our guns with us. It was while staying in Marbleshwar that we discovered a smaller hill station higher up in the Ghats called Panchghani and this soon became our favourite resort not only because the hotel there was more friendly and cheaper than Marbleshwar but the two brothers from Goa who owned it served a fantastic Vindaloo, which was their house speciality. The hotel was built on a plateau which had a panoramic view over the ghats and the area is now popular with hang gliders, although in our time it was virtually undiscovered. It was quite a steep climb by car to get to Panchghani and we often used an old model Singer which belonged to Ben, one of the senior bachelors, who we called Doc because of the bottles of pills he kept on his office desk. We always broke our journey at the Wellington hotel in Poonah, not only to refresh ourselves but also to allow the Doc's car to cool down before attempting the steep assault up the hill. Invariably steam would then start pouring out of the car's radiator so the Doc would stop the car and loosen the radiator cap and we would all sit by the side of the road waiting for the radiator water to cool down before we could continue, and this would happen several times before we reached our destination. Although this annoyed us somewhat the Doc was entirely philosophical about it, he refused to get his radiator repaired, and he insisted that he was the only person who fully understood his car, and that all that it needed was a rest from time to time.

Another popular place to visit was Elephanta Island and this could be reached in about an hour by ferry from the Gateway of India which was an ornamental arch built in front of the Taj Mahal hotel in 1924 to celebrate the 1911 visit of King George V. Apart from the boat ride the attraction of Elephanta was the Shiva cave temples dating back to 600 AD and the huge carved figures of Hindu Gods and Goddesses inside the caves were quite outstanding. Sadly much of their disfigurement had been caused by the rifles and pistols of early Portuguese settlers who had used the statues for target practice.

On one weekend when it was the turn of the bachelors for the Juhu bungalow we decided to invite most of the married officers and their wives to a Sunday curry tiffin party and in preparation we obtained a large quantity of coconuts which we filled with a mixture of gin and home made plum brandy. The party was so successful that after lunch all the bedrooms were occupied by the married couples who told us that they needed to "sleep it off". We thought no more about it until almost a year later when several of the married couples reciprocated by inviting us to Christening parties. The Manager expressed surprise that the wives of so many of his married officers were having babies at the same time, only to be told that it was due to the coconuts that the bachelors had given them some nine months earlier!

The bachelors took it in turns to meet the P & O ships calling at Bombay with newly appointed foreign staff officers on their way to the Chopping Desk in Hong Kong. It was our job to entertain these new officers and the bank paid for this so it was a popular pastime. One of the places that I always took my visitors to was the infamous Cages on Falkland Avenue and Grant Road where the prostitutes behind the cage bars would try to entice customers inside, and although most of the girls were positively repulsive a few of the younger ones were quite attractive, but sadly there was no age restriction in those days and many of the girls inside the cages should have been at school. As one progressed from Grant Road towards Lamington Road the cages gave way to brothels in old wooden houses and the higher class ones at the top of Lamington Road had French madams and Anglo-Indian girls, their window shelves had aspidistra plants and their lounges had pianos. This was where stag parties would often end up.

It was some time after I had arrived in Bombay that my lifestyle there was to undergo a complete change. I cannot remember the exact circumstances under which I first met Vardhini but I think it was at a private party given by one of my Indian snag bills customers, although I cannot be certain about this. In any event Vardhini was the daughter of a well known Maharaja and her circle of friends were entirely separate from the group of people with whom I spent most of my leisure time, who were predominantly bank people. Our friendship developed quite rapidly and it was not long before I was joining Vardhini in the Owners Box at the races and this did not go unnoticed by my Manager and his wife Heather who were both keen race goers but who sat in the Members Box underneath me. This situation became even more difficult when we used to inspect the horses to evaluate their chances before each race and this I did with Vardhini in the Owners enclosure, and I could see Francis glaring at me from the Members enclosure on the other side of the paddock. This situation was not helping my career in the bank.

The Obedient Banker

Vardhini's Birthday Party

Vardhini's friends were a cosmopolitan group and I particularly remember the Consul General for Costa Rica whose name was Makani, and he had evolved a system of weighting each horse according to its placing and I followed this system with some quite favourable results. One day however Makani told me to put everything I had on an aging mare called Isphahan who had been held back on previous races until she had become a rank outsider, and her owner had now decided that the odds were long enough to stop holding her back and it had been arranged for Isphahan to win a short eight furlong race at the next meeting. I followed Makani's advice and as soon as the tote opened I put all the money I had on Isphahan to win and I managed to get odds of thirty three to one. Soon after this I noticed that the bookies were lowering their odds and I considered this to be normal after they noticed the heavy betting and when the betting continued to increase they had panicked and partially covered themselves by putting a large portion of their clients' money on the tote for Isphahan to win, and this caused the final collapse. I was congratulating myself for being able to obtain such long odds when Makani rushed up to me and told me not to bet on Isphahan because the odds had shortened to such an extent before the owner had placed his bets that he had changed his mind and his horse was to be held back again.

I was devastated, and when the horses took off there was Isphahan in an early lead and I waited for her inevitable slowdown but instead of being overtaken she gradually increased her lead eventually winning the race with all the other horses trailing behind her. Makani rushed up to me and I asked him what had happened. "The jockey was told to lose the race" he said "but like yourself he had already put all his own money on the horse to win, so he disobeyed the owner's instructions and made himself a pile. He will lose his job, but I don't think that that will worry him very much". This was only one example of the manipulations which existed in Bombay's Turf Club. At a previous race meeting an objection flag was raised before a winner could be paid and when the club's vet took a swab of the winning horse's saliva it was declared that the horse had been doped and the objection was sustained. Another objection was immediately lodged, the vet's swab was examined, and it was discovered that the swab had the dope added to it before the saliva was tested, so the sustained objection was itself overruled. Betting on the races in Bombay was full of surprises.

As Bombay was considered a hardship post we were allowed to take two weeks local leave after one year and I decided to drive my Morgan to Aurangabad in the neighbouring state of Hyderabad, where I booked myself into a local hotel for a week's stay. The reason for choosing Aurangabad was threefold. The first reason was the absence of prohibition, the second was it's proximity to the famous Ajanta and Ellora caves which were major tourist attractions and the third reason was that the surrounding area provided some good shooting opportunities. My holiday therefore was a mixture of culture and recreation and while out shooting partridge and jungle fowl I was on one occasion joined by the two sons of a local doctor who were on their Christmas school holidays and they became my constant companions showing me each day where the best game was. Peafowl are now a protected species in India but in those days they were a delicacy and I shot a number of them on the wing in the ruins of a temple which they frequented. When in flight peafowl appear to be slow and ungainly birds but in fact they can fly very fast and I learned to shoot in front of them in order to bring them down, and although I gave some of the bag to the hotel most of it was given to the doctor's family.

In the meantime my friendship with Vardhini continued, and on one occasion she asked me if I was considering marriage and when I told her that this had not crossed my mind she said she fully understood this and that she would probably marry a German friend after I had left India, but in the meantime she would like to continue our relationship, and I was very pleased with this arrangement. In due course the Manager of the bank threw a large Cocktail Party and all bachelors were invited to give him the names of their girl friends for inclusion in their invitations, and I duly submitted Vardhini's name. A few days later the Accountant called me into his office and showed me the guest list. "You can't invite an Indian girl to the Manager's cocktail party" he said "look here, your friend has an Italian girl but Paula is the Italian Consul General's daughter and another bachelor has invited the Colonel's daughter so please try to find somebody else to invite instead of Vardhini. After all there is no point in upsetting the Manager more than necessary". I knew Mike from my time in Japan and he liked Vardhini and I knew that he was trying to help me. I told him that I was sorry but I could not withdraw Vardhini's name and I reminded him that not only was she a Maharaja's daughter but that her brother was the managing director of a large Indian shipping company with whom the bank did business. I had stuck my neck out and I would now have to wait and see what the consequences of my action would be.

A few days later I was again summoned to the Accountant's office. "Jerry" he said "I have spoken to Francis about Vardhini, and I was wondering whether or not she would be prepared to perform her famous Dance of the Seven Veils that she always does when I am invited to your flat?" The dance that Mike was referring to was a mini floor show that Vardhini liked to perform, by placing a crystal glass of whisky on her head and then picking up a silk handkerchief from the floor with her teeth, which was no mean feat considering she always wore a full length sari. My response was immediate: "It would be difficult to stop Vardhini from doing her favourite dance" I replied. "Good show" said the Accountant "then that's settled, but don't forget to tell her". Vardhini duly attended the cocktail party and her act was warmly applauded, but I never told her the circumstances under which the invitation had been issued.

The months passed by and in due course I was making preparations for my second year's local leave and I had in fact already made a preliminary booking for a houseboat in Kashmir when the Accountant called me into his office and told me that I had been transferred to Singapore. Many people thought that I had arranged for a posting out of Bombay by dating an Indian girl, but this was untrue. I myself initially thought that the Manager had moved me on because of my friendship with Vardhini but this was only partially correct because the Accountant showed me the semi-official letter from Head Office which was responsible for my transfer. Surprisingly Hong Kong had not singled me out but they had simply told the Manager that they considered his office to be over-staffed and that he should select whichever one of his foreign staff bachelors he wished to go to Singapore. It was no surprise therefore that he chose me, and the snags job in Inward Bills would now be taken over by the Head of the department, who should have had the job in the first place.

I remember asking the Accountant if I could still go to Kashmir for my local leave, but this was not permitted and I was told to complete a Singapore Immigration form and to be prepared to leave as soon as my entry into Singapore was approved. The form was a little complicated and I remember asking my friend the Doc what word I should write in the space for Race and he told me that the correct word to use was Caucasian. The form was then returned by Singapore who replied by telling me not to be facetious but as they did not tell me the correct word I simply inserted White in the new form and this appeared to be acceptable because my application for a Singapore work permit was approved, I sold my Morgan to a Colonel in the Royal Engineers, said goodbye to Vardhini, and off I went to Singapore on 2 December 1958 on the P & O s.s. "Carthage".

The "Carthage" was the third P & O liner that I was to travel on but she was an older ship than either the "Canton" or the "Chusan" and was destined to enter a scrap yard in Japan two years later. There were only two ports of call between Bombay and Singapore and I was entertained ashore in both Colombo and Penang. I particularly remember being taken to the Penang Swimming Club for dinner by some of the bachelors and there were a large number of very attractive Chinese-Malay girls there in sarongs and I remember dancing with several of them. This was in striking contrast to the Breach Candy club in Bombay which at that time had a strict "Whites only" rule, and it was a welcome prelude to yet another new lifestyle that I was about to experience in Singapore. There was not enough time to settle down on board so the trip served as a brief but pleasant respite between jobs, and it enabled me to put India behind me, at least for a while.

My arrival in Singapore on 10 December 1958 came at a time of political change and the events that I was about to witness would entirely reshape Singapore's future. Singapore had been a British colony since 1867 but in its first General Election in 1955 the pro-independence party candidate David Marshall came to power but when talks with the U.K. Government broke down he resigned and his position as Chief Minister passed to Lim Yew Hock. Then, almost six months after my arrival, elections were held on 30 May 1959 and Lee Kuan Yew, who was the leader of the People's Action Party, was swept to power and he assumed his duties as Singapore's first Prime Minister on 3 June, and Britain's Governor Sir William Goode resigned his post to become Singapore's first Yang di-Pertuan Negara. In 1963 Singapore merged with Malaya, Sabah and Sarawak to form Malaysia but two years later Singapore broke away from Malaysia and became an independent republic with the PAP still in power with Lee Kuan Yew at the helm, and Lee remained as Singapore's Prime Minister until 1990.

When the Accountant Derek introduced me to my new Manager, Ian looked me up and down a couple of times before he said anything. "So you are the new Caucasian" he said to me, and I noticed that he was not smiling when he said this, so I told him that I had used the word in good faith in my work permit application. He replied by telling me that Singapore was going through a period of emerging nationalism and that I must be very careful not to offend the authorities, as the last thing he wanted was an irresponsible junior jeopardising the reputation of the bank. I immediately realised that my new Manager was yet another product of the old school but in fact I saw very little of him while I was in Singapore, because once again I was to be a small fish in a big pond. When we left the Manager's office Derek told me not to worry too much about being a Caucasian because the matter would soon be forgotten when they found something better to joke about in the Senior Officer's Lunch Room.

With the decline of business in China, Singapore had replaced Shanghai as the second largest of the bank's branches in Asia after Hong Kong, and we had four appointed officers, the Manager, the Assistant Manager, the Accountant and the Sub-Accountant, as well as a number of Regional Officers, and most of the junior foreign staff worked in either the Cash or Current Accounts departments. There was a distinct and obvious gap in our senior foreign staff officers who were effectively divided into two groups, the pre-WWII staff and the post war staff and this was because there was no recruitment of foreign staff between 1939 and 1945. As and when the "old school" bankers retired their positions were occupied by younger post war staff and this transition was taking place during my early years with the bank. Both the Accountant and the Sub Accountant in Singapore were post war foreign staff.

I was told by Derek that my assignment to Singapore had not been specifically requested by them and that there was no particular person for me to take over from, so I was placed in Inward Bills as Number Two and I was also to assist the Telegrams Officer who was a Regional Officer. As our second tours had recently been reduced from four to three years I only had about one year to go before I was due for home leave, and the Imports job was fortuitous and without it I would probably have spent the remainder of my tour in either Cash or Current Accounts. Inward Bills was the most important department in Singapore and the officer in charge was the most senior of all the unappointed foreign staff, and I was very fortunate to work under him, I had a lot of respect for Peter's banking ability, and he was extremely helpful to me in every way.

My previous experience in Inward Bills in Bombay was useful but I was now also involved in the opening of Letters of Credit which was new to me and I found this work to be fascinating and it also brought me into direct contact with our customers, as we would have to discuss all aspects of the importation before the Credit was opened. Another job that the head of the department gave me was the diamond section as we had recently agreed to have the bank's name added to a short list of designated banks who were authorised to handle the import of diamonds on a consignment basis, and not every bank was prepared to do this because it was time consuming and specialised work, although it was very remunerative because of the large commissions we charged both the exporter and the importer.

Diamonds on consignment were mailed to the bank under double registered and insured mail and after we received the documents and the arrival notification I would collect the diamonds from the Post Office in the bank's cash van under armed escort, they would be placed in my safe and I would inform the prospective buyer that they were ready for inspection. When the jewellers arrived we were locked in a vault, the diamonds were checked against the invoice and then minutely inspected by the prospective buyers. These men were professionals, they screwed magnifying glasses into their eyes, weighed the stones on little scales which they brought with them and each diamond had to be removed from its tissue paper wrapping with tweezers and when the examination was complete, the diamonds had to be rewrapped and replaced in their original envelopes. As often as not the customer would decline to accept the diamonds because the clarity, density or integrity of the stones did not meet his expectations, in which case he would simply pay us an inspection fee. We then advised the exporter of the position and we either returned the diamonds or waited to show them to alternative buyers. All consignments of diamonds were handled as Bills for Collection and they were never shipped under Letters of Credit.

Most of the foreign staff lived in a large estate known as Sri Menanti and there were two bachelors' messes there, the Junior Mess and the Senior Mess. The majority of the houses in the compound were well constructed buildings in the Colonial style with large verandahs and wicker furniture and all the rooms had ceiling fans and the bedrooms had mosquito nets. The landscaped gardens were full of trees and this was a great advantage until later when the bank tried to sell the estate to a developer but the sale fell through because Lee Kwan Yew's wife had all the trees numbered and they could not be cut down.

One of our favourite downtown venues was the *Pasar Malam* at Bugis Street where we would enjoy our drinks with s*atay ayam* or *nasi goreng* while watching the never-ending parade of transvestites, and it was not unusual to see rows of Europeans in dinner jackets and evening gowns seated on restaurant balconies enjoying their late night Singapore Gin Slings. However after Lee Kwan Yew came to power he wasted no time in closing down Bugis Street by converting it into a shopping centre. He also introduced restrictive hours for the sale and consumption of alcoholic drinks and many of our favourite haunts were closing their doors at about the time we were ready to go there. Private clubs were not affected, and I remember joining an establishment called the Golden Dragon Club simply to circumvent the new restrictions. The Tanglin Club was universally popular and Thursday evenings were Guest Nights when dinner jackets were compulsory. I remember taking a foreign staff friend and his wife to the Club while they were passing through Singapore on a P & O ship, but by the time we got back to the ship it had already sailed. I put my friends up for the night and then took them into the bank in the morning to book them a flight to Penang where they could rejoin their ship, and this created quite a stir in the bank because both of them were still in evening dress!

Our main branch in Singapore was in Collyer Quay and although we generally used the junior officers' luncheon room for our tiffins we sometimes lunched elsewhere, and the Singapore Cricket Club was both convenient and economical. After lunch there we would often play the club's fruit machines and on many occasions this activity would more than cover the cost of our drinks and the meal, and there were two reasons for this. The first reason was that the machines were programmed to operate with a very small margin of profit for the club and the second reason was that we had to be back at our desks by 2 pm, so we had no option but to take our winnings with us rather than to put them back into the machines.

Also close to the bank was Raffles Place with Robinsons department store and leading down to Marina Boulevard was Change Alley, where one could buy almost anything from the stalls on either side of the narrow pathway, and we often visited these areas during our luncheon breaks. However on alternate Wednesdays a small group of us would reserve a table in the Elizabethan Room in the Raffles Hotel and I can still remember the crested silverware, the Melba toast and crispy fried onion which we sprinkled on our mulligatawny soup and the pink gins that we drank out of ornate crystal glasses. We then had to slip back into the bank one by one to avoid detection, and during our absence our desks had been looked after by our supervisors.

On weekends we would often venture up-country by driving our cars into Malaya, and Malacca was one of our favourite destinations as my 1952 companion on the "Canton" was there and Harry and his wife Betsy would serve us delicious curries. I had an ancient Chevrolet in those days and I remember while driving back to Singapore late at night we broke down in the jungle, it was pitch dark and there was no sign of life and no traffic, so two of us decided to take a torch and walk down the road until we got to the nearest village where we could get help. Eventually we spotted a light in the distance and it turned out to be a roadside store where the owner allowed us to use his telephone. We phoned the Mess in Singapore and a friend agreed to drive his car out to get us, and I shall forever be grateful to Mike for his help particularly since one of my passengers Brian had a pregnant bank wife in the car and there were still some bandits left in the Malay jungles. The roadside store had all sorts of amazing things for sale and I noticed a rusty tin of Carr's biscuits and several bottles of Guinness on a top shelf which we took back to the car and which we consumed while we were waiting for Mike to take us back to Singapore. The biscuits were stale and the Guinness was flat but we enjoyed them nonetheless.

My original posting to Singapore had been changed to Bombay while on leave because I was in the wrong place at the wrong time and I had later been sent to Singapore because I was no longer needed in Bombay. Now things were to be reversed because I suddenly found myself to be in the right place at the right time, and it all happened without any warning. The Manager of Ipoh, which was one of our small up-country branches in Malaya, was suddenly taken ill and a replacement Manager had to be found at short notice. The man chosen to fill the vacancy was the head of my department but someone had to take over his job first and Peter recommended me. I was therefore called in to see the Manager and he asked me if I was sure that I could take charge of the department in 24 hours and then run it properly, and I assured him that this would be no problem. The Accountant later told me that the Manager was very hesitant in giving me the job but he had given in when the head of the department told him that in his opinion I was the only person in the office capable of taking over the job at such short notice. As soon as this became known several of the senior officers who were in charge of smaller departments thought that they should have been given the job and they petitioned the Manager accordingly, but he refused to change his mind and I remained in charge of Inward Bills until I went on leave.

It was shortly after I took charge of Inward Bills that I was asked by one of our important customers if the bank would consider helping him with a very complicated transaction which involved the netting of prawns in the Indian Ocean with trawlers, the shelling and de-veining of them en route to Japan and the subsequent transhipment and importation of the processed prawns into the U.S.A. I suspect that my customer had already mentioned this proposition to my predecessor, who might have been reluctant to pursue it, but I was very excited by it as the value of the overall transaction was large, the profit element was considerable and our customer offered to pay us double the commission that we normally charged on back-to-back credits, which was the method to be used in the operation. Back-to-back documentary letters of credit are tricky and potentially dangerous and Thomson's Dictionary of Banking defines a back-to-back credit as one arranged in favour of the original supplier of the goods on the strength of a credit already opened in favour of the middleman by the ultimate purchaser. When the goods are first paid for the middleman substitutes his own invoices and the documents are presented for payment at the bank of the ultimate purchaser, the middleman's profit being the difference in price, less expenses, and in this instance the middleman was of course my customer.

There are two important golden rules when dealing with back-to-back credits and the first rule is that all aspects of the master credit should be repeated in the secondary credit and that no additional aspects in the secondary credit should conflict with any of the provisions of the master credit. The second golden rule is that the shipment and expiry dates of the respective credits should be sufficiently spaced to allow both for transhipment of the goods as well as the preparation, negotiation and dispatch of the new documents for the master credit. In the case of the prawn shipment there were two obvious deviations to the first golden rule, because the secondary credit would cover fresh prawns, whereas the prawns to be imported into the U.S. under the master credit had to be shelled and de-veined. The second deviation was that the master credit called for a certificate of Japanese origin and although the prawns were to be transhipped in Kobe they would actually have been caught in the Indian Ocean so their country of origin was obscure, to say the least. The transaction was further complicated because Singapore was neither the point of origin nor the destination of the goods and although it would be my department who would open the secondary credit it would be our Outward Bills department who would have to negotiate the substituted documents drawn under the master credit and then send them to the paying bank in the States in time for the prawns to be cleared and paid for at their destination. I therefore discussed these arrangements with my opposite number in Outward Bills and Mike agreed to handle the negotiation on the understanding that I took full responsibility for the entire operation.

My department was under the direct control of the Assistant Manager and all Letters of Credit which were signed by me were rechecked and countersigned by the Assistant Manager. In the case of unusual credits, such as Nemazi's back-to-back prawns, I would of course discuss the proposed operation with the Assistant Manager before taking any steps to open the credit. I warned Maurice in advance that I had a complicated back-to-back proposal and he told me that he would be pleased to discuss it with me as soon as I had complete details. It was with some trepidation that I entered his office a few days later, I was told to sit down, and Maurice then asked me the same questions that I had asked Nemazi and I gave him the same answers that Nemazi had given me. "What happens if the trawlers don't catch any prawns?" he asked. "Then both credits will expire unutilised" I replied. "How can you be sure that the prawns will be properly peeled and de-veined before they arrive in Japan?" "The Indian fishermen will be paid extra cash to do this en route to Japan". "How can we be sure that the Certificate of Japanese origin will be issued?" "This has already been arranged with an official in MITI (Ministry of Trade and Industry) in Kobe". It was obvious to me that the Assistant Manager was reluctant to approve the operation but he eventually agreed to it provided we allowed more time in the intervals between transhipment and negotiation, and although this meant an extension to the master credit and a longer period during which the prawns could deteriorate, as events turned out it was a wise decision.

The Obedient Banker

We duly opened the secondary credit and I was kept informed of developments on a regular basis. To begin with everything went according to plan until Nemazi told me that his contact in Kobe was experiencing difficulty in getting MITI to issue the certificate of origin and that he was flying to Japan to try to sort things out. At this stage Maurice told me that he was having second thoughts on the soundness of the operation but fortunately Nemazi returned to Singapore with the certificate of origin which was immediately given to Mike in our Outward Bills department. The substituted documents were then negotiated in terms of the master credit with only a week to go before its expiry date, and when they were accepted and paid for by the American importer we all breathed a sigh of relief. Nemazi invited the Assistant Manager and myself to a celebratory Chinese banquet and the featured main dish was several huge pan fried jumbo chilli tiger prawns served on a sizzling platter. Although Maurice congratulated me on the successful conclusion of the operation he asked me never again to recommend any further back-to-back credits of this nature. I was half expecting this because Maurice had a reputation as an experienced but cautious banker, and it was not long after this that he was transferred to our Head Office in Hong Kong where he was appointed the bank's Deputy Chairman.

The bank's senior bachelors in Singapore in 1959. L to R: Peter Wrangham, Jerry, Billy Young, Robin Campbell, David Livesey, Roy Gault and John Knight

It was not long after the prawn shipment that I was given another lucky break but this time it was to affect my accommodation and not my work in the bank. A new influx of junior bachelors had overstretched the capacity of the senior mess in Sri Menanti so two of us were asked by the Accountant if we would like to move into a bank flat in Macdonald House above our Orchard Road branch which was normally occupied by a married couple.

Billy and I had no hesitation in accepting the offer to move and the arrangement worked out very well for us as our new flat was both comfortable and centrally situated, and we considered ourselves very fortunate to have a flat to ourselves, rather than having to share the facilities of the Senior Mess. It was while I was living in Macdonald House that I met an American girl who had recently arrived in Singapore to take up a position with the U.S. Information Service in their Consulate General. I was already dating a girl from the Consulate at that time but this came to an abrupt halt after I met Virginia and it was not long after we met that she became my fiancée, even though I realised that I was on the rebound from an earlier infatuation that was not to be. Gini had been married previously and was five years older than me but we got along well together at that time and as I was approaching the end of my tour we agreed to get married in Singapore just before my departure.

Although engaged, I was still frequenting my favourite bars with my friends and it was not long before I began to notice that I was being followed by the same man each time I went into a different bar, so one evening I decided to put a stop to this annoying situation. When entering a new bar therefore instead of going inside I hid behind the door and when my tail walked in I stepped out in front of him and asked him why I was being followed. He immediately showed me his ID which indicated that he was a Marine corporal attached to the American Consulate and he told me that his job was to check out my nocturnal activities to ensure that I was a suitable person to marry a USIS officer. He went on to say that his investigation was now complete and that his report would be favourable, so I told him that I would send him an invitation to our wedding.

The marriage took place on 16 January 1960 in the Singapore Wesley Methodist Church with my flat mate Billy as Best Man and the reception was held in the Sub-Accountant's residence in Sri Menanti, and I was most grateful to Norman and June for letting us use their house on this occasion. There were almost as many American diplomatic staff at the reception as there were British bankers, but fortunately for me all the champagne consumed was from the Consulate's duty free PX and my friends took full advantage of this. Our honeymoon was spent on the m.s. "Oranje" which was the Nederland Line's flagship, and this was to be one of her last voyages before her refit in Amsterdam.

The "Oranje" was a very friendly ship with a predominantly Dutch and Indonesian crew and the stewards allocated to our first class cabin were a husband and wife team who served us breakfast in our cabin each morning. After we had set sail I discovered that I had been selected to be the organiser of the passengers' deck sports and when I asked the Purser why I had been chosen he told me that the position was always taken by a Briton and they had very few young British passengers on board. Before disembarking at Southampton we had a Gala Dinner followed by a Fancy Dress Parade and I won first prize by putting on a wig and entering the competition in drag as an Indian prostitute with a cushion and a couple of oranges pushed under my sari, and nobody knew who I was until I took off my wig when accepting my prize from the Captain. This was not the last time that I was to choose an alternative line to P & O, and the bank allowed this provided the cost of the voyage was within the P & O equivalent.

CHAPTER FIVE

COLOMBO AND CALCUTTA

The m.s. "Oranje" arrived in Southampton in February 1960 and initially my wife and I stayed with my parents but this was not a very satisfactory arrangement so I rented a caravan which we kept in a campsite in Selsey, and this gave us more independence than we would have had staying with my parents, and we did quite a bit of travelling in the U.K. meeting different friends and relatives My new posting had not yet been advised to us, so we bought the cheapest tourist class tickets we could get on the Cunard R.M.S "Queen Mary" from Southampton to New York, arriving there on 3 May. We stayed in New York for several days and we had already purchased visitors $99 coast-to-coast Greyhound Line coach tickets before leaving England and these tickets took us all over the States including a visit to my new father-in-law Dr. Dyer who was the Principal of a college in Oklahoma City. We even managed a diversion to Las Vegas as well as visiting my new brother-in-law Chuck in New Mexico and we stayed with him in his house in the atomic missile site complex in Los Alamos where he was one of the architects who had designed the original secret launching pads there. I was then advised of my next posting which was Colombo, and although I had a travel allowance equivalent to the first class P & O fare from the U.K. to Ceylon, this was not nearly enough to cover the cost of our travels so rather than retrace our steps to Europe we bought tickets for a cabin on a Dutch cargo ship the s.s. "Bengalen" which was sailing to Colombo from San Francisco and which we thought would get us to our destination in time.

The ship was taking on a deck cargo of dynamite and the longshoremen who were loading it in San Francisco when we boarded went on strike, and our sailing was badly delayed so we used the ship as a base going ashore each day until the ship finally sailed. There were only ten passengers, a missionary and his wife occupied one cabin and their two children were in another cabin. The other two couples spent all their time playing bridge together and it was twelve days before we reached Manila, which is the longest time I have ever travelled on a ship without the sight of land. We seldom ever saw another ship and in fact the ocean was so deserted that the Captain allowed one of his officers to fire off two distress flares to celebrate the fourth of July to the delight of the American missionary family. The Captain also had a canvas swimming pool erected on the deck which was mainly for the use of the crew although we could use it at certain times of the day, but we were not allowed to smoke on deck because of the dynamite.

When we were first shown our cabin I asked the steward if there was any brandy on board, because that was my favourite drink at that time, and the steward replied that there was only the Captain's Rémy Martin and I told him that was fine by me. Captain Van, as we called him, was a disciplinarian, and dinner was served promptly at 6 pm each evening with Captain Van and his officers at one table and the passengers eating separately at the remaining tables. After dinner we would all adjourn to the lounge where the Captain would often join us for drinks, the missionary family would go to their cabins and the bridge group carried on with their never ending card game. Fortunately there was enough Rémy Martin on board for the both of us. Captain Van constantly told me that it was a waste of good brandy to mix it with soda water and each time he told me this I replied that I would be happy to drink three star brandy with my sodas, which I normally did ashore, but since there was no three star brandy available I was obliged to use Rémy Martin and this made my brandy sodas taste even better.

We did not reach Manila until 14 July and because of the delay I was forced to leave the ship there where I to went into our branch and asked the Accountant to book me on the next flight to Colombo, and Peter managed to put me a on a KLM flight the following day. Virginia decided to stay on board the ship until it reached Colombo but I was lucky to arrive there just in time to take over the Remittances department before the officer in charge went on leave. Interestingly we kept in touch with Captain Van for some time after we arrived in Colombo and whenever the "Bengalen" was in port we would serve Captain Van a curry in our house, which he really enjoyed, and in return he always brought ashore a bottle of Rémy Martin for me to enjoy.

My predecessor in Remittances department was a bachelor who was several years senior to me and we also moved into the house that he occupied, and Arthur and I had lived in the same Mess together in Kobe. Apart from inheriting his house we also inherited his servants who were paid by the bank. In those days most of the bank houses in Colombo were rented and we were very happy with the large old house in Skelton Gardens which was on the outskirts of Colombo and fairly close to Mount Lavinia. The house had a large garden which was so overgrown that it resembled a tropical jungle and it was full of animals and insects. There was a coconut tree and several banana trees which attracted rats as well as a huge banyan tree in a corner of the lawn which had an amazing creeper growing up the trunk and one only had to look at it to imagine Tarzan swinging from bough to bough.

On the first morning after my wife had moved into the house the phone on my office desk rang and it was my wife: "Jerry, there's a huge animal here that looks like a dragon and it's walking across our lawn. Shall I call the police?" Arthur was sitting next to me and I asked him what my wife should do and whether or not she should call the police and Arthur replied: "It's only a thalagoya, which is a cross between an iguana and a giant lizard, and he lives in the top of the banyan tree. He is quite shy and entirely harmless and he only comes down from the tree when nobody is around. Please don't let your wife call the police because they will simply kill the animal to sell the skin, which will then be used for shoes or belts".

Shortly after Arthur had left Ceylon we invited the Accountant for dinner in our house and we purposely seated his wife in an old battered sofa which had seen better days, and almost immediately a mouse jumped out of the sofa and ran across the room. The Accountant's wife then decided to change places, but as soon as she sat down in one of our armchairs her dress caught on a broken spring which was protruding through the faded upholstery, and my wife and I apologised profusely. The next morning I was called into the Accountant's office, and Ken came to the point immediately. "I have changed my mind and your request for a new suite of living room furniture which was turned down last week is now approved". I had been with the bank long enough to know how to get sub-standard house furniture replaced.

Ceylon obtained its independence from Britain after peaceful negotiations in 1948 with Senanayake as its first prime minister, it then became known as the Commonwealth of Ceylon, and it was not until 1972 that it became a republic within the Commonwealth and changed its name to Sri Lanka. My arrival in July 1960 coincided with the appointment of Sirimavo Bandaranaike as the first female prime minister and head of government in post-colonial Asia. This was at a time when restrictions on foreigners and foreign companies under the terms of the Colombo Plan were very evident, and imported items were becoming more expensive and more difficult to obtain, and high levels of taxation were being introduced.

Most of us switched from imported beer to local beer and the best local beer at that time was from the breweries in Nuwara Eliya, the highest town in Ceylon some 2000 feet above sea level where many of the tea plantations were situated. Nuwara Eliya beer came in large green reusable glass bottles and the secret was to first remove the cap to determine whether or not the bottle had been previously used to store kerosene. If not, then the open bottle was placed upside down in a bucket of water and all the glycerine, which was heavier than the beer, would then flow out of the bottle and after half an hour the bottle could then be placed in the frig and was ready for consumption.

One of the delights of Ceylon was the lush vegetation and the profusion of plants and animals, and this made a pleasant change from the more arid and Spartan countryside that I had experienced in India. A second delight was the beaches and the bank owned a beach bungalow to the south of Colombo at Bentota where we would spend weekends whenever it was our turn to use it, and this retreat was commonly referred to as Bentot. In fact Bentot was very basic having no electricity and few other amenities, but this was more than compensated by the clarity of the sea water and the vast stretch of sand fringed by palm trees which was virtually deserted apart from the occasional fisherman. The nearest resort to Bentot was Hikkaduwa which one could reach by walking along the beach, and the main attraction there was to go out to sea in a glass bottomed boat to watch the turtles and occasionally we got glimpses of them mating.

The Bentot bungalow was run by a cook boy called Bailin who was a protégé of the Manager's wife and there was a list of rules and regulations and Bailin took great pleasure in reporting minor infringements and this could lead to a temporary suspension in use of the bungalow, thus allowing the senior management to use it more often! I recall one weekend at Bentot when two of us paid some fishermen to take us in their boat to an outcrop of rocks at low tide where Roy and I collected over 100 minute oysters using knives to prize them off the rocks, and our wives helped Bailin to cook us a delicious oyster pilau for dinner.

We could also visit beaches closer to Colombo for evening swims, and Mount Lavinia Hotel was only a short distance from our house. It was there that we could sit out on the lawns which overlooked the beach sipping our sundowners after a hard day's work in the office, although Sunday afternoon tea with sandwiches was a specialty of the hotel. The Galle Face Hotel was another place we went to on special occasions, especially for traditional British roasts, but we always chose curries at the G.O.H., and I have to admit that the Grand Oriental Hotel, which dates back to 1875, was one of my favourite spots. Almost as close as Mount Lavinia was the seaside town of Negombo which was north of Colombo and we would often drive there directly from the office and dive into the sea from the overhanging cliffs, taking care to avoid the rocks below. At high tide this could be quite dangerous because of the numerous caves beneath the cliffs and many swimmers were known to have been sucked into these caves without their bodies ever having been recovered.

Social life in Colombo was more integrated than in the other branches I had worked in up to now but in many ways it could be surprisingly formal and I often found that sometimes my sense of humour was either not appreciated or not understood. Although my supervisor in the bank was a Tamil, most of our local friends and neighbours were Sinhalese and a few were the descendants of Dutch Burghers. An example of not being entirely understood occurred once when we were invited to dinner by an army officer. How and when we had first come to meet Captain Bandaranaike, who was a cousin of the prime minister, I cannot now remember, but Bandy was a renowned womaniser and he used to flirt blatantly with foreign wives and this we tolerated. Anyway we were having pre-dinner drinks in his regiment's Officers Mess and when I ordered a whisky soda the steward filled up my glass halfway with whisky before he added the soda. I then turned to Bandy and said jokingly "That was a mean drink", meaning of course that the steward had been over generous with the whisky. Bandy then reprimanded the steward telling him to give me more whisky, and no matter how often I told him that my remark had been intended as a compliment and not as a complaint, he refused to believe me. Bandy might have learned some useful military strategy at Sandhurst, but he was not familiar with the humour that can be concealed in an Englishman's over statement.

In Japan the polite form of address was the suffix *San* (thus Tait-San) and the equivalent in Ceylon was the prefix *Sri* (thus Sri Tait), although the word Sri is actually Sanskrit for venerable or sacred. Sri can be used in Ceylon in a great many different ways, and it was also used while I was there as part of a car's registration number. I had purchased an Australian Holden car from a distributor who was one of the bank's customers and the dealer had advised me that the current Sri-3 plates were shortly to be replaced with a new Sri-4 series, and that cars with a Sri-4 plate would have a higher value than the Sri-3 cars. He therefore advised me not to register the car in my name until the new Sri-4 plates were available, so I accepted his advice and continued to drive my unregistered car on the temporary dealers' plates that the garage let me keep. Imagine my dismay when several days later I read in the newspaper that the import duty for all new cars not registered by midnight the day before would be increased by 33 percent. I immediately phoned the dealer and he told me not to worry because the Minister for Transport was using an unregistered Holden that he had bought from him at the same time that I had bought my car, and the deadline for registration without penalty was now to be extended by 24 hours. Not only did I save the extra import duty, but I also got one of the first new Sri-4 license plates.

After about seven months in Ceylon we had settled in nicely, made a number of friends, and were really beginning to enjoy life when I was told that I was to be transferred to Calcutta. In those days this sort of thing could happen at any time without warning. Apparently the officer in charge of the Securities department in Calcutta had suffered a severe injury on the rugger field, and I had been chosen as a suitable replacement. This transfer would mean a better job but my previous experience of India had not impressed me and I was not at all happy with the transfer but I had little option but to accept it gracefully as an obedient banker. In actual fact I was at that time in the final stages of acquiring the accounts of the American Embassy for our bank, as our neighbour was the Political Officer in the Embassy and we had become good friends mainly because my wife was an ex-employee of the American Consulate General in Singapore, and there were no American banks in Colombo at that time. My pending transfer however interrupted the negotiations and we were unable to obtain the Embassy accounts before I left Ceylon. As expected I sold my car at a small profit and as a concession my wife and I were given permission to book a passage on the P & O s.s. "Himalaya" to Bombay where we would take an overnight train to get to Calcutta. This was an unusual concession for the bank to make not only because my presence was needed urgently in Calcutta but also because the "Himalaya" was a one-class vessel and we were normally expected to travel first class.

We sailed from Colombo on 14 March 1961 but I cannot remember anything particularly exciting about our short trip on the "Himalaya" apart from the fact that the atmosphere on board was very jovial and relaxed, and this may have been because the ship was on the last cruise of that particular run. I recall the ornate wooden carvings above the main bar of the ship and the generosity of the officers who were constantly buying us drinks but all too soon we arrived in Bombay, and it was time to disembark.

What I do remember very clearly was the long line of coolies we had with us on the platform at Bombay's Victoria Terminus. All our belongings had been taken off the "Himalaya" and put in a lorry to get from the port to the VT railway station. We had several steamer trunks and a number of wooden crates containing our worldly possessions and these were carried by the coolies on bamboo poles along the platform and placed in the goods van at the rear of the train, and I was given a signed copy of the manifest. We ourselves would be travelling in an air-conditioned class sleeper carriage and the journey from Bombay to Howrah railway terminus in Calcutta took two nights and one day or two days and one night depending upon the time one left, and our journey was to be for two nights and one day. The food and drinks available on the train and at the stations we stopped at were of dubious quality so the bank gave us a huge icebox which was placed in the centre of our carriage and this icebox contained enough provisions and drinks to last us during our journey, and the ice box was one of several that bank officers and their families used each time they took train journeys.

This was my first experience of travelling on the Indian railway system and anyone who has read John Masters' book "Bowani Junction" or seen the film will have an idea of the thrill derived from this mode of travel. The sheer mass of humanity that is crammed onto the platforms of the stations where the train stopped or passed through is overwhelming, and everywhere we looked there were crowds of hawkers with trays of food and merchandise, and there were even barbers with stools on the platform where you could sit and get a shave before continuing on your journey. Railway police, stray dogs, beggars, porters and an occasional sacred cow completed the picture, and to draw back the window curtains to view this bedlam from the tranquillity of your private carriage is an experience never to be forgotten. At larger stations the train would stop for up to half an

The Obedient Banker

hour and five minutes before departure passengers were advised by loud speakers to return to the train, and as soon as it left the ticket inspectors did their rounds, and I think we had our tickets clipped at least a dozen times.

Calcutta owes its origin to the East India Company, and the city was founded in 1690 at a point in the River Hooghly where the company's clippers could no longer continue their journey up stream due to the silt in the river. This spot therefore was where the EIC were forced to unload their cargoes and the fact that the area was inhospitable swampland below sea level made no difference to the traders, and warehouses were constructed on the riverbanks to store both the imports and the exports. After discharging their cargoes the ships were then re-loaded with cotton, silk, indigo, saltpetre, tea and opium before returning to Europe, and later on to the Americas. Calcutta then expanded rapidly and soon became the capital city in India during the British Raj until 1911, and it is still one of the largest cities in India and is the capital of the State of West Bengal. When the bank opened its branch in Calcutta in the late 1860s West Bengal was a major centre for jute production and the surrounding mills processed the jute that was traditionally shipped to Dundee in Scotland. The bank became heavily involved in financing this trade but by the 1950s the market for jute had declined due to the emergence of synthetic fibres such as nylon and polythene.

Upon arrival we were told that there was not yet any accommodation available for us but arrangements had been made for us to move into a guest room with the Accountant and his wife in Sunny Park. I had served with John in Osaka and he and Janie were very hospitable and did their best to make us comfortable but the arrangement was restrictive to say the least, so under pressure from my wife I asked the Manager for an alternative and it was agreed that we could move into a downtown boarding house. Here the situation was not that much better because the place was primitive and we were obliged to hire a bearer to take care of us and he had a charpoy in the corridor outside our room door on which he sat during the day and slept on during the night. We were not at all happy and we were missing our old house and garden in Colombo, but eventually a bank flat in Middleton Mansions became available, and we moved in.

Middleton Mansions was a block of flats close to Calcutta's main thoroughfare Chowringhee which the bank shared with the Chartered Bank and the National Bank of India and although adequate our accommodation in no way compared to the house we had occupied in

Colombo. Our servants were supplied and paid by the bank and when we moved into our flat they were already living there and they treated us almost as intruders. This was our first major encounter with Bengalis and it was not a particularly pleasant introduction to our new lifestyle. The main problem centred on the kitchen which the cook considered to be his private domain and although my new *memsahib* was welcome to inspect his kitchen from time to time she had no right to interfere with how he had organised things there. My wife had other ideas and eventually with the help of two other bank wives living in the same block a compromise was reached until we were able to get a new cook.

The bank's branch in Calcutta was its main office in India and it was an imposing building on a corner of Dalhousie Square. The Securities department was an important department for the branch because many of our customers were members of the Indian aristocracy and much of their family fortunes were deposited in our vaults, including those of the old Nepalese Royal Family. My Vault was lined with steel cabinets with lockable sliding drawers reaching half way up to the ceiling and on one side were the Safe Custody items, which were free of any lien or encumbrance, and on the other side were the Securities items which were mainly collateral for the branch's loans and advances. At that time bearer debentures were a very popular form of investment and since they were not registered their ownership was unknown to both the issuing authority and to the government, and dividends therefore could not be individually allocated. For this reason all the bearer debentures had detachable coupons and it was my job to detach these coupons from time to time and to collect and distribute the dividends to the beneficial owners as and when they became payable.

All stocks and shares pledged as collateral to secure advances were registered in the names of the bank's nominees rather than remaining in the names of our customers, and the Accountant and I were the appointed nominees of the branch. This meant that not only did we both have to sign blank transfer deeds to be kept with the share certificates in order to make them marketable but we also had to register our powers of attorney, and sometimes the powers of attorney of past nominees, with the respective companies whenever shares were bought or sold. Since the Calcutta Stock Exchange was very active at that time and as our customers often asked the bank to place their buy and sell orders on their behalf, we were kept very busy and we allocated the actual purchase and sale part of this business to brokers and we split the commission with them. In retrospect the entire procedure was archaic but there was nothing that I could do about it at the time.

The Securities department operated under a system of dual control whereby all deposits and withdrawals were checked and signed for by both the Accountant and the head of the department, although the contents of the vault were under my sole signature. When I arrived in the branch I had no department head to take over from and it was necessary for me to physically check the entire contents of my Securities vault and this task took me almost two months to complete. Fortunately this did not extend to the majority of the sealed parcels and boxes in Safe Custody which we accepted on a "Contents Unknown" basis, but in cases where the bank had given receipts for specific items I had to check them and I have never before nor since had my hands on such a huge collection of jewellery, gold bars, title deeds and bundles of shares and debentures.

The Securities Vault had a massive reinforced steel door with two combination locks, one combination being held by the Accountant and the other by myself. Inside this outer door was another grille door also with double locks for which both the Accountant and I had separate keys. During the day I was constantly entering and leaving the vault and whenever I needed access I had to ask the Accountant to open up the grille door for me and as soon as I entered the vault the Accountant locked the door behind me. When I was ready to leave the vault I pressed a bell on the inside wall and the Accountant would then open up the vault to let me out at the same time checking whatever I was removing from the vault and initialling the corresponding voucher. This same procedure was followed for everything new that was taken into the vault. When I questioned the necessity of this complicated arrangement with the Accountant John told me that it was standard procedure for a securities vault under dual control, that it had been in use for over fifty years and that I should adhere to the system without any deviation, as had numerous Securities officers before me. Once again I was to fulfil my role as an Obedient Banker.

John was an effective Accountant with a positive attitude, he and the Manager Joe were a close team, and John was later to assume the Manager's job before his promotion to Deputy Chairman. Pay day in Calcutta at the end of each month was presided over by the Accountant, and as few of the local staff maintained current accounts most of them had their salaries paid to them in cash and after they assembled the Accountant would call out their names and one by one they came forward and signed for the cash they received in a leather bound register.

Three of my department babus' names were *Dickshit* and John took great delight in calling out their names "Dick Shit Number One" "Dick Shit Number Two" and then "Dick Shit Number Three" with a deadpan expression. Although I found this amusing to begin with I changed my mind when the senior Dickshit told me that his name in India was pronounced *Dikkit* and it was only our Anglicised spelling that produced an unfortunate association of words, and would I please ask the Accountant to use the Indian pronunciation of his name in future. When I relayed this request to John he answered me as follows: "I read it as I see it. Their names are Dickshit, so Dickshits they shall remain". John could be stubborn at times and he was a formidable man in many ways with only one eye as he had reportedly lost his second eye in a game of conkers at school and this had been replaced by a glass eye which could be quite disconcerting. John knew that his nickname was "Cyclops" after the mythological giant with a single eye in the middle of his forehead, and it is possible that this had something to do with his attitude although this did not affect the respect that the staff had for him as an efficient administrator. In the difficult conditions that prevailed in India sometimes a sense of humour was essential in order for the foreign staff to maintain our equilibrium.

The climate in Calcutta was generally hot and humid, with heavy rain during the monsoon season, and although the winter months were much cooler this was when the street sleepers lit cow dung fires not only to keep warm but also to cook their evening meals. The pungent smoke from these fires then mingled with the fog that drifted in from the surrounding swamps, and from the mist that the Hooghly River produced, and the resulting smog that hung over the city was unpleasant in the extreme.

West Bengal is the most densely populated State in India and one aspect of Calcutta was that it was virtually impossible to get away from people and wherever we went we were followed by beggars, hawkers, children and dogs and whenever we stopped anywhere crowds would gather. Unlike Bombay there were no beaches or hill stations nearby so clubs and cocktail parties formed a major part of our leisure activities, but fortunately we did not have prohibition to contend with. The Bengal Club was for *burrasahibs* and the Calcutta Club was for *chotasahibs* so I joined the Saturday Club commonly known as the Slap and the Light Horse Bar there, with its famous relics and trophies soon became one of my favourite watering holes.

Despite the active social life, Calcutta could be claustrophobic and most of us felt the need to get away from things whenever we could, particularly at the weekends. Unlike many of my colleagues I did not at that time play golf, but as Calcutta was surrounded by paddy fields and scrubland there was some small game to be found there, so I gradually started to spend more and more of my spare time out shooting, and snipe and duck figured prominently in my bag. This activity did not appeal to my wife so I used to join several friends for weekend shoots and we pacified our wives by bringing back the day's bag for an evening meal.

A German friend of mine with BASF was a constant companion on these shooting expeditions and we used to go duck shooting together on a small nearby lake. The best time for duck was at dawn when flocks of them rose from the water and we would then try to bring some of them down before they got too high. This required an early Sunday morning start and Werner had a company Mercedes and driver and he would generally pick me up from Middleton Mansions at around 4 a.m. I remember on one occasion I had settled in his back seat and was about to resume my sleep when Werner decided to open all the car windows. "Why did you do that Werner?" I asked "I'm trying to catch up on my sleep after a heavy session at the Slap, and I need to see what I am shooting at". Werner's reply was not very helpful: "You've had so much whisky that my car smells like a distillery, so I am going to wake you up with some clean Calcutta smog"

Werner always took his pith helmet and a shikari with him when we went shooting and the shikari would decide where we should stop the car. We would walk along a narrow mud bank, with paddy fields on either side, until we reached an area of the lake where the duck were resting and we would then lie down and wait for the sun to rise. When dawn broke the duck took off and the sound of their wings was like a train going through a tunnel and the sight of the silhouettes of these birds against the background of a rising sun is something I shall always remember. We often had competition in the form of fishermen who had small boats, and they laid nets on top of the water which they attached to the tops of bamboo poles sticking out of the water. When the duck took off they pulled on ropes they had attached to their nets and several duck were caught in the nets before they could take off from the water. When our bag was meagre or the birds we brought down could not be retrieved we would give our shikari a twenty rupee note and he bought as many duck as he could get from the fishermen, and we hoped that our wives would not notice the absence of any lead shot when the birds were later cooked.

When in season snipe provided a more exciting and rewarding pastime than duck and we would walk them up in a line without beaters and sometimes the birds were only a few feet in front of us before they took off. You have to be alert when shooting snipe. Early in the season the young birds are very agile and they fly extremely fast in zigzags, constantly changing direction, so you also have to be careful where you shoot. Later in the season the snipe are slower in flight and they are also larger in size, but in order for us all to get a decent meal we needed to bag at least six brace per gun. When we returned to our cars we were caked with mud, but the cold beers in our freezer boxes made the excursions even more enjoyable. It was the Indian Army who originally coined the word "sniper" which derived from the ability of a few of their soldiers to bring down these illusive birds with their rifles, and to achieve this with a single bullet would have been no mean achievement.

My Securities job was relatively easy and I was fortunate to have an excellent supervisor and many of the branch's senior *babus* were in my department because of the confidential nature of the work they performed. The office itself however was not without clerical staff problems and the influence of Jyoti Basu, who was then Leader of the Communist opposition party in the West Bengal Legislative Assembly, was very evident. Our Union organised several demonstrations while I was in Calcutta including some "pens down" and "go-slow" strikes and although the labour unrest we experienced was not significant, it was an indication of the problems that the branch would have in the future.

One of my departmental tasks was to maintain the Guarantees Outstanding registers, and our branch in Calcutta had an unusually large number of Letters of Guarantee outstanding. Guarantees are generally issued in order to avoid the payment of a debt and they are therefore contingent liabilities with contra accounts in the bank's balance sheet. Although each guarantee had a clause stating that it was conditional upon a claim being received within three months after the expiry date, our lawyer had warned us that this clause was of questionable legality and one of my jobs was to try to remove as many expired guarantees as I could from our books.

I remember two particular guarantees that I was able to get rid of, on the basis that they could no longer be considered as contingent liabilities. The first guarantee was an undertaking from the bank that twenty dozen rolls of pink Harrods toilet paper would not be resold and that the rolls were for the personal use of the wife of a previous branch manager. The toilet paper had apparently been discovered during a routine customs inspection of the luggage of an incoming manager upon arrival in Calcutta and it had been given a resale value five times that of Indian toilet paper, and a substantial import duty had been levied, the levy being waived on receipt of the bank's guarantee. I made the point that even if the *burramemsahib* had only used one roll of toilet paper per week the entire stock would have been exhausted well before the end of her husband's three year tour, my recommendation was accepted, and it was agreed that this particular Guarantee Outstanding could now be reversed.

The second guarantee I remember was a little bit more complicated, but it was also in favour of the Calcutta Customs and Excise Department. One of the bank's customers had imported a horse as a domestic pet and domestic pets were allowed into the country without the payment of import duty. The authorities had suspected that the horse was to be used as a race horse, so the bank had issued a guarantee undertaking that the horse would not be used for gainful purposes, and the horse had been given an inflated value. As with the toilet paper guarantee, this guarantee had no collateral deposit securing its issue, so our customer would not be unduly concerned about it. I remember being particularly intrigued by this guarantee, so I decided to telephone the owner of the horse and I told him that I was conducting a routine check on the whereabouts of the horse and I was told that it had died some six months previously. In my report on its death I added that even if the horse had still been alive it would have been too old to race, so approval was given to remove the guarantee from our books. The reversal of such guarantees might seem to be a matter of common sense, but the bureaucratic red tape that prevailed in India coupled with the fact that the Reserve Bank of India inspectors paid particular attention to our guarantees in their inspections, put these guarantees into a class of their own.

The political scene in India in 1961 was unstable and New Delhi's Congress team of Jawaharlal Nehru as Prime Minister and Krishna Menon as Defence Minister was unpopular both at home and abroad. The Chinese had for some time been building up a presence in Bhutan and Sikkim and in November, when they made incursions into Ladakh, Nehru ordered the Indian Army to block the Chinese advance, which they were unable to do. Then, on 12 December, the Indian Army itself entered the Portuguese enclave of Goa and the Governor, upon instructions from Lisbon, surrendered the Colony to India's armed forces without a single shot being fired. I remember the next day in the bank's officers' luncheon room asking our senior regional officer what he thought about his army's successful invasion of Goa. "Oh" replied Vesuwala "you mean the liberation of Goa. It should have happened in 1947 when you guys handed our country back to us." I was a good friend of Vesuwala, and in order to keep our future conversations amicable we both agreed to refer to the change in power in Goa as an annexation.

Six months later in June 1962, Indian and Chinese soldiers clashed for the first time on the N.E. border and the Chinese unexpectedly withdrew. India took this as a sign of weakness sending their own troops into advanced positions and the Chinese, who considered the Indian action as aggression, then crossed the disputed border known as the McMahon line on 20 October. Some skirmishes between the opposing forces ensued, and Nehru advised General Kaul that it was OK to fire on Chinese troops. A battle then took place and on 26 October India proclaimed a state of national emergency and called on the U.S. for assistance. The Chinese had three well equipped regiments in place but instead of confronting General Kaul's single battalion they deployed south on either side of the Indian troops and the entire Indian battalion was completely cut off and surrounded.

At this stage in Calcutta we were following the conflict with growing anxiety and in the first week in November the British decided to evacuate their women and children from Assam. My wife and I attended an emergency meeting in the Slap convened by the British High Commissioner in Calcutta and we were among several expatriates who volunteered to accommodate a group of British refugees in our flat. We were given several mattresses which we put on our living room floor and the refugees moved in a few days later, the wives bringing their jewellery and silver with them and their children carrying their favourite toys. On 15 November Chinese troops attacked and overran a large area north of Bomdila and on 18 November the town itself was captured. The headlines in Calcutta newspapers read "Chinese Expected in Darjeeling by Christmas" and a full scale attack on India appeared imminent, but on 21 November China suddenly withdrew its forces, declared a ceasefire, and returned its prisoners as they had achieved all that they wished to achieve in India.

Neither India nor China had formally declared war on each other but the conflict was recorded as the Sino-Indian War of 1962, and whereas China's casualties were 722 killed, 1047 wounded and 1 captured, India lost 3128 men, 1697 were wounded and officially 3123 soldiers were taken prisoner, although China claimed to have returned over 4000 POWs. This was a humiliating defeat for India and although the causes were thoroughly investigated and are contained in the Henderson-Brooks-Hagar Report, this report was suppressed by the Indian government and was never made public, and it is still a classified document. When the PLA retreated they left their newly constructed roads behind them and these were the roads on which they had brought in their tanks and artillery which had threatened India's northern states and had caused us considerable concern in Calcutta.

In the midst of all this turmoil and after one year in Calcutta I had become due for two weeks local leave and I decided to go on a shooting expedition with a small group of friends, and Werner was one of them. Another in the group, who was also named Jerry, was the son of a Calcutta broker and he had a girl friend in the American Consulate and it was through Joan that we were able to reserve a shooting block in the nearby state of Bihar. Indiscriminate shooting of wild animals was by now well under control in India and District Officers had been replaced by Forest Officers whose main task was conservation. The block we had secured had been a protected block meaning that it had not been shot over for some time, and we were told that it could contain a large variety of game.

Shortly before our shooting expedition and on a weekend visit to Calcutta's Alipore Zoo I noticed my German friend Werner standing in front of a tiger's cage. "Why are you looking at the tiger like that?" I asked Werner, and he replied "I am watching his movements very closely to understand the animal better, but I am also deciding exactly where to aim my rifle in case we meet a tiger on our expedition".

We had three cars on our shikar, including Werner's Mercedes, and several women including my wife and Jerry's American girl friend, and we would be staying in a remote Dak bungalow in the forest where the girls would do the cooking. While driving to our destination we reached a spot where the road crossed a river bed, but recent heavy rain had flooded the crossing. Two of our cars which were lightweight and locally manufactured made it across the river without difficulty, but Werner had installed a heavy steel plate on the bottom of his Mercedes for protection and when his driver reached the water the sheer weight of the car brought it to a standstill, the engine flooded, and we were unable to move the car out of the swirling water. The PWD were working on the roads nearby and they brought up a jeep and winched Werner's car to the other side of the river, and Werner gave the PWD officer in charge a handsome reward for rescuing his car.

While we were waiting for Werner's car to dry out we talked to the gangs of PWD workers who had collected around us and we discovered that they were being paid 25 naye paise a day, which is a quarter of one rupee. We needed beaters for our shikar so we offered them 50 naye paise a day or a share of the kill whichever they preferred, and we duly selected 20 out of the 50 or more applicants. When we reported to the Forest Officer and showed him our permit which was in the name of the American Consulate he told us that he did not condone the shooting of animals but as we had a proper permit he had no option but to allow us to proceed and he allocated us a Forest Guard who would monitor our activities, although it would be our own shikari who would plan and organise the entire operation. We then assured the Forest Officer that we only shot for the pot and that we would respect his feelings, and we all had a drink together.

During the first few days of shooting we had a mixed bag of rabbits, jungle fowl and partridge and this was sufficient to feed both ourselves and our beaters and their families. We then reached a particularly dense section of our block and our shikari suggested that the guns should wait in line in a forest clearing while the beaters would approach us from the opposite end of the thicket and walk towards us thus driving all the game in the thicket into the clearing where we would be waiting for them. This method is naturally not very popular with beaters because it means that they are walking directly into the line of fire, but it is a very effective method of preventing any animals from escaping. The beaters took a narrow path to get to the back of the thicket and I was in the middle of the line of guns standing underneath a tree in order to get some shade, and our Forest Guard was with me. As the beaters approached us several jungle fowl and a couple of rabbits ran out of the thicket and into the clearing and we picked them off one by one by shouting out "Mark" before firing our guns.

At this stage the beaters were quite close to us and I had just reloaded my gun with another cartridge when there was a crashing sound in front of me and a fully grown wild boar emerged from the thicket and started to charge towards me. The Forest Guard climbed up the tree and I instinctively fired my left barrel which contained a number four cartridge, but this did not deter the animal who was still coming straight at me. My rifle was behind the tree with the rest of my gear but as a precaution I had placed a cartridge with a lead ball in the spare barrel of my gun, and this was nothing less than a miracle. The boar was now just a few feet away from me and I can still see his beady eyes and ugly snout between a pair of tusks as I gently squeezed the trigger. My lead ball hit the boar full in the face and his head literally disintegrated and the animal dropped dead in front of me. Apart from target practice this was the first time I had ever fired a cartridge with a lead ball at a living animal and I was amazed by its effectiveness. I had mixed emotions after killing the wild boar, but I had done so in self defence.

Werner was one of the first people to congratulate me and our beaters were absolutely delighted. We told them that we wanted to keep one of the boar's hind legs for ourselves but they could have the rest of the animal. Our beaters were Bengali Muslims and although the pig is forbidden food they all opted for a share of the kill rather than the 50np alternative. Most of the beaters carried bows and arrows and all of them had knives and in less than ten minutes the animal's blood had been poured into skin pouches, all its flesh had been removed from its bones, and each beater had a large packet of meat wrapped up in a palm leaf secured with twine, which they hung around their necks. I was the hero of the day. There was no refrigeration in our bungalow nor did we have any rock salt and there was no time to hang our leg, which is what it needed, so we therefore roasted it over a log fire for our dinner and although the meat had a delicious flavour it was very tough so we put the rest of the uneaten meat into a curry.

Two days before the end of our shikar we had experienced a lean day's shooting so to supplement the kill we drove slowly along a forest path at dusk with our headlights on. Werner and I were sitting on the bonnet of his car with torches strapped to our guns and we were picking off enough hares on the sides of the pathway to satisfy the needs of our beaters and their families, and our rifles were in the back of the car. Although not illegal this form of hunting is frowned upon in some circles but in our case expedience prevailed. If we tapped the bonnet once this meant that the driver should stop the car and if we tapped the bonnet repeatedly this meant that the driver should increase speed. It was beginning to get quite dark and we were on the point of calling it a day when a large animal suddenly appeared on the side of the pathway and we first noticed it by the reflection of our headlights in its eyes. When the animal started to run along the path in front of us we hit the bonnet repeatedly in order to catch up with it. "It's a cow" I shouted to Werner "No, it's a deer" replied Werner, and the shikari then shouted from the front seat of the car "Sahib, Sahib, tiger, tiger!" When we hit the bonnet, the driver applied the brakes abruptly, and we were both catapulted towards the tiger which had now stopped and was facing us on the pathway. I have always insisted that what Werner and I then did is what any normal person would do in similar circumstances. We fired our guns at point blank range at the tiger knowing that we could not kill it with lead shot but desperately hoping that it would run away without attacking us, and we then flung ourselves into the back seat of the car and I even left my empty gun behind me.

Our Forest Guard had witnessed the entire incident, and he now took charge. After satisfying himself that the tiger was no longer around, he tied several strips of cloth to the branches of a tree to identify the exact spot where we had last seen the tiger, and he then told us that we must report the incident immediately to the Forest Officer. The very last thing the Forest Officer wanted was a wounded tiger in his district so after telling us to return to our bungalow he took the Forest Guard and our shikari in a jeep to inspect the area. An hour later he returned to our bungalow, and he was nothing but forthright. "You idiots have not only shot and wounded a tiger in my district but you chose a tigress with three cubs that she was training in what should have been a safe block for them. Under the emergency powers vested in me by the Commissioner of Forests you are hereby detained and you are required to assist me in tracking down the wounded animal. A curfew has been imposed and at dawn we shall drive a herd of cattle along the tiger's tracks, and if she is still in my district the cattle will detect her presence". I set my alarm for 5 am and when I went to sleep Werner was cleaning his rifles and sorting out a selection of ammunition.

We had no difficulty whatever in following the tracks of the tiger and her cubs and I was very relieved when our shikari told us that the traces of blood were becoming fewer and fewer which indicated that our buckshot could not have inflicted much damage. After two hours the Forest Officer announced that the tiger was no longer a threat, that its wounds were only superficial and that it was no longer in his district. As a result of this the curfew was lifted and we were free to return to Calcutta. This was a huge relief to me, as at this stage I had become somewhat disillusioned with the whole idea of shooting, but it was quite evident that Werner was very disappointed with the outcome when we returned to Calcutta.

It was in 1962 that the Indian government introduced a Gold Control Order whereby all privately owned gold over 14 carats would have to be declared, and thereafter it would be regulated by the central government in a manner yet to be determined. I became aware of these restrictions before they were implemented and I asked the Accountant whether we should warn our customers of the impending legislation because I knew that there was a lot of privately owned gold in safe custody in my Vault. In due course I was instructed not to advise our customers of possible restrictions on their gold because our lawyer felt that we should be careful not to pass on to our customers any information that we might have received in the form of confidential directives from the Reserve Bank of India. I was also told that as our custodian business was remunerative I should not in any way encourage our customers to remove their gold from the bank. I gave these instructions considerable thought and I eventually decided that as and when customers who had declared their gold to us came into the bank then I would talk to them and give them the opportunity to transfer their gold to a "Contents Unknown" parcel, and several customers did this and they later had good reason to thank me for my advice. I was giving my instructions the widest possible interpretation, but I was still an Obedient Banker.

Inevitably in November the bank received a directive from the Reserve Bank of India stating that all gold held by us was confiscated and we were given a deadline by which to hand it over. By then only one large gold bar was held by us so I took the heavy brick into the RBI who verified it and then gave me a 15 year Government of India 6.5% Gold Bond in the name of our customer, and this was duly placed in her Safe Custody file in my Vault. I later learned that the 1982 Gold Control Order had netted the central government 1670 tonnes of gold but that ninety percent of this was confiscated gold and that only ten percent was surrendered voluntarily. The Order was later acknowledged to be a failure, and it was not perpetuated.

Towards the end of 1962 I had been in Calcutta for about a year and a half and I had another year or so to go before I was due for home leave. My experiences in Bihar had put me off shooting so I decided to take up golf and I joined the nearby Tollygunge Club. The premier golf club in Calcutta was the Royal Calcutta Golf Club and they had two 18 hole courses, the Old Course and the New Course. I was occasionally invited to play there but the Royal had numerous water hazards known as tanks and my golf balls invariably ended up in these tanks. Although the forward caddies, known as *agiwallahs*, would often recover my golf balls for a small fee, it was very embarrassing each time I submitted my score card at the end of the round, so I much preferred to play the easy course at Tolly.

I was not very good at golf and I never managed to break my 24 handicap. My friends and I preferred four ball games and as this slowed down other players we invariably waved them on and two ball games had the right to overtake us anyway. We did not mind this at all because the holes at Tolly had numerous shamianas where we would stop to quench our thirsts but staying too long in the shamianas often provoked complaints from other members which we tended to ignore. One of my favourite holes was the long third which was a par 5, and when approaching the green we used our number 7 irons to drop our balls into a group of vultures who frequented the green because it was under the shade of several large banyan trees, but we never managed to secure a direct hit.

The nearest beach to Calcutta was further south at the coastal village of Digha which was close to the border dividing West Bengal from Orissa. Although Digha was only 250 kms from Calcutta it was a tiring six hour journey by car on the Grand Trunk Road via Kharagpur, and the road was always heavily congested with columns of lorries. We then discovered a shorter coastal route where the road met an estuary and then continued on the other side and there was a makeshift ferry there consisting of two boats lashed together which could take our car across the water, so we made several weekend visits to Digha using this route and we stayed in a beachside bungalow overnight. Digha had a long and almost deserted sandy beach fringed by a plantation of Casuarinas and we buried our bottles of beer in the sand at low tide to keep them cool. It was on one of our weekend trips to Digha that we discovered a much better beach in Orissa called Puri, and although it was too distant for weekend trips we decided to spend our next local leave there.

In March 1963 we took our car to Puri and we stayed in a guesthouse on the beach where the waves were strong and there was good surfing. Apart from the beach there was plenty of culture nearby and we visited the Sun Temple at Konark, the Barbati Fort at Cuttack and the Lord Shiva temple at Chandaneshwar. However it was the State capital of Bhubaneswar that intrigued us the most, and after visiting the Jagannatha's temple we had an interesting and rewarding experience in the Orissa State Museum. When we had completed our tour of the museum and admired its exhibits a guard came up to us and told us that the Curator of the Museum would like to see us in his office. We sat down at his desk and the reason why he had asked to see us soon became clear to me. "It is so gratifying to see foreign visitors in my museum" said the Curator "and I can see immediately that you are a keen collector of art and that the treasures we have here are of great interest to you. It so happens that we recently had an inventory taken of our exhibits but by mistake one or two items were overlooked". The Curator then opened his desk drawer and took out a palm leaf ink drawing and what resembled a small oblong concertina with strips of bark between two wooden covers. "This is an antique family bible and as you can see the calligraphy is not Oriya but it has been written in an earlier script which is now a dead language. Perhaps you would be interested in accepting these two little items as a personal gift from me. All I would ask for in return is that you would consider a small donation to the upkeep of this museum, say fifty rupees". I still have the palm leaf drawing hanging in my living room and the bible is in a nearby cabinet.

It was not long after our visit to Puri that we were invited to dinner by my German friend Werner, and the reason for the dinner was to view a tiger skin that Werner had mounted on his bedroom wall. Apparently Werner had finally shot a tiger in Assam but as he did not trust the local people to skin the animal he had placed it in a wooden crate full of rock salt which he then put in the goods' van of a train going to Calcutta, and he had told his driver to take the car back to Calcutta. However halfway to Calcutta a guard knocked on the door of Werner's air-conditioned carriage and told him that as the passengers further down the train were complaining about the smell coming from the goods' van Werner's tiger was to be removed from the train and deposited at the next station. Werner did not tell me how much he had to give the guard to keep the animal on the train, but I suspect that he had acquired a very expensive trophy.

I was due for home leave in July 1963 but my departure from Calcutta was delayed due to the lengthy handover of my department to my successor, and I have never been more ready to go on leave than I was then. I chose to return to the UK on board the Flotta Lauro line s.s. "Sydney" which was to depart from Bombay on 22 September, and we took the 36 hour train journey from Calcutta to Bombay, where we spent the night before joining the ship the following morning.

CHAPTER SIX

HONG KONG, AND PROMOTION TO MANAGER

Our ship the "Sydney" had recently been refurbished and although it could accommodate 994 tourist class passengers the first class complement was only 92 passengers, and when we looked down from our spacious first class decks up forward we could see the cramped conditions in the stern of the ship. The majority of the officers and crew were Italian and our facilities were lavish, to say the least. We had been allocated a small table in the first class Dining Room and when I sat down on our first evening aboard I discovered that I was sitting next to the Roman Catholic Bishop of Bombay who was on his way to attend a Vatican Ecumenical Council meeting in Rome that Pope Paul VI would convene. When we were all seated the Bishop introduced himself and told us that he had a favour to ask us. "Apart from being a servant of God" he told us "I am also an amateur connoisseur of wine. I have discovered that this ship has a small supply of vintage Brunello di Montalcino from Tuscany and I have taken the liberty of securing it for our table, and I would like to invite you to help me finish the wine before we reach Naples". I became a good friend of the Bishop and he told me later in the voyage that he also had several bottles of Brunello in his cabin and this helped him in the evenings while he was composing his Vatican dissertation.

We passed through the Suez Canal on 29 September and after a day ashore in Messina on 3 October we disembarked in Naples, where we had first class rail tickets on the old Rheingold Express to London, which since 1962 had become known as the Trans-Europe Express. What I remember best about this train journey was the magnificent dining car where each table had ornate Tiffany lamps and the meals we had there were a far cry from the meals we had eaten from the bank's ice box on the Indian trains, and it was not until 16 October that we arrived in the UK, which was about a month since we had left Calcutta. I think that this journey was one of the most pleasant trips in my life and the entire cost was well within the bank's travel allowance.

Our previous home leave in the UK had prepared us for our time in Europe and once again I rented a caravan although this time instead of it being a trailer we had a Dormobile and we lived in it on and off until 27 December. We had planned an ambitious winter holiday in France, Spain and Portugal and we initially took the ferry to Boulogne on 1 November. As it was fairly cold in France we headed down to Spain as fast as we could and I remember reaching Andorra on 7 November where I posted all our Christmas cards because I wanted the envelopes to have Andorra stamps, but the mountain pass beyond Andorra was blocked by heavy snow and the police sent us back to France and we entered Spain by a different route. We enjoyed our time in Spain and we stayed in camp sites as close as we could get to the major cities we visited. I remember that we stayed in Barcelona for quite a long time and it was when we were having lunch in one of our favourite restaurants off Las Ramblas that our waiter came up to our table with tears in his eyes and told us that President Kennedy had been assassinated, because he knew that my wife was American.

It was in Portugal however that I was to have a far greater shock. We had finished a dinner of fresh sardines in our Dormobile and before going to sleep I paid a visit to the camp's nearby toilet. I had previously heard a lot of noise coming from the direction of the toilets but I thought nothing of it because this sort of commotion was not unusual in caravan camps. When I entered the toilet the first thing I saw were the legs of a man sticking out under the door of a toilet cubicle and there was a small river of blood running across the floor from the body. The cubicle door then swung open and I could see that the dead man's throat had been cut. What to do? Rightly or wrongly I decided to go straight back to my Dormobile and say nothing to my wife about the incident. Shortly after I switched out the lights I looked out of the window and saw a police car and an ambulance arrive and the ambulance then took away the body from the men's toilet. For some time I watched as the police walked around the camp, but they did not interfere with any of the caravans. The next morning I told my wife that we were going back to Spain because I had had enough of Portugal and as we were heading towards the border I noticed that we were being followed by a police car. When we reached the border we had to go through customs and immigration and I fully expected to be questioned by the police but nothing happened and we were allowed to enter Spain without any difficulty. Viva España!

It was not until 30 November that we arrived back in the UK and during the month or so that we were there I completed writing an article on our camping holiday entitled "November can be Fun" and this article was duly published in the Motor Caravanners magazine. Once again we had decided to visit the States and we were also going to the Bahamas to view a small plot of land I had bought there while I was in Singapore. We booked ourselves on a U.S. Lines freighter sailing from Southampton to Baltimore on 27 December and after spending Christmas with my parents in Sussex we said goodbye to our rented Dormobile and boarded our new ship.

U.S. Lines was a "dry" shipping line so we had been advised to bring our own alcohol with us and I had therefore placed an order with the agents and my liquor selection was waiting for me in our cabin when we came on board. When we set sail the First Mate told us that when unloading a crate of Budweiser beer, which was the ship's cargo on arrival in the UK, the crane's faulty net had broken and the cans of beer had been placed in the galley and that we could help ourselves to them at any time during the day or night without charge. As the First Mate was smiling when he told us this, I could not help but wonder whether he had anything to do with the faulty net. He also warned us that the ship had received a severe gale warning and that as their new cargo was a load of British sports cars the ship was riding very high in the water and we could be in for a rough crossing.

In the event the 1963 winter storms were the worst to hit the Atlantic and the eastern US seaboard for many years and our ship was tossed around on the ocean like a cork and most of the passengers and many of the crew were confined to their cabins. The captain threw a party on New Years Eve but it was so rough that we were all given ropes which we could attach to parts of the ship to prevent us being thrown around. Worse than this the ship was being driven north by the gale force winds and we were told that it would be impossible to make it back to Baltimore, so we arranged for the wireless officer to cancel our Bahamas flights and hotel booking. Finally, on 9 January, we docked in Boston and our 6 day Atlantic crossing had taken us 13 days.

The Obedient Banker

A U.S. Lines representative then came aboard and he told us that he was authorised to give us travel vouchers to get to Baltimore by either road, rail or air but that as the roads were impassable, the railway tracks were blocked by snowdrifts and the airport was closed he would also give us hotel vouchers to stay in Boston until we were able to leave the city. We already had coach tickets from Baltimore to Miami so we were given connecting tickets from Boston to Baltimore. After three days we managed to get to New York but we were then confronted with 20 feet snowdrifts so we once again used the US Lines vouchers to stay in a New York hotel and it was not until 18 January that we finally arrived in Nassau.

After leaving the Bahamas we visited my wife's father in Oklahoma City and it was while we were there that I was advised that my next posting was Hong Kong and this was good news that I had half expected anyway. My wife decided to stay on for a while in Oklahoma with her father and she would fly out to Hong Kong to join me there some weeks later. By this time my travel allowance was a bit thin so I booked myself a cabin on a Norwegian freighter the Barber Wilhelmsen Line s.s. "Troubadour" sailing from Los Angeles on 24 February. What I remember most about the "Troubadour" was the lavish buffet smorgasbord lunches and I have never in my life eaten so much fresh lobster.

When we arrived in Manila on 5 March I went ashore and met up with my old Bombay friend the Doc who was at that time working in the bank's Manila office. In the evening the Doc took me to an unlicensed club on Dewey Boulevard, now known as Rochas Boulevard, and we knocked on an unmarked door on the second floor of a seedy looking building, and after the Doc had identified himself we were allowed to enter. Inside the doorway was a small table with an assortment of pistols and above the table was a notice reading "Check you firearms here". We sat down at a five card draw poker table and after about an hour I had accumulated enough pesos to pay for our dinner so we then beat a hasty retreat. In those days Manila was something like Chicago had been in Al Capone's time.

When the "Troubadour" arrived in Hong Kong on 10 March we were not allotted a berth and the ship was secured to a mooring where the cargo would be discharged onto tenders and the passengers and crew went ashore in launches. It was the bank's custom to meet all arriving officers and a junior member of the foreign staff came on board and introduced himself and we then boarded the bank's own launch the "Wayfoong" which took us ashore, much to the surprise of the ship's crew.

The following morning I was taken to see a sub-manager of our Main Office who told me that there was no specific job set aside for me and that I would be temporarily placed in Inward Bills as Number Three until a more suitable job became available. A couple of weeks later I was again summoned to his office and he told me that there were now two suitable jobs available and that I could choose whichever job I preferred. Although not without precedent, to be given a choice of jobs was nonetheless unusual so I immediately asked the sub-manager what the alternatives were. "Well" he replied "you can either step up to Number Two of Inward Bills, which is one of our most important departments, and which I recommend. Alternatively there is a vacancy in our Mongkok branch in their Books department, but as this is not considered to be a full time job you would have to look after the branch's sub-branches and help with an experimental mainland branch expansion programme". I already had a good working knowledge of Inward Bills procedure and the Mongkok proposal sounded interesting so I knew instinctively that the Mongkok job was what I wanted and I told the sub-manger so immediately. "Ah well, Jerry" he replied "it's your choice and I wish you well, but I'm sorry to have you leave our office".

As events turned out later, I had made a very fortunate decision because I was approaching the end of my period of automatic pay rises based on length of service and I would soon be entering the area where seniority was unimportant and one's salary depended upon the job, and this required an "appointment". All appointments had to be approved by the Board of Directors, but once one had become appointed then all future appointments would be paid at the same or a higher level. Having survived the automatic progression system for almost twelve years I was well aware that I was now approaching a crucial stage in my career where ability as well as obedience would be important factors in shaping my future. Two other factors helped, the first one was being in the right place at the right time, and the second one, for lack of a better word, was patronage. Patronage exists and has existed in all walks of life from time immemorial, and the Hong Kong Bank was no exception. Although in principle I disagree with patronage and I never sought nor encouraged it during my time with the bank, I have to admit that a happy office was generally a successful office and that any conflict or incompatibility between officers was detrimental to the bank and should be prevented or corrected whenever possible. Some managers therefore asked for staff they knew well and this in itself was not necessarily a bad thing.

Upon arrival in Mongkok I discovered that their Books department had for many years employed a Russian Senior Supervisor who was not only an expert in accountancy but whose knowledge of the bank's bookkeeping system was unrivalled, so although I was in charge of the department it was Yvanovitch who was its mainstay. The hub of any Books department is its General Ledger from which the Balance Sheet is prepared and a large number of Subsidiary Ledgers are maintained separately the balances of which all appear in the General Ledger, and it was not until some years later that these accounts were transferred to computers. It was my job to review the monthly, quarterly and annual results of the branch with the Manager and as Mongkok was going through a period of remarkable expansion at the time I was there, these results continued to improve each time I was summoned to the Manager's office. I remember on one occasion he brushed aside the Balance Sheet and asked instead to see the comparative tables for Commission Received and Interest and Discount Received, both of which were Profit and Loss accounts. Fortunately I had anticipated this and I gave him the papers I had prepared for him. After he had perused the totals of these accounts he grabbed me by the arm; "Jerry, just look at this, these two accounts are the pulses of our branch, and it's good to see them both throbbing madly". Martin was shortly to be promoted to a senior position in Head Office, and I too was soon to get my first appointment.

The bank had a large and modern compound on Fei Ngo Shan Road off Clearwater Bay Road on the mainland and this was occupied by many of the married officers of both our Kowloon and Mongkok branches, including my own Manager and Accountant. I was given one of the semi-detached houses in this compound and although it was a little remote the accommodation was spacious and comfortable and provided a totally different style of living to that of the huge blocks of flats that many of our junior officers occupied on the mid levels of Hong Kong island, which was already becoming congested. When my wife arrived from the States she was very happy with our new accommodation, and the atmosphere in the compound was friendly with lots of parties in each others' houses.

Shortly after moving into the Clearwater Bay compound a number of the Chinese servants there quit their jobs, and our cook boy told me that the cause was bad *feng shui*. *Feng shui*, which literally means wind and water, is an old Chinese belief that is based on harmony and balance, particularly where the positioning and design of buildings and structures are concerned. Our compound was on the top of a hill with an excellent view of the sea and when it was built care was taken not to disturb a number of Chinese graves that were on the site. My cook however was adamant that the spirits in these graves were restless and he told me that he had seen *kwais* floating around the compound, and that the best time to see them was at midnight when there was a full moon.

I decided to test my cook boy's theory and I waited until the next full moon and at 11.30 pm I took my brandy and soda out onto my verandah, switched off the lights, and I then waited for the ghostly *kwais* to appear. To my amazement at exactly midnight I noticed a white figure slowly passing through the compound, and every so often the figure stopped for a short period before continuing its journey, and eventually it disappeared over the top of a mound at the far end of the swimming pool, which was where the graves were. I then went to the spot where I had last seen the figure and there was our night watchman in his white uniform inserting his watchman's key into a time clock at the most distant of his routine check points. I reported the incident to the Accountant next morning and the Manager later called me into his office. "I really have to thank you for taking the trouble to investigate the complaints of our servants" Martin said to me, "I think you have solved the *kwai* problem, but don't ever underestimate the importance of *feng shui*".

Although I enjoyed my work in Books department it was my job with the sub-branches that was both exciting and challenging. When I first arrived in Mongkok I had five sub-branches with Chinese managers under my control and it was my job to monitor their activities and assist them with any operational problems they might have. I would visit my sub-branches every afternoon and I undertook routine checks of their ledgers and I would periodically count their cash.

The main activity of these sub-branches was their Savings Bank accounts and these deposits were used to finance factory loans in Mongkok. The bank's Compradore would provide the staff for all new sub-branches and our Property department would provide all the equipment ranging from furniture and stationery right down to kitchen utensils, as each branch had on site cooking facilities, but there was no clear procedure in force for selecting sites for new branches. I was therefore asked to assist with this and I started off with a street map of our area on which I marked my five existing branches and I divided the map into separate sections which I thought would be suitable for new branches. I then visited each section until I found a vacant shop house or a suitable site, and as soon as I had identified myself as an officer of the Hong Kong Bank the owner would become very excited because he knew if we opened a sub-branch in his premises it would increase his prestige and all the surrounding stores and shops would benefit by having a branch of the bank nearby. All that I then needed to do was to give details of the site to the Manager of our Property department, and the rest would be up to him.

It may seem strange that such a basic procedure was all that was needed but the circumstances at that time were favourable and in less than one year our Property manager Norman and I had opened no less than ten new offices and I then found myself in charge of 15 sub-branches with a small group of Chinese clerks as my assistants, and I had unwittingly created a miniature Sub-Branches department in Mongkok office. I remember the Compradore, who was then known as the Chinese Manager, coming up to me at a bank cocktail party, and I wondered what on earth he had to say to me. "Could you try to keep your new branches down to one a month" Peter said to me, "because I am beginning to run short of staff". The new branch opening procedures followed a routine pattern, and an auspicious time and date were chosen for the ceremony, and I would inform the police. We invited about fifty guests, we all wore red and white rosettes, the fire crackers were lit and we generally had a lion dance, a red ribbon across the entrance door was cut by a pair of scissors which I handed to a local dignitary, and we followed the new manager into his branch where drinks and small chow were served.

Urban Councillor Elsie Elliott being introduced to Jerry at a sub-branch opening

During this time the Industrial Banking department in Mongkok was rapidly expanding and although a large number of businesses were prospering it was inevitable that a few of them would not survive the prevailing boom. I well remember one occasion when all the foreign staff officers in Mongkok were invited out by a customer who owned a fleet of tug boats. One of these boats had been converted into a pleasure launch and we were taken on a scenic tour of the harbour while drinks were served before securing alongside the Jumbo Floating Restaurant in Aberdeen harbour where we enjoyed a fabulous seafood dinner. The next morning our host of the previous evening walked into the bank and handed over control of his tug boats to the bank before declaring bankruptcy.

It was also towards the end of 1964 that a lack of confidence in a number of Chinese banks saw the beginning of a bank run and in January 1965 the Ming Tak Bank closed its doors followed by the Canton Trust and Commercial Bank in February, and even the large Hang Seng Bank started to experience liquidity problems that would lead to its eventual take over. The continuing withdrawals caused a shortage of cash within the Colony and as we had insufficient un-issued notes in our vaults to meet the emergency we chartered a plane and flew a large quantity of Bank of England sterling notes into the Colony which the Hong Kong Government declared as legal currency on 9 February. I remained in Mongkok office throughout the night to supervise the unpacking of these notes from tin lined wooden crates. These notes were then distributed to my sub-branches in cash vans throughout the night but the announcement of their availability was sufficient to end the bank run, and the new notes were never used.

By early 1965 the Mongkok office manager had been transferred to our Head Office and his job had been assumed by the Manager in Osaka. I was called into his office and I thought that it would be to discuss my sub-branches which were now taking up more of my time than my job in Books department, but I was mistaken. "Congratulations, Jerry" Guy said to me "you have been appointed Manager of Kwun Tong branch and you are to select one of your sub-branch Chinese managers to take over your job which will now become Manager Sub-Branches". Kwun Tong was a rapidly expanding industrial township close to Kai Tak airport and not far from our compound on Clearwater Bay Road, and I was absolutely thrilled to get my first appointment. It was while I was taking charge of my new branch that I learned of my father's death in England, and the branch take-over prevented me from attending his funeral.

I was fortunate to have an excellent team to support me in Kwun Tong. A senior officer of our Portuguese staff was in charge of our Inward and Outward Bills departments and Vickers' experience was invaluable as most of our major customers were mill owners who were continuously importing raw material and new machinery and then exporting their finished products. I had also been given a Chinese Business Promotion Officer, later to be called a Business Representative, and John not only acted as my translator but also as an adviser in the running of my office.

An example of the importance of this relationship was when I had to turn down a loan request from the owner of a textile mill who I considered was over extended. I had been studying Cantonese for the past year but this was useless to me because both John and our customer were from Shanghai and spoke an entirely different dialect. The three of us discussed the loan request for a while and I asked John to tell our customer that I considered his proposed expansion unjustified due to an inadequacy of orders. After John had finished explaining things our customer jumped up with a big smile on his face and literally embraced me, and he invited us both out for dinner that evening. After he left I asked John why our customer was so pleased to learn that his loan had been turned down, and John explained the reason. "I told Wong that you were very impressed with his business and that in about three months time you would probably be in a position to approve the loan. In the meantime I shall provide him with the names of several importers so that his order book will be expanded when he comes back to see us".

I could never have achieved this result by myself, and although the study of Cantonese was obligatorily for me at that time, the use of a translator was often more satisfactory than an imperfect attempt to communicate in Cantonese, which would have resulted in considerable "loss of face". In fact my knowledge of Cantonese never developed much beyond the conventional greeting of *nei ho ma* and asking the cost of something which was *gai doh cheen*, and I was never able to achieve the six different inflections given to each Chinese syllable.

John and I were constantly being invited out to Chinese dinners by our customers who would invariably come to the office the next morning with requests for increased facilities and I told John that in future I would first discuss any increase in facilities with the customer and if he then wanted to invite us out after a decision was made, then I would be happy to accept the invitation. John immediately told me that this was not the way that Chinese conducted business, but I was adamant and John told me later that not only did our customers eventually accept the new arrangement but they also approved of the change.

A normal Chinese *chow* would consist of up to twelve separate courses and these banquets took place in large neon decorated restaurants with dance floors and the girls who were often provided sat with us at our round revolving tables. Large lobsters with flashing coloured light bulbs in their eye sockets were a favourite dish and shark's fin soup, which I liked, and abalone, which I did not like, were almost always served. In between courses, when we were not on the dance floor, our host would often reach over and top up our glasses from the bottles of whisky and brandy which were on the table and John and I were then subjected to the *yum sing* routine, which is literally "bottoms up", and this required us to drain our glasses together with our host. Sometimes our host would use professionals to perform this ritual and these men were known to swallow glasses of olive oil before the toast, and this lining in their stomachs enabled them to consume large quantities of liquor before feeling the effects. As a countermeasure, we would often respond by asking for a *yum ching* instead of a *yum sing,* and this involved lifting up one's glass with one, two or three fingers level with the top of the contents, and then consuming exactly the correct amount to bring the level of the drink exactly to the bottom of one's fingers, and I soon became very adept at this feat.

Another Chinese custom that could be embarrassing was the giving of presents particularly over Christmas, and this was known as *cumshaw*. The fact that *cumshaw* was generally given to branch managers and heads of departments inevitably linked the gifts with the granting of facilities and the bank decided to monitor all *cumshaw* in accordance with the guidelines of I.C.A.C., the Independent Commission against Corruption. We were told not to refuse to accept *cumshaw* as this could offend our customers but we had to submit lists of all the gifts we had received and the bank would decide whether or not the gifts could be retained. I remember that one of my Mongkok sub-branch managers had listed a fifty Hong Kong dollar department store gift voucher as *cumshaw* and I had told him to spend the coupon and then put whatever he had bought on his list, as the acceptance of any form of cash was forbidden. The Chinese Manager then took my instruction rather too literally and when he re-submitted his *cumshaw* list he had reported a gift of fifty cans of Carnation evaporated milk instead of the gift coupon; as he had five small children he had bought what his family most needed, so I decided let the matter rest there.

The Obedient Banker

In my own case in Kwun Tong John had told me that a grateful customer had suggested giving me a bottle of one hundred year old brandy for Christmas, and would I like to receive this. I replied jokingly that I would prefer one hundred bottles of one year old brandy and John and our customer must have discussed this together and reached a compromise because just before Christmas a miniature wooden barrel on a pedestal containing Courvoisier VSOP cognac was delivered to my house, and I threw a New Years Eve party to which I invited the donor and his senior staff and we ceremoniously broke open the barrel and by the time the party was over the barrel was empty.

Alongside the thriving businesses in Kwun Tong, which were predominantly in the textiles sector, our Savings Bank deposits were increasing daily and I had to have our counters extended and employ additional staff in order to cope with the growing numbers of our depositors. I had noticed that the counters and the rubberised floor tiles in the customers' area were badly burned by cigarette butts so I had a number of sand boxes placed at the foot of our counters in between the spittoons. Many of our customers were mothers and amahs with babies slung across their backs and as soon as they discovered my new sandboxes they allowed their children to relieve themselves in these boxes. The junior foreign staff officer who was in charge of our Cash and Current Accounts departments and whose name was Colin, then suggested that the sand boxes should be removed but John told me that the boxes were actually attracting more new customers to the bank, so I ordered additional sand boxes for our banking hall and arranged for the sand to be replaced regularly.

We had numerous gimmicks as give-aways and these included key chains incorporating imitation metal coins depicting the bank's building, but these key rings had to be withdrawn when large numbers of the imitation coins were discovered in the Colony's parking meters. The most popular gimmick however was a red plastic money box in the shape of the bank's building which we displayed on our counters and the demand for these money boxes was so great that even after we started charging HK$5 per box, we were still selling over one hundred boxes each week. Needless to say we maintained special children's savings accounts and when the boxes were full of coins we unlocked them and removed the coins which were then credited to the child's account. Chinese New Year was traditionally the time when outstanding debts are repaid and small monetary gifts are exchanged and these transactions made use of small red paper envelopes with gold lettering called *lai see* packets. The bank printed hundreds of thousands of these little packets and we handed out bundles of them free of charge and the production costs were more than offset by the publicity, because Wayfoong's *lai see* packets were highly prized.

Living on the mainland had its advantages and although I was already a member of the Hong Kong Football Club and the Cricket Club on the island I also joined the United Services Club in Kowloon where the bank had been allocated a limited number of associate memberships, and we used this club for many of our social activities. My main recreation however was a Chinese junk which I purchased jointly with the sub-manager of the Nederlandsche Handelsbank in Hong Kong, and we moored our boat at the Hebe Haven Yacht Club along Hiram's Highway on the Sai Kung peninsula, which was close to our flat on Clearwater Bay Road. Louis and I with our wives and friends spent many enjoyable weekends on the "Sea Witch" and there were several small outlying islands with sandy beaches within Hong Kong's territorial limits which we could visit and we often spent the night on the boat or on the beaches in our sleeping bags.

It was at this time that the Hong Kong government required all operators of motorised craft including junks to hold both navigators and engineering certificates and as neither Louis nor I possessed these certificates we always took our binoculars with us on the "Sea Witch" and we were careful to avoid being caught by the Marine Police who regularly patrolled Hong Kong's territorial waters, until we obtained our certificates of proficiency. We used our junk regularly for almost a year until the "Sea Witch" was sunk in a typhoon, and our insurance company initially refused to pay our claim by asserting that our boat had not been properly secured to the pontoon. We appealed and a claims adjuster's investigation later ruled in our favour as their diver had discovered part of the Hebe Haven Yacht club's pontoon still attached to a portion of the bows of our boat. I had not been a Leading Seaman in the Sea Cadets at school for nothing, and I had secured our boat with a conventional knot known as a round turn and two half hitches.

Typhoons occurred fairly regularly in Hong Kong and they were all given female names in alphabetical order. When the Hong Kong Observatory raised the number one signal we would often ignore the red flag which was simultaneously raised on the beach at Big Wave Bay because the surfing there was too good to miss. However when the higher number signals were raised it was time to bring in all the pot plants from our verandahs and balconies and to secure the purpose made wooden typhoon shutters that the bank supplied for all exposed windows. Although destructive,

The Obedient Banker

typhoons were not altogether unwelcome in Hong Kong because they helped fill up the reservoirs at Tai Tam, Pokfulham and Aberdeen, as water shortages were a problem until China agreed to the laying of a pipeline parallel with the Kowloon Canton railway track.

My position as manager of the bank's branch in Kwun Tong gave me some recognition within the community and it was not long before I was appointed to the committee of the Kwun Tong District Kai Fong Welfare Association which was a singular honour for a foreigner and although I attended their meetings regularly I did not participate to any great extent in their deliberations although John kept me advised of what was going on in order that I could cast my vote when required to do so. It was due to my activities with the Kai Fong that I became a member of the Council of the Children's Meals Society, and my main job there was to help supervise the distribution of cooked lunches to the schools in our area. My real involvement in social work however was when I was elected a Director of the Discharged Prisoners Aid Society and I soon discovered the main reason for my selection.

The majority of discharged prisoners in Hong Kong were either prostitutes or drug addicts and often both, and our job was rehabilitation. We had case workers who would visit Stanley Prison and when the prisoners were released our case workers would meet them with cars at the prison gates but as the pimps and the drug dealers were also there the discharged prisoners would have to decide whether to come with us or whether to revert to their former activities. Our Society had one of the highest records of drug rehabilitation in the world and this was because we only selected prisoners who genuinely wanted to get rid of their addiction and we used padded cells and the controversial drug methadone to achieve this. I myself was not directly involved in the drug side of our operations but I was put in charge of a hostel that we had in Kwun Tong where we housed the discharged prostitutes until we could find them jobs, and it was because of my success in achieving this that I eventually ended up as Vice Chairman of the Society. It was not my idea originally but it was logical that as and when the factories in Kwun Tong expanded they would need to employ additional staff on their conveyor belts. Therefore whenever I advised my customers that their factory expansion loans had been approved, I would also ask them if they would take on a group of unskilled workers on their conveyor belts, and in this way we achieved a remarkable turnover in our hostel.

Jeremy Tait

I was fortunate to have been sent to Kwun Tong at a time when the Colony was going through a period of expansion and increasing prosperity, but not all our experiences were without complications. Refugees were pouring into Hong Kong and Chairman Mau's Red Guards and their sympathisers were becoming more and more evident and there were riots and demonstrations and even some minor border clashes. But despite this threat Hong Kong's businesses were thriving and there are two particular incidents with my work in the bank during this period that I particularly remember.

The first incident involved a good customer of mine who was an importer of general merchandise which he stored in his godowns and later distributed to mainly small Chinese retailers in the Colony. The tetra-pack had just been introduced in the UK and somehow or other my customer Soo had managed to secure a contract with Express Dairies whereby he would import their tetra-packs of milk to supplement the existing limited supply of fresh milk that came from cows in the New Territories. Long Life milk was at that time unheard of in Hong Kong, and the loan that Soo wanted would be secured by his stocks of this milk under letters of hypothecation to the bank but the amount required was in excess of the limit of my authority so I discussed it with the Branches Manager in Hong Kong and Johnny approved it in principal, subject to the submission of a Loan Credit Report. In those days we did not yet have Loan Committees but my LCR was approved by the Manager Branches, Vickers opened a revolving letter of credit in favour of Express Dairies and Soo had no difficulty whatever in finding retailers for his new milk. We were all congratulating ourselves on the successful outcome of this project when the unexpected occurred. The first indication of any problem was when Johnny phoned me to tell me the facilities that he had approved had created a "conflict of interests" within the bank and that I would shortly receive a phone call from the bank's Chief Accountant asking me to attend a senior management meeting at which he would also be present.

The meeting was presided over by the Senior Manager of our Hong Kong office and Roy came to the point immediately. "We have nothing against Kwun Tong's milk facility which is sound in itself but we must all realise that the Dairy Farm group of companies are one of our most important customers and they have traditionally been the suppliers of all of the colony's milk for many years. The company was therefore very surprised to discover stocks of Long Life milk in some local grocery stores and they were even more surprised when they found out that it was their own bankers who were financing the import of this milk in direct competition to their own fresh milk which is now overvalued as a result. The Kwun Tong facility must now be cancelled and the purpose of this meeting is to decide how best to do this". I was completely stunned by this, but there was absolutely nothing that I could do about it. As I remember Soo refused to sell out to Dairy Farm, our facility was withdrawn and Soo had no difficulty in renegotiating similar facilities with another bank. I had lost one of my best customers through no fault of my own, but the Obedient Banker had learned a lesson that he would remember for a long time. This type of situation can occur with decentralisation as a result of expansion, but specialisation would later be introduced to prevent similar conflicts of interest.

The second incident involved another important customer of mine who was later to become the Colony's largest exporter of towels. Lee imported all of his raw cotton from Japan under an exclusive contract with Mitsubishi and this contract also required him to buy all his new machinery from the same source. He had huge orders for his towels mainly from large department stores in the US such as Sears and Montgomery Wards, and we were constantly giving him new manufacturing loans which themselves required new machinery loans. On one occasion a US buyer had offered to triple his order in return for a one third mark down in the price, and although Lee figured that he would still make a sizeable profit if he accepted the offer John and I advised him against it and he took our advice. It was at this stage that I told Lee that I thought that the time had now come for him to diversify and he then told us that he was also in the precious stones business and that he owned a jewellery shop in Hong Kong. As a result of this I agreed from time to time to permit Lee to open Letters of Credit with us for the import of precious stones and although Vickers pointed out that Lee's Letter of Credit facility was for textiles I told him that I would allow Lee to open occasional LCs for precious stones in the interests of diversification provided they were paid off promptly.

At one stage John told me that Lee had recently flown to Rangoon to attend the last public auction of raw jade in Burma. In those days jade was auctioned off in blocks of stone and the quantity and quality of the jade inside these rocks was a matter of guesswork, although each bidder thought they could determine the contents either by gently tapping the rocks or by holding them up to the sunlight. In any event Lee had been the successful bidder for a particular block of granite and the terms of the sale required the production of an authorised bank's irrevocable letter of credit. The amount was considerable but Lee had sufficient credit in his import line and although

Vickers was reluctant to open the LC he agreed to do this when I told him that Lee would be paying us three times the normal opening commission.

The rock duly arrived from Rangoon on a CPA fight and it was put into a safe in Lee's office and I asked John why it could not be broken open and the jade sold in order to retire the outstanding letter of credit. John then replied that the rock could not be broken until the time was auspicious and this was a form of *joss* that had something to do with *feng shui*. I had no option therefore but to retire the credit and to transfer the value of the rock to Trust Receipts Outstanding and I asked John to try to come up with an auspicious date as soon as possible as I could not keep the merchandise under Trust Receipt indefinitely. When John came into my office a few days later I could tell from his face that he had something else to tell me about the rock, and I was not mistaken. "What Lee did not tell me" John said "was that he had a partner when he bought the rock and this partner has now opted out and Lee has bought his half share in the jade. He now wants a small loan to pay off his partner because next week there is an auspicious day to open up the rock".

At this stage my last resort was to transfer the jade from Trust Receipts Outstanding to a Loan against Imports and the new LAI would have to be repaid within a month. I then granted Lee the loan to help him pay off his partner within my authorised limit but I was beginning to suspect that there was no such thing as an auspicious day and that Lee had simply kept the rock in his safe until his partner could no longer bear the suspense and had agreed to sell his share. Be this as it may, the auspicious day finally arrived and John left the office early in order to witness the opening up of the rock which was to take place at 5:30 pm. I told John that I would stay at my office desk until he phoned me with the result. I had just poured myself a second brandy soda when shortly after 5:30 my phone rang, and it was John. "It's pure imperial green jade and worth a fortune" John said "and it's going to take a while to use it up because it is so pure it can only be used for rings. Lee will pay off all his loans with the bank next week, but in the meantime take the next ferry to North Point where a car will be waiting to take you to a Night Club. Lee and I will meet you there and you had better tell your wife not to expect you back until late, because we are planning a very special celebration".

I had completed almost three years of my third tour when I was told that the Chief Manager, who had now become the bank's Chairman, wished to see me. I had no idea why, and when I reported to his Private Secretary, Margaret gave me no indication of the reason for the interview when she ushered me into the inner sanctum. Jake Saunders, later to become Sir John, had succeeded Sir Michael Turner as the bank's Chief Manager in 1962 and he had been a Colonel in the army during the war. He had a youthful appearance and a pleasing smile, which at times could be deceptive. Jake had evolved a series of signals when interviewing people whereby Margaret would know whether she was to remain in his room and whether or not the person being interviewed was to be seated or kept standing. In my case I was given a chair and Margaret left the room, so I knew that at least I was not about to be disciplined, but I noticed that the Chairman had my personal Staff file in front of him.

"You've had a pretty varied career so far" the Chairman said to me "but now you have a more specific job to do and we are sending you back to Calcutta as the Accountant there, but with the rank of Junior Sub-Manager". I immediately told the Chairman that I did not enjoy working in India, which was an acknowledged hardship post, and that I would much prefer to have a different posting. "Don't you want the promotion?" "I didn't say that, sir" I replied. "I get the distinct feeling that you do not want the promotion, is that right?" and Jake looked at me with one of his ingratiating smiles. "Oh no sir" I replied "I would definitely like the promotion." "Good, then that's all settled. Now here are the arrangements". In a nutshell he then told me that I was being sent back to India to prepare the way for a full scale integration of the three separate banks which were part of our Group there. I was to get rid of as many outdated systems as I could in our own office but more importantly I was to persuade our local staff that integration was in their long term interests and in particular I should try to get our three separate unions to merge. If I could achieve this I was promised a job much more to my liking, and I walked out of the Chairman's office with mixed feelings, because I was uncertain as to exactly what I had let myself in for.

Within days of my interview with the Chairman I was told to hand over my job to Vickers and to proceed on leave and we chose the Lloyd Triestino ship the m.v. "Victoria" which would take us from Hong Kong to Venice with the usual ports of call including Djakarta, Karachi and Brindisi, and this was to be the last sea voyage that I would take between postings. After arriving in Venice we stayed on in Italy for a short holiday before flying to the UK, where we arrived on 23 April. By 11 May we were in France with a rented caravan and once again we visited Spain and Portugal before returning to the UK on 12 July, where we stayed for a further two months before flying to Calcutta on 19 September.

CHAPTER SEVEN

CALCUTTA AGAIN, THEN CALIFORNIA

Life in Calcutta as the bank's *chotasahib* was a distinct improvement on the conditions I had experienced some five years earlier. I had expected to occupy the house at Sunny Park which was traditionally the Accountant's residence but integration of the bank's properties had already started, my Manager was now living in Sunny Park, and I was given an apartment in Judges Court Road which was a Mercantile Bank property. The flat was modern and spacious with central air-conditioning and the complex had its own tube well which meant that we did not have to rely upon the municipal water supply which was contaminated because the city's parallel sewerage and water pipes, which dated back to the East India Company, were full of leaks. I was also given a bank car and a driver and my wife could use the car for her shopping trips and coffee parties while I was in the office.

The political scene in Calcutta in 1967 however was chaotic and in February West Bengal had formed a United Front coalition government and the Communist leader Jyoti Basu had the Finance portfolio, and would later become Chief Minister. On 22 November, some two months after my arrival, there was a mass rally on the Maidan followed by a two day general strike and when a Civil Disobedience Campaign was launched on 18 December there were 3500 arrests including 14 members of the Legislative Assembly. The situation then worsened and in January 1968 President's Rule was declared in West Bengal.

This was not an easy background for me while I was attempting to implement the instructions I had been given by the bank's Chairman. Our Manager had been given the job as Calcutta's *burrasahib* after he had been forced out of Indonesia due to *Konfrontasi* and he was awaiting retirement. Apart from handling customers' facilities and the foreign exchange and supervising the imports and exports, Tom left the running of the branch to me and after lunch he generally returned to Sunny Park where he was a keen gardener having been awarded several prizes for his roses by the Calcutta Horticultural Society.

Citibank had recently tried to install NCR teller machines in their Calcutta branch with disastrous results and they were engaged in a full scale confrontation with their Union. Our own teller machines had arrived and were awaiting clearance but I was reluctant to install them until I had reached some sort of agreement with our Union. I therefore visited Citibank and met with their Operations Officer and by the time I sat down with our Union I knew exactly the problems that I would encounter, and I had evolved a compromise solution. Each of our teller stations was manned by three *babus* who performed the manual procedures involved in accepting, recording and issuing receipts for customers' deposits, but the new machines could handle all three of these operations and they only needed a single operator, thus making two *babus* redundant in each teller station, and this would be the crux of the problem with the Union.

My proposed solution took our Union completely by surprise and I told them that if they agreed to the installation of the new machines then they should select the most capable of the three *babus* who would be promoted to machine operator and the other two *babus* would assist him until he moved on at which time an assistant would assume the job until there was only one *babu* left as a single machine operator. The Union were very happy with this proposal, and although it would create a temporary moratorium on new employment it caused no redundancy, and it worked perfectly even though our customers' receipts would now have an officer's signature as well as a machine imprint for a short period of time. Several other banks in Calcutta wondered how we had managed to mechanise our teller operations so easily.

The bank's Christmas Party at the Manager's residence was a traditional event and it was primarily intended for our more important customers and local dignitaries, and I was duly given a copy of the previous year's guest list to approve. The bulk of our customers were Indian and there were hardly any Indians on the guest list and many names on the list were tea planters and others who were no longer our customers. I therefore gave the Manager a list of our more important Indian customers for inclusion on the guest list and I also put a cross against the names of several guests who I thought should be excluded. Tom was astounded and he told me that to invite so many Indian customers to his house was out of the question, and I replied that not to invite them would make a mockery of the whole concept of an annual party for our customers. Tom and I actually got on very well together and we were known as the Cat and Mouse team because our names were Tom and Jerry. Tom eventually agreed that we should invite our more important Indian customers and he asked me if I would like to have my own Christmas party to which our Indian customers could be invited, while he would have his own guests at a separate party. This was agreed and although the allowance for the *chotasahib's* party was one third of the allowance for the *burrahsahib's* party, this was more than sufficient because most of our Indian *customers* did not drink alcohol, and the *chotasahib's* Christmas party then became an annual event because of its popularity with our customers.

It was a tradition with the staff in Calcutta office that the *burrasahib* be treated with the greatest respect at all times and the bank's carpenter had constructed a wooden platform which was placed on the pavement between Tom's car and the bank's entrance during the monsoon period so that Tom would not have to step in the muddy water when getting out of his car. Tom appreciated this and he was escorted into the bank under the shelter of several umbrellas which our sepoys held above his head. One morning Tom told me that there was a sepoy who always carried his briefcase for him into the bank when he was stepping out of his car and that this particular sepoy was so obliging that Tom thought that he should be promoted to a more senior job. As we employed almost a hundred sepoys in Calcutta, who were classified as subordinate staff, I naturally asked Tom if he knew the name of the helpful sepoy and Tom told me he had no idea who he was. I therefore asked our *Jemedar*, who was in charge of the subordinate staff, to identify the sepoy and the next morning it was my sad duty to inform Tom as follows: "Tom" I said "I'm afraid we can't promote your sepoy for the simple reason that he is not a member of our staff. In fact he works for one of the brokers who queue up outside your office each morning and the reason he carries your briefcase into your office is because this enables his employer to go to the front of the brokers' queue". This incident is only one of many that illustrate the conditions under which we worked and which still existed in India in the late sixties. The main duties

The Obedient Banker

of the sepoys were to act as messengers and to carry all the departmental registers, ledgers, cash boxes and office equipment to and from the vaults and strong rooms. It was one of my tasks to reduce their numbers by not replacing sepoys when they retired and the last thing I needed was to perpetuate an archaic situation with an unnecessary promotion.

As branch Accountant my desk and cabinets were inside an air-conditioned glass cage from where I had an unobstructed view of the office and one of the duties that I enjoyed the most was managing the branch's money, which was basically squaring off our daily position while at the same time maintaining our statutory liquidity and reserve positions. Like most business procedures in India this was a complicated task but my predecessor Roger had created a chart onto which I would enter estimates of the branch's daily liabilities such as our inward clearings and pending remittances, and these would be offset by incomings such as maturing loans and outward clearings. The result would give me an estimate of the amount of overnight money that I could either lend out or that I would have to borrow, and these short loans were negotiated by me over the telephone with brokers.

From midday onwards nobody was allowed into my glass cage because it was then that my three telephones would start ringing. When money was tight the overnight rates would rocket upwards and that was the best time to be a lender. When money was plentiful the rates would drop but sometimes the entire position would change at the last minute when the second clearings came in as several banks would have overestimated or underestimated their positions. Some banks were cautious and started to square their positions early while others were reckless and left it to the last minute in the hope that there would be a surplus of money if they were borrowers, or a shortage if they were lenders, but even this could change at the closing. For some reason or other the Japanese banks were always late comers so my favourite broker David would tell me whether he thought that the Bank of Tokyo for example would be lending or borrowing and this would help me to decide at what stage I should enter the market. My friend Ian, who was the Manager of the Eastern Bank, operated in much the same way as I did and we often found ourselves in competition with each other, as we used the same broker David. By far the largest participator in the money market was the State Bank of India and when I had occasionally left it too late to square my position David would negotiate an emergency contract for me with his friend in the State Bank.

Calcutta was one of the few branches in the bank that had its own in-house lawyer and Parry was also our senior Indian officer who had initially been appointed as the bank's Legal Adviser in India specifically to look after our accumulated Bad and Doubtful Debts. As our Union were constantly consulting Parry he soon assumed an unofficial role as their adviser. Later the bank was told that we should appoint an Advisory Committee whose Chairman must be an Indian citizen and we nominated Parry, and this was approved by the Reserve Bank of India, which was the regulating body. Parry now had a conflict of interests, so I was given his Bad and Doubtful Debts files to administer, although I could of course still seek his advice.

This additional task then gave me another opportunity to get rid of some of the deadwood in our office. There was very little that I could do about the debts under litigation but I was able to write off a number of loans where eventual recovery was obviously impossible, and I also eliminated a few smaller debts by reaching compromise agreements with the debtors and then providing for the shortfall, and some other debts were settled by arbitration. One of our larger debts however needed urgent attention. As a result of a failed agricultural project in the United Provinces, now known as Uttar Pradesh, the bank had found itself in possession of a large quantity of Eastern European road rollers and these had been placed in an open compound with armed guards but some of them had been stolen and their value was depreciating while the debt was increasing.

Fortunately for us the dispute between India and Pakistan over Kashmir had recently entered a critical stage and India was constructing roads up to the Kashmir border and they needed extra equipment for this work. I had already given details of our road rollers to the Ministry of Agriculture and as a result of this we were contacted by the Ministry of Defence. As I recall instead of buying them from us the Ministry of Defence requisitioned them, but in any event the compensation we received was sufficient to repay most of the debt.

One of the largest and certainly the most intriguing of our Bad and Doubtful Debts was a loan that the bank had granted many years previously to a timber company engaged in logging in the Andaman & Nicobar Islands. The Andamans were colonised by the British in 1858 and were used as a penal colony until the islands were occupied by the Japanese in WWII. They then became an Indian territory in 1950 with a local Administrator appointed by West Bengal who had jurisdiction over the territory but as more and more settlers were sent there the islands experienced a gradual breakdown of law and order. The bank had a registered wrap-around Debenture over all the assets of the timber company and included in the charge were the elephants that the company had brought into the islands to assist them in the felling of the trees. When the company went bankrupt they abandoned their sheds and machinery and they released the elephants into the dense forests on Interview Island, and the bank had apparently given up all hope of realising anything from the company's assets.

I was not convinced, and after having studied the Debenture carefully and verifying its validity with the State Registry office in Calcutta I asked the Manager for permission to visit the Andamans to see if there was anything of value there. I was advised that the journey was too dangerous for me to undertake but I was able to arrange for the Securities supervisor Subodh to undertake the trip to Port Blair. Subodh had previously been my Number Two in Securities department and when he returned to Calcutta he told us that all property of the defunct company had long since disappeared but the elephants had multiplied over the years and there was now a huge herd of them running wild on Interview Island, and this area was later to be designated as a wild life sanctuary. I therefore recommended that we should file a claim on the elephants with the Administrator and when the claim was rejected Parry agreed that we should go to court and the judge would then have to decide whether or not the offspring and descendents of the original elephants could be considered as legal property of the bank.

The counsel for the defence argued that the elephants were wild animals and that they had inherited their freedom as descendents of elephants who had been given their freedom in much the same way as slaves had been given emancipation, and as such the bank could not claim ownership of them. Our lawyer however had discovered an obscure clause in the wording of the Debenture that gave "all liens, rights and privileges of whatever nature to heirs or assigns in perpetuity" and the judge ruled that if the Andamans Administration repaid the loan and the bank then relinquished any claim on the elephants, then the lien would cease to exist. One more of our Bad and Doubtful debts had now been resolved.

Our social life in Calcutta during 1968 was very active. Although I was still a member of the Saturday Club I had also joined the Calcutta Club and we went out almost every evening. We enjoyed eating in local restaurants although three days of the week were designated as meatless, fishless and riceless days, and these restrictions were intended to conserve food. The owner of one of my favourite restaurants was very understanding and on meatless days I could have a brain curry, because brains were not meat, on fishless days I would have a prawn curry because prawns were not fish, and on riceless days there was always some rice left over from the day before!

Sometimes a small group of us would gather together underneath a giant banyan tree on the Maidan, which was a huge open area in the centre of Calcutta, and we would pour ourselves whiskies and brandies before debating obtuse subjects such as the meaning of life. We called ourselves the Calcutta Transcendental Society and in retrospect this activity was a harmless means of escape from the somewhat artificial life we were forced to live in Calcutta. On one occasion the discussion was to discover the most important thing in life and after discarding health, money and sex we ended up with happiness and enjoyment. Most people then opted for happiness but I preferred enjoyment, because some people enjoy being unhappy. The vote for enjoyment was then carried unanimously.

After a year in Calcutta I was due for two weeks' local leave and we chose the classic tourist golden triangle of Delhi, Agra and Jaipur and to make it more interesting we included Benares, now known as Varanasi. Initially we flew to Benares where we had a reservation in Clarks Hotel and when we checked in we were told that for an extra twenty rupees we could have the same room and double poster bed that President Kennedy and Jackie had slept in, but we later discovered that there were several double poster beds in the hotel and that the receptionist made the same offer to all arriving foreigners and this could net him at least one hundred rupees a day.

The holy city of Benares is a very old city with narrow streets and numerous temples, many of which we visited, but the main tourist attraction is to take a cruise down the river Ganges and the best time to do this is at dawn. We were absolutely astounded by the number of bathers and worshippers standing in the dirty shallow water and the stone lined bank of the river had over one hundred ornamental ghats some for bathers and others for cremation, and it was the burning ghats that we were most interested in. After Benares it was time to move on to Delhi and although our hotel was in New Delhi a visit to Old Delhi is a must when in India's capital. It was there that we enjoyed a meal in one of the world's most famous Indian restaurants the Moti Mahal where we ordered Tandoorie Chicken and a cheese and peas curry which were served on traditional metal *thalis*, and the accompanying *nam roti* came on a banana leaf.

The Obedient Banker

The express train journey from Delhi to Agra can now be made in two and a half hours but in the 1960s the elegant way was to take the overnight train which could be boarded at 6 pm in order to have dinner in the dining car before the midnight departure, and the train would slow down to a snail's pace during the night in order not to arrive in Agra before 8 am. We had an excellent meal in the dining car and by the time we returned to our air-conditioned carriage the steward was turning down the sheets on our beds. In Agra we did everything that tourists do by visiting the Taj Mahal in the morning, taking in Agra Fort in the afternoon, and returning to the Taj in the evening in order to see it by moonlight. The next day we visited the abandoned city of Fatehpur Sikri which had been built by the Emperor Akbar between 1571 and 1585, and the city had later been evacuated for lack of water.

Our travel agent in Calcutta had arranged for a private car to drive us from Agra to Jaipur, also known as the Pink City, and we stayed at the Rambagh Palace Hotel which was a former residence of the Maharaja and our garden bungalow there had a shamiana where we were served by bearers in turbans who brought us our drinks on silver trays across a lawn that was full of peacocks, and this was India at her best. Our tour of the city included a visit to the Hawa Mahal, the Palace of the Winds, and we decided that Jaipur was one of the nicest cities we had seen in India and we had several more days in Rajasthan including a visit to the romantic city of Udaipur, before flying back to Calcutta.

It was in early 1969 that our manager went on leave and this coincided with the leave of Mercantile Bank's senior manager in Bombay. During Tom's absence I was appointed Acting Manager Calcutta and as both managers refused to change their leave dates I was also appointed Acting Chief Executive officer in India for all three banks. Jyoti Basu had by then become West Bengal's Deputy Chief Minister and our Union were becoming more active in their demands, so when they began a go-slow strike I was forced to enter into head-on discussions with them. The more moderate of our staff had formed a splinter Union which we did not recognise and this was an added complication, so I met with them on an informal basis and convinced them to join forces with the official Union, and this had a dilutary effect.

Some of our Union's demands were legitimate because they were provided for in the new conditions of service and pay as laid down in the Shastri and Desai Awards and one of the requirements was the creation of three grades of clerical staff with a minimum pay scale for each grade, and the majority of our splinter Union's members would be eligible for the top A grade due to their seniority. I had a list of our Union's demands and after consulting our Legal Adviser, Parry and I selected the demands that we considered justified and in particular we chose a large number of our senior staff for inclusion in the new Grade A category, and this would result in an increase in their salaries. We considered this a wise move because the Awards made no provision for promoting B grade clerks to A grade level, so when A grade staff retired there was no obligation to replace them.

I then gave our Union an ultimatum. As Acting CEO I would approve about one third of their demands on the condition that the Unions agreed to form a central unit with whom the management of all three banks would negotiate. The alternative was that I would resign my position as Acting CEO in which case the new CEO would be the Mercantile Bank's manager in Calcutta, which was the very last thing that our Union wanted. To reinforce my offer I gave the Union several photocopies of my letter of resignation which had been prepared for me by Dolly Majoo the Manager's secretary, and I also gave them a list of their demands that I would approve. I then closed the meeting by telling the Union that if they did not accept my ultimatum by 10 am the following morning, my letter of resignation would become effective and I would advise the manager of the Mercantile Bank in Calcutta that he was now in charge. On arrival at the office the following morning Subodh was the first to tell me that the Union had agreed to my proposal and I breathed a sigh of relief because I had not yet decided exactly what to do if the Union's decision had been otherwise.

Calcutta was an unhealthy city and illnesses were commonplace so we contracted a local doctor who visited the bank each day, and free consultations were provided to all members of our staff. Dr. Das had been a Colonel in the medical division of the Indian Army and although his services were primarily intended for our local staff I visited him regularly for minor ailments, and I had discovered that his home-made concoction for upset stomachs and common colds, which I also used for hangovers, was particularly effective. We called the mixture Hooghly Water because it had the appearance and consistency of Calcutta's main river and the bottle had to be shaken vigorously before use in order to mix the sediment with the brown liquid inside and the medicine had a strong herbal smell and a vile taste. Before I left India I asked Dr. Das for a prescription for his Hooghly Water to take with me. "There is no way I can give you my recipe" Dr. Das replied, "because half of the twenty or so ingredients are indigenous to India and would be unobtainable elsewhere, and quite frankly I myself have no idea which of the ingredients are the most effective, so I have to include them all to be on the safe side". From the taste and smell of the mixture I knew that it contained ginger, eucalyptus, peppermint and cloves but the other contents were a mystery and would probably not have been acceptable to the B.M.A. Nonetheless I took several bottles of Dr. Das' Hooghly Water with me when I went on leave.

One of our larger customers had a distillery and we financed the production of their locally made spirits, the most popular of which was Haywards Gin. The company then decided to expand their business by adding liqueurs to their products and also by introducing a new table wine which was to be called Golconda. When I visited the Shaw Wallace distillery on a routine inspection I was somewhat surprised to discover that the same base liquor that was used in their spirits was also used in their liqueurs and that the only difference between each liqueur was the artificial flavouring and colouring that was added to each vat. Golconda wine itself had a fascinating label depicting a bunch of grapes with drops of rain water on each grape and although we regularly served Golconda at our dinner parties, the word went round that the closest that a grape ever got to a bottle of Golconda was on the label.

Shortly after Tom had returned from leave and reassumed his duties he called me into his office and showed me a semi-official letter from Head Office appointing me as Vice President and Manager of our Los Angeles office, and I could hardly believe that I had received such an exciting and welcome posting. The Chairman's promise to me some two years earlier had been kept and we flew out of Calcutta on 9 June 1969, which was two days after my thirty eighth birthday.

I had been told to report to Hong Kong after leaving Calcutta and we stayed in a bank flat in the Head Office building for about a week while I was given a briefing on the situation in California as well as several files to read to prepare me for my new job. I could have entered the States on a Treaty Trader Visa which would have been valid for the period of my assignment but as my wife was American I preferred to apply for a Permanent Immigration Visa and this was granted without any difficulty. After leaving Hong Kong we broke our journey in Bangkok, Beirut and Athens and we did not arrive in the UK until 29 June.

As I had been in Calcutta for less than two years I had been given just over three months leave before I was to arrive in Los Angeles and I decided that it would be a good idea to spend part of this time in the States in order to familiarise myself with the country and its customs before taking on my new assignment. After a few weeks in the UK we therefore flew to Trinidad for five days where we stayed with my sister Gillian, whose husband was in charge of Universal Studios and Paramount Pictures on the islands, and we arrived in Miami on 29 July.

My first task in Miami was to purchase a car which we would drive to Los Angeles. The 1970 models were already appearing in the showrooms and I found a heavily discounted new 1969 yellow Plymouth Barracuda with a black vinyl hardtop and I asked the salesman for insurance cover but as I had no credit rating in the States the best he could do for me was to get me third party cover to the Florida state border. I then phoned our Manager in Los Angeles and he immediately arranged a fully comprehensive motor policy for me and I paid for the car out of a bundle of American Express traveller's cheques, much to the surprise of the dealer. I had been in the States for less than a week, but I had already learnt a lot. It took us over a month to reach Los Angeles and we zigzagged across the States and I was amazed by the variety of the people we met and the scenery we passed through, which ranged from the jazz bars of New Orleans to the magnificence of the Grand Canyon and from the solitude of the deserts to the glitter of Las Vegas, and by the time we arrived in Los Angeles we had seen a very good cross section of America. We stayed mostly in motels and I remember that I had figured the cost of the trip at about thirty dollars a day, ten dollars for food and drink, ten dollars for lodging and another ten dollars for travel expenses including petrol. By the time we reached LA I had acquired a taste for bourbon.

The bank's Los Angeles office was downtown at the junction of Spring and 7th and it had a small clock tower on the sidewalk in front of the entrance and above the clock face was a sign reading Hong Kong Bank. I found the bank without difficulty and after driving my Plymouth into the parking lot behind the office I went inside and introduced myself to the Manager. Bill looked me over and after welcoming me to Los Angeles he said he had something very serious to tell me. "Jerry" he said "there are three things you have to do before anything else, if we are to keep our customers. The first thing is to get you a new car, because even my tellers don't drive Plymouths. The second thing is to get rid of your bryllcream, and the third thing is to get yourself a new suit". Bill was a dour Scotsman, but I now knew that he also had a keen sense of humour, so I replied. "This suit was hand made for me by Goulam Mohammed who is one of the best tailors in Calcutta, and besides it's a Prince Charles plaid". Bill looked at me again "Nobody here wears double breasted herringbone anymore. Sears has a weekend sale and I'll take you there myself on Sunday". I still had a lot to learn.

Bill already had a house for his retirement so after we had settled into the bank residence in San Marino, which was half an hour's drive from the office on the Pasadena freeway, he moved out and we were very happy with our new residence, which had a secluded back yard and a large swimming pool. My takeover of the office however was not quite so simple. Bill had been Manager there for a long time and he was well liked by both his staff and his customers, so to begin with I was treated a little bit like an outsider, but this did not last for long as I got to know both my staff and my customers. It was a friendly office, and I enjoyed working there, but little did I know that it would not be for long.

The past performance of the bank in California had not been very satisfactory. Although the San Francisco Agency had been opened in 1875 its activities had been restricted because it was excluded from accepting resident deposits, and its advances were dependent upon overseas deposits or inter branch borrowing. In 1955 a wholly owned subsidiary bank was incorporated in San Francisco under State banking law and a year later the Los Angeles branch was opened, but loan losses in San Francisco necessitated increased capital and the bank had never been able to obtain the trade financing business that had been its prime objective. Such was the position when I assumed control of the Los Angeles office, and unlike Calcutta I had not been given any specific objective to achieve other than a reminder that foreign trade was a priority, although this was to change very shortly when it was decided to purchase a local bank in an effort to expand our presence in California.

I had only been in LA for a few days when I was instructed to report to the Los Angeles office of the Selective Service System, and I was then registered for military service and given a Reserve card with a V2 category. I asked the registration officer what V2 meant and he told me that it was Veteran Class 2 which meant that I could be called up in the event of nuclear war or an invasion by aliens. I then asked the officer what would happen if the UK went to war with the US, as I was a UK citizen, and he told me not to worry. "We have lots of very comfortable prisons here, as our Japanese residents discovered after Pearl Harbour". I left the SSS office somewhat confused, but it was I who had decided to apply for permanent immigrant status and not the bank, and I was beginning to learn quite a lot about American democracy.

We were a sub-clearing bank in Los Angeles and when I took over the branch we were using the United California Bank to handle our clearing and they invited me to lunch in the hope that I would agree to renew the clearing house agreement we had with them. It so happened that I had recently applied for a credit card and I had used a UCB application form but my request had been declined because I had still not established any credit rating. The UCB luncheon room was full of Vice Presidents and towards the end of the meal the bank's President asked me if I was happy with his bank's services and if I was ready to renew our contract. This was the moment I had been waiting for, and I handed the President my rejected credit card application which had a UCB letterhead. The VP in charge of card services was at the lunch and the President gave him the letter and told him to give me a credit card with the same preferential terms and conditions that were used for their own senior officers. The clearing house agreement with UCB was renewed, my credit rating was established, and I had learned a little more about American business procedures.

After Bill retired, I decided to conduct a customer survey in our office with a view to improving our business and I inserted questionnaires with our checking account statements asking our customers why they kept their accounts with us, rather than with other banks. As I expected most of the replies gave convenience as the answer, meaning that they worked nearby, but some of the other replies were helpful and one particular reply was very revealing, and it read as follows. "Where else could I get cheques from a bank with 64 separate letters in its name, the Stars and Stripes alongside a Union Jack, my own name in Chinese characters and with Mount Fuji in the background? Whenever I use one of your cheques to pay for my groceries the supermarket check-out lady holds it up and says 'Is this for real?'" The name of our bank at that time was The Hongkong and Shanghai Banking Corporation of California Incorporated, but we changed this to The Hongkong Bank of California in 1970, and now the Group is simply known as HSBC.

I was just beginning to really enjoy life in Los Angeles and I had settled in sufficiently to start expanding our activities when the situation suddenly changed in much the same way as it had done when I was in Colombo. Our new President in San Francisco had been told by Head Office to look for a suitable small bank in California for acquisition in order to accelerate our expansion, and in 1970 it was decided to take over the Republic National Bank and Trust Company of Beverly Hills. I had nothing to do with the acquisition of RNB and in fact it was the intention of our President to leave me in charge of own downtown LA branch and to retain the services of the existing Senior Vice President of RNB as Manager of the Beverly Hills branch which was to be our new regional headquarters in Southern California. I was later to discover that it was our Head Office in Hong Kong who refused to agree to this and when our President suggested that I should join Jim Carpenter as a joint manager, this was also unacceptable to Head Office. Eventually Jim agreed to continue as Manager of Beverly Hills as a Vice President and I was given the job of Senior Vice President in Beverly Hills in overall charge of all six of our branches in Southern California, which now included North Hollywood, Encino, Silverlake and Carson. I was of course pleased to get the promotion but I was not prepared for the problems that I was about to experience. I handed over the downtown LA branch to my Assistant Vice President and Operations Officer Mike who was promoted to Vice President, and fortunately my secretary Aurora agreed to come with me to Beverly Hills.

I had no reason to complain about the lavish facilities in our Beverly Hills branch, which occupied most of the ground floor of our own building at 9300 Wilshire Boulevard, but the running and control of my new branches was a nightmare. Head Office had accepted that it would not be possible to install the bank's standard operating and reporting procedures into the new branches overnight but I was nonetheless inundated with semi-official letters from our Overseas Operations department in Hong Kong about so many trivial matters that it was very difficult for me to achieve the integration that was so badly needed. I had been told that our previous President in San Francisco Gordon, who was a Scotsman, had travelled each week to Sacramento on a Greyhound bus while negotiating the opening of the bank's new branch in the State capital but such behaviour in Beverly Hills would not have been appropriate. I myself was driving a Lincoln Continental Mark III and our new President Colin used a gold coloured Cadillac from our Leasing department's fleet whenever he visited Southern California. Given that much in Beverly Hills was artificial, the only way to survive there was to go with the flow.

I was now working a long way away from the bank's house in San Marino and although I generally avoided rush hours by getting into the office early and leaving late, a single journey sometimes took me up to two hours of driving on three different freeways so I naturally asked the President for permission to sell the bank house and to purchase a new one nearer to our office. We found a suitable residence in Bel Air next to Zaza Garbor's house but Colin told me that for some reason or other our

Head Office had not approved the exchange of houses. Some years later in Head Office my curiosity got the better of me and when I had located the relative S.O. correspondence I noticed that an officer had written a remark in pencil in the margin reading "Who does he think he is? Errol Flynn?" and several other officers had initialled this remark in agreement, and an Assistant General Manager had added in pencil "Block it!" Commenting in pencil on circulating S.O. correspondence was an effective method whereby AGMs could ascertain the opinions of their junior officers, but such remarks were generally erased before the S.O. went to Filing. An element of jealousy coupled with a lack of understanding would result in my wasting hundreds of hours on freeways over the next four years – and I never got to meet Zaza!

As a result of our acquisition of RNB we were now a full clearing bank and I was elected a Member of the Beverly Hills Clearing House Association. I was already a Member of the Foreign Trade Association of Los Angeles as well as being a Director of the British American Chamber of Commerce and I joined the Beverly Hills Club where I generally took my customers for lunches until the club closed down in order to make way for a block of apartments. I now needed a new club for official entertainment and I asked Colin if he would approve my membership of the Playboy Club in nearby Century City and he had no objection to this. I made full use of the Playboy Club which was very popular with my guests and I was eventually given gold card membership status which had certain privileges.

Two of my favourite areas were Marina del Rey and Newport Beach both of which were close to Beverly Hills and I often took my customers out to meals at a restaurant in Newport Beach called the Abbey where the waiters were dressed as hooded monks and we sat at rustic wooden tables with clusters of candles which the monks would ceremoniously light when they took our drink orders. An evening hangout was a Polynesian restaurant at the end of the pier and they served margaritas which we drank with straws out of a large bowl which was placed in the centre of our table.

During this time I was not only working long hours but I was also heavily involved in business entertainment which was of no interest to my wife who preferred to stay at home. The rift between us widened and we then separated under a Marriage Settlement Agreement which culminated in divorce, and she moved into her own apartment and obtained a secretarial job. I was once again a bachelor.

The Obedient Banker

I took full advantage of the long weekends with no work on Saturdays and as most public holidays were on Mondays, these long weekends were often spent in Las Vegas which was a four or five hour drive from my house. I can remember a particularly enjoyable weekend when I was playing blackjack in the Riviera which was one of my favourite casinos. Whenever I won I would increase my bets and I suddenly found myself on a winning streak. "Playing green" shouted the dealer, which meant that I was betting with twenty five dollar chips which were green in colour, and the Pit Boss got off his pedestal and came over to our table to watch my play. "Playing black" shouted the dealer, and this meant that I was now using one hundred dollar chips. I continued to win and during a pause while the cards were being shuffled the Pit Boss asked if my partner and I would like to accept a complimentary room for the night in the Riviera hotel. "No thanks" I replied "We have already booked into Caesar's Palace". "OK" said the Pit Boss "then how about a complimentary dinner for two at Delmonico's?" As so often happens, when the deal recommenced my luck ran out so I cashed in my sizeable winnings and we went straight into Delmonico's where we ordered Pacific Coast Lobster Tails which we dipped in drawn butter, and a medium rare centre cut Prime Rib. When the champagne arrived I removed one of my partner's shoes from which I pretended to drink the champagne, and we were given an ovation by the other guests who were witnessing our celebration.

For normal evening entertainment I had a wide choice of the venues surrounding the office or those in the neighbourhood of my house. After my marriage broke up I would often stop off on the way home at a popular singles bar called Heckles which catered to divorcees in their mid-thirties and which was conveniently situated at the Pasadena freeway exit which I used to get to my house. Heckles had a long curved bar with girls seated at every other stool so I was generally able to choose which two girls I wished to sit next to. If you fancied one of them then you offered to buy her a drink, but if one of the girls fancied you then she would buy the drink, but buying your own drink meant that either you were not particularly interested in striking up a conversation, or you were playing hard to get. Such were the rules of the game. After a conversation had started one of the first questions asked was "How many do you have?" and I soon discovered that this meant children, and when the word got around that I had no children my popularity increased. Most of the Heckles girls were working mothers and it was not long before I was dating a very attractive blonde who worked as a secretary in a Pasadena transport company and who lived nearby. After a couple of dinners out together I was invited to a home cooked meal in the girl's house and the main purpose of this was to meet her children. The next day the blonde phoned me and said that as her eldest son did not approve of me it was no longer possible to continue to see each other but I did not tell her that I had also reached the same conclusion after meeting her children. I then crossed Happy Hour at Heckles off my list, and I started to go to the new topless bars that had recently opened in North Pasadena but the area was very run down and there was no variety in the floor shows, so I then spent most of my leisure time in the area of Beverly Hills.

The night clubs on Santa Monica Boulevard were a bit risky as the area was popular with the gay community and there were places where you could participate in mud wrestling with well built coloured ladies or the early equivalent of chat rooms where you could discuss your fantasies with a partner while watching an explicit movie. I much preferred the more sedate night spots on Wilshire Boulevard and although I never found Hollywood itself to be particularly exciting there was an Arabian night club on Hollywood Boulevard called Ali Baba's which featured belly dancing with audience participation and this was one of my favourite places.

Jerry with Ali Baba's belly dancer in Hollywood

We had some Armenian customers who imported Persian rugs and they sold them through a small chain of stores known as Carpet World. I was entertaining the Hasserjian brothers one evening and we decided to go to Ali Baba's, and Ted's wife who was English, came with me in my car to keep me company. I must have been driving somewhat erratically because the police stopped me on Hollywood Boulevard and I was obliged to take a sobriety test. California law in those days gave me three alternatives, either to be breathalysed, or to touch your nose with your index fingers, or to walk in a straight line, and I chose the latter option. I did this twice and when the policeman asked me to do it a third time Ted's wife told the sergeant that this was harassment and if I was not allowed to continue my journey she would file a complaint against the cop. The police sergeant then told us that we were free to go but if I continued to drive the car he would follow us, so Ted's wife wisely moved over into the driver's seat and she suggested that I conserve my energy for the belly dancer.

When I had first been given the California posting I had the option of taking one month's local leave each year or two months home leave after two years in which case the bank would pay for the airfare to the UK or equivalent, and I opted for home leave. However after a year in Beverly Hills I discovered that it was a State Banking Department regulation that I should vacate my job for at least one week each year so each intervening year I took an extra week's holiday in Mexico, and I was thus able to visit Acapulco, Mazatlán and Puerto Vallarta on three separate occasions.

It was in 1972 that our Executive Vice President in San Francisco Mike was replaced numerically by a junior foreign staff officer and I was then given the position of Executive Vice President and although I remained in Beverly Hills I had to fly up to San Francisco regularly for Board Meetings and I would take the Senior Trust Officer with me. We were experiencing considerable problems with our Trusts in Beverly Hills and we had to change the Senior Trust Officer twice before we found someone capable and when Ben came to us from Security Pacific Bank he reorganised and expanded the Trust Department in a very efficient manner. By far the largest trust account we had acquired from RNB involved the Miramar hotel in Santa Monica and the administration of this Trust was complex and several law suits were involved. Ben worked very closely with our lawyer Chuck and eventually they were able to sort things out, but it was not an easy task. We were fortunate to have retained Chuck as our legal counsel and the Miramar hotel was only one of many of the bank's problems that he was able to resolve for us.

The situation with most of the business we had purchased from RNB was not good. In his History of the bank Professor King refers to RNB's questionable assets and undoubted liabilities, but this was not our only problem. Our purchase of the bank had been subject to elimination of those loans and advances that our internal auditors in Hong Kong decided to exclude, and what was left after they had finished was a shell and to replace the stripped loans was not an easy task, and we encouraged our branch managers to actively seek out and submit quality loan proposals.

As Executive Vice President of a new oriental bank in Beverly Hills I was constantly interviewing all sorts of strange people with unusual proposals, most of which were entirely inappropriate, but there was one meeting that presented me with what I thought to be an excellent loan opportunity. The men who entered my office identified themselves as agricultural scientists who needed substantial finance for a hydroponics project in Arizona, and they were part of the Howard Hughes Foundation who would guarantee the facility. I asked them why they had chosen to approach the Hong Kong Bank and they told me that although the Foundation had extensive facilities with all the major American banks their policy was to diversify their banking business and their financial director had selected us, and I considered this explanation to be entirely plausible.

The actual project was to grow vegetables hydroponically in temperature controlled greenhouses in the Arizona desert on beds of impregnated gravel, and a crop of at least 300 tons of tomatoes per acre was projected as compared with the normal agricultural average of 50 tons. However the best part of the proposal was that the facility would be fully secured by the unconditional guarantee of the Howard Hughes Foundation and it would absorb a large portion of our unutilised deposits. Our President agreed with me but as the facility was way above our limits we referred it to Head Office in Hong Kong for approval. We fully expected the loan to go through without any problem but we were amazed when Head Office refused to approve the facility on the grounds that it was far too much money to advance on a project which was outside our geographical area and we were told that we should try to keep our advances within the State of California.

After the rejection of the hydroponics loan it was with some trepidation that I recommended approval of a large loan to a chicken farm in Kansas called Egg City and Colin agreed somewhat reluctantly to sign the application that we sent to Hong Kong, but at this stage we were desperate to find an outlet for our surplus deposits. Hong Kong did not turn down the application but they asked me why Egg City was situated in Kansas and not in California and I replied that not only was Kansas a major poultry farming State but geographically it was centrally situated in the USA. As such, every evening a fleet of trucks left Egg City with several hundred thousand freshly laid eggs and these trucks headed north, south, east and west and by dawn all their distribution centres throughout America had supplies of fresh eggs which could be retailed within 24 hours of laying. Head Office was obviously impressed by my explanation and they exceptionally approved a very large out of State loan.

All went well with Egg City for several months until one morning I received a telephone call from their President. "Which do you want to hear first, the good news or the bad news?" he asked me, and I told him to give me the bad news first. "My chickens have contracted Newcastle disease and the Department of Agriculture and the Food and Drug Administration have ordered that all of them are to be destroyed. This is the end of Egg City". My first thought was that this was also the end of my career with the bank, but I asked the President to give me the good news. "Do you remember when you set up the loan for me you insisted on an insurance policy in favour of the bank for 110 percent of the value of my hens, and I almost took my business elsewhere? Well, I am flying to Los Angeles this afternoon and I will bring you the insurance company's cheque to pay off the loan because your collateral has been destroyed, so please book us a table for dinner tonight and line up the dancing girls." I took him to the Abbey in Newport Beach where the monks lit the candles on our table and I ordered one of their famous Crab Louis salads followed by roast duckling, and we ended the evening with a Polynesian floor show at the end of the pier. In one way it was a happy ending, but the bank was back to square one insofar as our surplus deposits were concerned.

Another interesting proposition was when a major distributor of imported food products offered me several tons of Libby's Mixed Fruit Salad at half price if I could find an overseas buyer, and as an incentive I would be paid a sizeable commission. These cans of fruit salad were en route to Los Angeles but they contained an artificial sugar sweetener called cyclamate which the FDA had just prescribed as a prohibited substance so the shipment would have to be diverted to a country where cyclamates were allowed. The distributor showed me the Bills of Lading and the documents of title to the goods and I then cabled details of the proposal to our Trade and Credit Information Department in Hong Kong and in order to save time and to avoid any direct involvement in what could become a questionable transaction I asked TCID to communicate directly with the importer, so I never discovered the precise outcome of this trade enquiry although I learned later that the goods were diverted to Mexico. Once again the distributor had come to us because of the reputation of our parent bank, and once again I had fulfilled my role as an Obedient Banker.

To partially alleviate our liquid position we employed a Loan Officer on contract and Max had a part time job as an Advisor with the Small Business Administration of the State of California and this generated a constant stream of small loans to an amazing selection of enterprises ranging from peanut vendors to motor vehicle repair shops, but in the event of default each loan was guaranteed by the State of California. One of our new customers dealt in men's neckties but most of his stock was very wide ties and as the new trend was for narrow ties when his stock was liquidated Max gave us all large quantise of neckties as presents and some years later when wide ties came back into fashion those of us who had not thrown away our wide ties had Max to thank.

It was not only our loans that were causing me headaches because one morning I received a telephone call from someone who wanted to talk with Martin Ackerman who was the previous owner of RNB. I told the caller that I was the new Executive Vice President and how could I help him and he told me that he was the sponsor of a large number of our customers' fixed deposits, known in the States as CDs, which were coming up for renewal and could he expect the same commission as previously. This was all I needed, so I passed him on to our President in San Francisco, and I had no desire to know how this phone call had been dealt with.

We had several visits from senior management in Hong Kong and when the bank's new Chairman himself came to Los Angeles it was decided to throw a Cocktail party in my house to which we would invite our most important customers and several local dignitaries. I used outside caterers to organise the party and the centrepiece was a champagne fountain where you could refill your empty glass by holding it under the cascading champagne. While waiting for our guests to arrive the Chairman asked me to show him the house and when walking back from the pool he turned to me: "Your pool has to be the largest swimming pool in the bank and it is even bigger than mine". "You may be right" I replied "but it is one of the smallest pools in San Marino". The Chairman pondered my reply for a while but as we entered the house Guy turned to me and smiled. "Jerry" he said "you have just made a very important point that I shall bear in mind". Towards the end of the party Ted Burnett, who was the Mayor of San Marino and a retired President of Prudential Assurance, came up to me and asked for volunteers to help carry his French wife to the bottom of the garden and put her over the wall into their back yard where her son was waiting for her. When the Chairman asked me what was going on I explained the position and I told him that this was a regular occurrence whenever I entertained the Burnetts because when Yvonne had had too much to drink it was easier to lift her over the wall rather than have Ted drive her back home, because although we were neighbours Ted's street entrance was a block away. Guy told me later that life in California was very different from what he had previously imagined.

Some months later we had a visit from the Deputy Chairman, who was later to become Chairman, and this time we decided to have a Reception in the Beverly Wilshire Hotel which was where he was staying, and after the party was over we all went out for dinner. There were two attendants dressed as Beefeaters standing on either side of the Ballroom entrance and our reception line was just beyond the Beefeaters. "What did you think of the Beefeaters?" our President asked the Deputy Chairman "it was not our idea but it was suggested by Hernando Courtright, who runs the Beverly Wilshire". "Nice idea" Mike replied "I have never ever seen black Beefeaters before".

In the meantime the bank's loan position was still unsatisfactory and it was decided to convene a Loan Committee in Southern California comprising the President, myself and Mike, who was our downtown Los Angeles branch Manager, but exactly how the Committee would operate was not specified apart from the fact that all three of us were expected to sign each Loan Credit Report after the respective loan had been approved. Most of the loan proposals we dealt with came to us from our branch managers and it was simply a question of whether or not we would approve them within our limits. However some new proposals were being presented by the President himself and if approved they were allocated to whichever branch the President chose, but Colin never told us where he got the proposals from, although I suspect that it was from some sort of loan placement agency.

At one Loan Committee Meeting we were discussing an LCR for a large facility to the supplier of home alarm systems whereby we would make advances against each individual contract and these advances would be repaid from the home owners' monthly instalment payments. Mike, who was previously a State bank inspector, refused to approve the facility because it was technically unsecured, and I agreed with him. Colin then told us that if he, as the bank's President, approved the loan then it would be sufficient if the two of us simply noted his approval of the facility on the LCR above our signatures, and after we agreed to this the same procedure was followed for several other facilities that we were unable to agree upon. The President chose our Encino office as the branch for the alarm systems facility and when the company declared bankruptcy, the circumstances under which the facility had been granted were investigated and it was discovered that our Loan Committee had not always been unanimous in their decisions. The rules may not have been broken, but they had probably been bent.

By 1974 I had been in California for over five years and although we were a larger bank our overall position had deteriorated as a result of the purchase of RNB, and a major policy decision was then finally taken to gradually scale down our operations in California which had not lived up to earlier expectations. I was tempted to switch jobs when I was offered a managerial position by a major American bank in charge of their International operations in Hong Kong but I did not fancy being in direct competition with the bank where I had worked for over twenty years. At that time the Chairman and the Manager of our Internal Audit department were in California conducting an investigation into our operations and I worked very closely with the Internal Auditor during his investigation, and the decision to scale down operations was mainly based upon his findings. Before returning to Hong Kong John asked me if I would like to join his department, which was being expanded, and he had told the Chairman that he would like to have me work for him, and the Chairman had agreed. Colin had already retired as President in San Francisco and had been replaced, and as I was also handing over my job I told John that I would be happy to accept his offer.

There were several farewell parties but the party that I particularly enjoyed was a small farewell dinner given to me by our International department which I had staffed and looked after during my time in Beverly Hills. The party was held in a Theatre Restaurant called "1520 AD" and we were served foaming jugs of ale by buxom wenches and Henry VIII made his nightly appearance. A photograph taken at this party with signed messages from members of my staff serves as a reminder of a celebration which marked the end of my frontline banking activities.

Jerry's farewell party in a downtown Los Angeles Theatre Restaurant

I flew out of LAX on 13 July on an overnight TWA flight to London, and the Obedient Banker was now about to enter into an entirely new phase of banking centred on supervision and control.

CHAPTER EIGHT

INTERNAL AUDIT, WORLDWIDE

On arrival in the UK on 14 July 1974 I had less than one month's accumulated leave and I chose Air France to get me to Hong Kong because this enabled me to stop off in Nice, Beirut and Bangkok en route, and these stop-offs would add considerable variety to my holiday and to some extent they were a substitute for sea travel which was no longer an option. In Nice I spent the daytime on the beach and in the evenings I went to the Municipal Casino which was conveniently situated on the Promenade des Anglais a short distance from my hotel, and both locations were popular gathering places.

In Beirut I checked into the Alcazar Hotel which was behind St. Georges Yacht Club where I was able to get a temporary visitor's pass. The club's swimming pool had a sun deck overlooking the marina and I invited one of the girls I met there to join me for a dinner show at the Casino du Liban later that evening. The floor show was one of Frederick Apcar's world famous revues with galloping horses and cascading waterfalls, and we enjoyed ourselves so much that my friend invited me for dinner the next day in a restaurant in Beirut's old quarter where we were served an assortment of over 25 different Lebanese dishes. In Bangkok I stayed with an old friend of mine in the bank and I remember on the first evening after a cocktail party Paul's wife Jacky allowed him to show me some of Bangkok's night life and we visited several bars in Patpong before taking in a floor show.

I assumed my new duties as an Internal Auditor in August and after about a month I had just about finished studying audit programmes and questionnaires in preparation for my first branch audit when the Head of Audit asked to see me. "We have had a nasty fraud in Indonesia" John said to me "and the Jakarta Manager has asked for our help. Their foreign currency cashier has absconded with some US dollars but they are uncertain as to the extent of the fraud. I am too busy to handle this myself so I want you to sort it out. Stay in Jakarta for as long as you have to, and give me a full report when you get back to Hong Kong". I was to go on a one man Special Investigation before I had even started auditing. The bank at this time owned 30 percent of Cathay Pacific Airways and we were required to fly CPA whenever possible but as there was no direct CPA flight from Hong Kong to Jakarta I was exceptionally allowed to fly Garuda with an open dated first class return ticket, rather than changing planes in Singapore. I had also arranged with our Travel department to book me a room in the Borobudur Jakarta Hotel for an indefinite period.

The first thing I did in Jakarta was to assess the situation. The missing cashier was believed to have flown to Kalimantan and the police had been alerted. The estimated amount of the loss was the total value of the US dollar notes recorded as being held by the bank at the time the cashier had absconded, but the loss could be considerably greater if the cashier had falsified entries in his Notes Purchased Register. I decided that the best way to verify the accuracy of the register was to check the bundles of daily vouchers in order to reconstruct all the purchases and sales of US dollar notes over the past few months and I was given several clerks to assist me in this laborious task. Eventually my reconstruction was complete and as I had not detected any discrepancies in the register I was able to confirm that the loss was limited to the balance of the Notes Purchased account.

There was however an anomaly. The bank's Standing Instructions required the foreign currency notes to be counted regularly by an officer and the total had to agree with the balance in the Notes Purchased account in the same way as Cash in Treasury was counted. So if as I suspected the foreign currency cashier had been dipping into his reserves why had this not been noticed on balance nights when the Head of Cash department, who was a foreign staff officer, had counted the foreign currency and signed a certificate to this effect? I confronted the officer concerned in the presence of the branch manager and I asked him several times whether he had in fact personally counted all the US dollar notes at the time he had signed the certificates and each time I asked him he admitted that he had not counted the notes as he had accepted the word of the foreign currency cashier that the amount was correct. I had given him an opportunity to retract his statement, but he had not done so. I mentioned this in my report and since his actions were not of a criminal nature he was asked to submit his resignation for personal reasons and his letter of resignation was accepted by the bank with regret. There was no other option. I delayed my return to Hong Kong for a couple of days because I wanted to complete my report before I left, but this also gave me the opportunity to spend two more evenings in the Ancol Recreation Park where the facilities included a casino and a night club called Dreamland, and I considered that after the stress of my first Special Investigation I deserved a little R and R.

After I returned to Hong Kong the Head of Audit congratulated me on my report and told me that he was leading an audit team to the Philippines in October and that I was to join his team. When we arrived in Manila John then set the audit in motion and after a week he returned to Hong Kong leaving his Assistant Manager in charge.

Jerry and Tony Dawson with their audit boss John Bray in Manila

The assistant manager Doug was senior to me and he was a Mercantile Bank man as our two banks were integrating our staff, and he was very helpful in explaining audit procedures to me. Although we were staying in the InterContinental Hotel in Makati, which was within walking distance of the bank's Manila branch, we ate most of our meals in the shopping centre mall where our hotel was situated and there was plenty of night life there to keep us occupied. Most of the bars had lots of attractive girls but for the most part they simply provided a pleasant background because if you got too friendly with them they would expect you to buy them lady drinks. My fellow auditor Tony called these girls sparrows and when I asked him why he replied "Because they twitter", and he was later to say the same thing in Jakarta, but occasionally in some bars we would invite a sparrow to join us.

I had discovered a bar that had a Happy Hour during which a naked girl would lie on a table with her body covered with hors d'oeuvres. We were very polite and would help ourselves to slices of salami and bits of cheese from each end but just as things were beginning to get interesting the owner of the bar would announce "Happy Hour finish. Come again tomorrow." It was a good beginning to our evening entertainment. On one weekend I visited the Pagsanjan Falls in Laguna some 90 kms south of Manila in order to shoot the rapids and the boatmen steered me downstream between rocks and boulders until our *barca* reached the main falls which we could view above us from a raft. When we had completed our audit of Manila Doug asked me if I would like to undertake the audit of our branch in Iloilo single-handed instead of with him, and when I agreed he said that he would fly there with me to help me set up the audit and then leave me to complete the audit by myself before returning to Hong Kong.

Iloilo City is the capital of a predominantly agricultural province of the same name situated in the south east portion of Panay Island and the terrain there is mainly marshland with numerous paddy fields. The reason why the bank maintained a branch in this remote area was the large amount of deposits that it generated, mainly in the form of savings accounts, and these funds were used in Manila to provide facilities to the bank's major customers in that city. The foreign staff manager of Iloilo was on leave at the time of my audit and I stayed in the only decent hotel in town and apart from the absence of any foreigners and the somewhat primitive conditions the main problem that I encountered was the difficulty in getting a proper meal. The food in the hotel was a total disaster, there were no restaurants as such in town and the dishes that the food stalls served were mainly *batchoy* or other mixtures of rice or noodles, and meat was hard to find. Eventually I discovered an establishment called Fatima's Bookshop that served adobo that was probably caribou but you had to join a queue to buy it and sometimes I joined the queue three times before my appetite was satisfied. I was the centre of attraction in Fatima's Book Shop and by the time the audit was finished I had become a regular customer and there was always plenty of adobo waiting for me at lunchtime. There was virtually nothing for me to do over the weekend so I asked the bank's acting manager where the action was and he told me that apart from the local cinema the only place to go to was the Salem Night Club next to the railway station, but he advised me against it.

The only meat I could get in the hotel was chicken but it tasted of fish because that is what the chickens were given to eat and even my breakfast eggs had the same taste. I ordered a bottle of local rum to help me finish my Saturday chicken lunch and after a siesta and a bath I asked the hotel to get me a taxi and I told the driver to take me to the Salem Night Club. To be the centre of attraction in Fatima's Book Shop was nothing compared to what happened to me after spending 25 pesos on an all night entrance ticket to the dance hall and this entitled me to unlimited dances with as many girls as I wanted, and only the drinks were extra. I did not return to my hotel until about noon the following day and when I walked into the bank on Monday morning the Manager asked me if I had had an accident because he noticed that I was having some difficulty in walking. "No Ramon" I replied "I disregarded your advice and I went to the Salem Night Club on Saturday, and I have never in my life danced with so many attractive girls". I then completed the audit and was glad to return to Hong Kong.

Accommodation in Hong Kong for an ever-increasing number of foreign staff officers was both expensive and in short supply and the majority of middle-management officers, such as myself, were given apartments in large blocks of flats on the mid levels of The Peak and I started off in one of the more congested blocks called Panorama. Most of the occupants of Panorama were junior married officers with young children and I therefore asked our Residences department if they could find me somewhere quieter to stay and I moved to Harbour View Mansions which was much more to my liking, and the absence of a communal swimming pool did not worry me. It was from my balcony in Harbour View Mansions that I would often check to see if there were any American warships anchored in the harbour because if there were then the Wanchai bars would be full of sailors, and one or other of my clubs would be a better choice for evening entertainment.

I had purchased a maroon MGB sports car and I had also acquired a one third share in a 36 ft motor launch with twin inboard engines and

I did most of my entertaining aboard this boat by inviting my friends out for evening dinners or weekend picnics. My partners were Chinese businessmen who I did not know, having bought my share in the boat as a result of an advertisement, and we used our boat on a roster basis. As I was a member of the Royal Hong Kong Yacht Club I had a mooring in Causeway Bay which my partners shared, and this considerably reduced my boat expenses. We also had a coxswain and a boat boy as well as a speedboat which we used to get to the beaches and also for water-skiing. Water-skiing at night was a particular pleasure of mine and often this would produce fascinating phosphorescence in the water which was caused by plankton. On one occasion I was caught up in some fishing nets while trying to avoid a swarm of jelly fish and I had to be rescued by the boat boy under the glare of the searchlight which was mounted on the bows of the speedboat. We always made certain that there was at least one other person in the speedboat apart from the coxswain in case of accidents when water-skiing. Towards the end of November it was time for me to go on another branch audit and it did not surprise me when John chose Jakarta because the earlier fraud there had suggested that a full scale audit of the branch was advisable and I was appointed Team Leader which apart from overall supervision included responsibility for the audit preparation, allocation of duties and production of the audit report. Internal Audit was previously known as Inspection and it is now referred to as Compliance, but the basic function remains much the same, no matter what it is called. One of our Assistant Manager's major contributions to Internal Audit was the completion of extensive programmes and questionnaires for use during audits and when John retired it was Doug who then took charge of the department.

Apart from following our programmes and completing our questionnaires the method of conducting audits was left pretty much up to the Team Leader and my experiences in the Philippines had given me a couple of new ideas so I decided to introduce them immediately. When we arrived in Jakarta I told my team that we must eat our first breakfast, lunch and dinner in the hotel's Coffee Shop and that any wine or liquor that we consumed with these meals should be paid for separately. Our dinners should consist of a prawn cocktail, sirloin steak and ice cream, or similar, the receipted bills should be stapled to a copy of the menu and the combined cost of the meals would then become the daily allowance that each of us could claim for our meals for the duration of the audit, regardless of how much or how little we actually spent. Not only did this arrangement work well but it was also very popular with my teams and when our branch managers occasionally complained about the cost I had only to show them the Coffee Shop menu. It then became standard administrative procedure for all my branch audits.

It was normal for the Team Leader to discuss the major problems and discrepancies that the audit had revealed with the branch manager at the conclusion of the audit, and this discussion could often affect the contents of the report. We already had a system whereby sensitive and potentially controversial material could be contained in a separate section of the report entitled "Senior Management Only" and this section was not sent to the branch manager, nor was it available to central bank inspectors or other regulatory bodies. Notwithstanding the SMOs I had noticed that the reporting of some deviations and contraventions in previous audits was in my opinion unnecessarily harsh and this often gave the impression that the auditors were trying to find fault rather than simply trying to improve procedures. I therefore introduced a new category of reporting which I called "Corrected During Audit", and this was my second innovation. In a nutshell this meant that instead of recording an irregular procedure in the report and then detailing the recommended corrective action to be taken, we would simply mention the irregularity and then state that it had been corrected during the audit and since the irregularity no longer existed there was no corrective action to be taken. Although this innovation was mainly cosmetic it had the effect of toning down the impact of the report without impairing the effectiveness of the audit itself. I made a point however of not using the CDA procedure too often and it would be up to me as Team Leader to decide where and when it could be applied.

It was on the first day of our Jakarta audit when we were counting the cash reserves in the bank's Treasury that I first introduced the CDA procedure, as I noticed that the branch's liquor supply was also stored in the same vault as the cash and this contravened a Standing Instruction which did not allow the storage of any inflammable material in the cash Treasury. I therefore suggested to the Accountant that he move the crates of liquor to a separate area and when we came to count the bottles of liquor which were collateral for an overdraft facility we found the liquor to be correctly stored and the only mention of liquor in the cash Treasury was a CDA in the Cash section of our audit report. This innovation was a useful tool and it could even be extended to more important irregularities such as when the debit balance of a current account exceeded the authorised limit on the first day of the audit but if the excess was then repaid a few days later then the overdraft would be within its limit at the close of the audit, the matter was a CDA, and no corrective action was necessary.

While we were in Jakarta we were invited to a party in the bachelors mess and to get there our car had to pass through an area that the bachelors referred to as the Cemetery because there were graves on either side of the road. The Cemetery was always congested and our car had to slow down and when it finally came to a standstill a couple of girls tried to climb into the back of our car. We mentioned this to one of the bachelors and he told us to be very careful in the Cemetery, and not to stop the car there. "Why so" we asked. "Well" he replied "the big problem with the Cemetery is that most of the girls there are not actually girls, and you'd be far better off in the Ancol Recreation Park".

Eventually it was time to leave Indonesia and we arrived back in Hong Kong in time for Christmas. Most of January 1975 was spent reorganising the department under new management and we had also taken on two new audit officers who were qualified chartered accountants, and they were employed as contract officers rather than being members of the Foreign Staff. Our next branch audit was Kuala Lumpur in Malaysia and once again I was given the job of Team Leader. During this audit I spent quite a lot of time in explaining the bank's procedures to our new CAs, which after twenty three years I knew pretty well, but I also took the opportunity to learn a lot from them regarding standard accounting practices and our team worked well together. I found conditions in Malaysia to be similar to Singapore only there was much more space and I spent one weekend at the mountain resort of Genting Highlands which I reached by helicopter from KL as the Skyway cable car had not yet been constructed. The Theme Park at Genting Highlands had been constructed by Lim Goh Tong in the late 1960s and it had a casino and many other amenities that attracted a large number of tourists, and I rediscovered a taste for *nasi goreng* in my hotel restaurant. The facilities in KL itself were a little more restrictive but I had reciprocal arrangements with the Cricket Club which I visited several times, and the bank officers themselves would often entertain visiting auditors in their homes.

I had only been back in Hong Kong for about a month and I was fully expecting to be sent on another branch audit, when an unexpected development took place which would provide me with the most exciting and certainly the most unusual assignment that I was given in my time with the bank. The Vietcong were moving into South Vietnam and when communication with our Saigon office was cut off we lost all contact with our branch and I was then given my second one man Special Investigation. I was asked by our Staff Controller if I was prepared to volunteer to fly to Vietnam as the Chairman's representative to assess the political situation there and to determine whether or not our Saigon branch should be closed. I was to take whatever action I deemed necessary, with a view to protecting the lives of our staff and their families, as well as the assets and properties of the bank. I was given some written guidelines which were then the equivalent of a branch closing procedure manual, and I was told to wear a pair of gym shoes, so I put my usual hip flask in my airline bag, and I flew to Saigon on 4 April where I stayed in the branch manager's house.

One of my first tasks upon arrival in Saigon was to personally deliver a sealed envelope to the manager of Citibank from their regional head office. I knew that the letter contained secret and detailed instructions as to what to do if Saigon fell into enemy hands, such as evacuating staff and burning code books etc. However, when I arrived at Citibank I discovered that the manager as well as all his American staff had left Vietnam on the plane that I had come in on the day before, and the branch was now under the control of their senior Vietnamese officer. I made a quick decision, and gave him the secret letter addressed to his predecessor, and I was later complimented on my action when I returned to Hong Kong. The situation with our own bank manager was very different; Ian was a bachelor and he had surrounded his house with sandbags, he had a Lugar pistol, and he told me that he was keeping his last bullet for his Doberman Pinscher.

I found the French banks to be far more helpful than most of the embassies, and it was by chance that I met up with a number of foreign journalists in a hotel bar one evening. After several days I had gathered sufficient political information to enable me to make the ultimate decision, which was to prepare for the inevitable closure of our bank, but how long could I safely stay in Saigon to achieve this? The decision was made for me when an American Lockheed C-5A Galaxy Transport plane involved in the evacuation process crash landed on the runway at Saigon's airport shortly after take off killing 138 passengers, an immediate curfew was imposed, and my promised jump seat on Cathay Pacific's last flight out of Saigon was no longer an option.

It was fortunate that I had used the French Embassy and the French banks as my main source of information because they were unanimous in their conviction that Saigon was about to fall. The CIA and the American Army Intelligence had published a report on 5 March stating that South Vietnam could hold out until at least the end of the year but this prediction was ill conceived. The decisive conflict which sealed the fate of Saigon was the Battle of Xuan Loc which lasted from 9 April to 20 April and this was more or less the period during which I was in Saigon. Unlike the Americans the French had no major evacuation plans and the reasons for this were threefold. Firstly, there were far too many French citizens in Vietnam to make this feasible, secondly the majority of French citizens were of Vietnamese origin and thirdly and most importantly they had little to fear from the VC, and this I learned from my discussions with the French Consul.

Having made up my mind that our branch must be closed, the next thing I did was to make arrangements with our senior Vietnamese officer Danny Mai whereby he would hold the fort for us as long as he could safely do so after I had persuaded our own manager to leave, as I considered that abandoning the office would have invited looting. We therefore secretly chartered a fishing vessel to take Danny and his family across the water to Thailand, where they could get down into Bangkok where they would be under the care of our branch there until we could get them visas to enter Hong Kong, and when I authorised the payments I wondered whether I was exceeding my authority. I calculated that in the unlikely event that the communists halted their advance before entering Saigon, then at least our branch would be in safe hands. In any event, there was plenty of cash in the bank's vaults, and I thought it better to use it in bribes, rather than to leave it for the Vietcong. Fortunately for me, not only did our Head Office subsequently ratify my action, but they also promoted Danny to manager Paris, after I had arranged his escape to Thailand.

My next step was to try to get possession of the bank's title deeds, which I intended to smuggle out of the country, but the manager refused to give them to me as I had no specific authority from Head Office to remove them from the bank's vaults, so I asked to see them instead. The details of the title deeds were meticulously recorded in the bank securities register and I noticed that the documents were not only for the bank building but also for the manager's residence and included separately were the title deeds for our Haiphong branch in French Indo China which had been closed many years previously. I then bracketed the ledger entries in the register with my green ink pen, which I used for audit purposes, and I wrote against the entries "Temporarily removed by Group Head Office Internal Audit Hong Kong for examination and return". I then signed the entry and put the bundle of title deeds into my briefcase, and when Ian smiled at me I knew that we had reached an acceptable compromise.

I spent a lot of my time in Saigon in the streets and although there were isolated skirmishes and some looting in the latter stages it was relatively safe to wander around in daylight. However the plight of the local people was absolutely appalling. Hundreds of thousands of refugees were desperate to leave the country, the value of the local currency had collapsed, there was a rampant black market and one US dollar would buy me a meal with as much wine as I could drink. I was inundated with pleas for help which I was unable to give and I myself was beginning to adjust my values. I had to think ahead, and in situations such as this when you are about to lose a banking business my guidelines had made me realise that assets can become liabilities, in other words it is better to be owed money than to have it taken away from you.

When the curfew was lifted and the airport reopened, the Vietcong were only a few miles from Saigon, so I flew back to Hong Kong with my precious title deeds, some bank silver, the pregnant French Vietnamese wife of Bob who was the manager's assistant, and a Ngor Bue lacquer painting, which was a gift from Danny and which I still have in my possession. Although my report was accepted by the bank's senior management it had to be approved by our board of directors before any formal announcement of the branch closure could be made in the form of a press release. I was therefore instructed to attend the board meeting and to be prepared to answer any questions that any of the directors might ask me. I took a copy of my report with me but instead of entering the boardroom I was told to wait outside the door until my presence was needed. After about half an hour the Chairman's Private Secretary opened the boardroom door and Margaret told me the board had unanimously approved the closure of our Saigon branch based on my report, and as nobody had any questions I could return to my desk.

By 27 April over 100,000 VC encircled Saigon, and on the following day three missiles hit the city, and the Americans began their huge and controversial evacuation entitled Operation Frequent Wind using helicopters and the seventh fleet, and this resulted in the evacuation of over 50,000 people. On 29 April the VC launched their final attack on Saigon with a heavy artillery bombardment and when South Vietnam capitulated on the afternoon of 30 April the dissolution of the South Vietnamese government and the withdrawal of all American forces had effectively ended the Vietnam War. My recommendation to close our branch had not been premature.

The Head of Audit had told me to get rid of the Saigon and Haiphong title deeds but I could not find a single department in Head Office that was willing to accept them, and even a friend of mine in Group Finances told me that they considered them to be more of a liability than an asset. In desperation I asked the Deputy Chairman for advice but as he was unable to help me I decided that the best thing to do was to dispose of them by secretly putting them into the archives section of the vaults, but there was to be a sequel to this. Seventeen years later in 1992, HSBC re-opened its branch in Saigon, then known as Ho Chi Minh City, and I was able to tell the bank from retirement in Spain, where in the vaults they could find my title deeds, and they were duly located. The episode was written up in the bank's magazine, and my decision to smuggle the title deeds out of Vietnam in 1975 was finally vindicated. I had done all I could be expected to do as a retired Obedient Banker, but I was never actually told whether or not my smuggled title deeds helped the bank in their compensation negotiations with Hanoi.

I barely had time to settle back into my Hong Kong routine when I was told to lead an audit team to Singapore and this was a relatively easy audit because I was familiar with many of branch's procedures. There was a general pattern to be followed in all our audits and the element of surprise was very important in order to prevent last minute "cover-ups" or window dressing. To ensure secrecy we were allowed to book our own flights and hotels instead of using the bank's Travel department and although the duration of each audit was estimated in advance the audits were always open-ended and it was left to the team leader to decide when to return.

In every audit the first thing to do was to count the cash and this could either be done in the evening or early morning the following day. I much preferred the early morning counting and I invariably adopted this method when I was Team Leader. It meant that we could settle into our hotel after our journey and next morning when the first officer arrived to open up the bank he found the audit team waiting by the front door. We would then take control of the safe keys and the vault combinations and after we had counted the cash we would count the travellers cheques and anything else that we could think of. I even told my teams to count the number of staff in the office and to repeat this several times during the day and the results could then be compared with such things as the payroll and the staff vacation lists and this innovation often revealed some surprises.

There were generally three stages to each audit, and the first stage was one of concern and uncertainty because of a natural fear that no meaningful lapses, irregularities or contraventions would be discovered. The second stage was one of complacency and boredom, because the audit had progressed sufficiently to enable the auditors to relax and get down to the more mundane tasks such as sending out balance confirmation letters. The third stage was more interesting because towards the end of an audit the problems and anomalies had been identified and the necessary corrective action had to be determined. It was during the second stage that I always chose a day that I referred to as "Audit of the Outside Office" and this would give us all a one day break from routine auditing, and it was in Singapore that I first introduced this innovation.

The Singapore branch had recently moved from Collyer Quay into the Ocean Building and we could find no noticeable aspects of the outside office that needed investigation. We had already examined the branch's opening up and locking up procedures and security was good so I decided to disguise myself as a customer in order to check out the branch's customer relations. I therefore walked into the banking hall with a false moustache and wearing a pair of sun glasses and a baseball cap and I approached a receptionist. I had an old cheque book from the days when I had maintained a current account in Singapore so I completed a cheque for fifty dollars and asked the receptionist to cash it for me. Eventually the girl told me that the account did not exist and after I told her to check this out again she told me that the account was a dormant account. I agreed that the account had not been used for several years but I would still like the cash and she told me that there was no money in the account because it had been transferred to Unclaimed Balances. I then told her that I would like to formally claim the balance but she told me that this would be impossible, because the account was no longer active. At this stage about half an hour had elapsed and as I was attracting a certain amount of attention the Accountant walked over to the receptionist and started to ask if he could help us. "Good grief" John exclaimed "it's Jerry", and he told the girl that I was the bank's internal auditor. I then removed my disguise and thanked the receptionist for her help, and I told John that I had simply been checking his customer services. As auditors we all had pocket tape recorders which we used for our reports and when I played back my recorded conversation with the receptionist to the Manager both Angus and John agreed to improve their customer services, so I gave the episode a CDA rating in my audit report before returning to Hong Kong.

Sir Robert Ho Tung had been the bank's Compradore in Hong Kong, and his family owned a mansion on The Peak called Ho Tung Gardens.

The Obedient Banker

When Sir Robert died in 1956 his estate was administered by the bank's trustee company and it provided for the bank to have first option to rent two self contained flats in the mansion. These flats were normally occupied by senior married officers but as the lease restrictions did not permit any children or domestic pets on the premises there were very few senior married officers in the bank who were eligible. Shortly after I returned from Singapore I was offered one of the flats, in much the same way as I had been offered a flat in Singapore in 1959, and I had no hesitation in accepting the offer.

The building in which my flat was situated was more like a castle than a mansion, and I had my own private entrance and a fantastic view of Hong Kong harbour. The grounds were absolutely fabulous with terraced gardens and an ornate swimming pool with a pagoda, which I was allowed to use, and there was also a huge marble chess board with almost life size pieces. The Ho Tung family spent a lot of their time in Taiwan but occasionally General Ho and The Dragon Lady (as we called her) would visit their mansion and I was then on my best behaviour. However on one occasion we had an unexpected visit from The Dragon Lady at a time when a group of us were frolicking in the pool and some of the girls had removed their bikinis, and this resulted in a complaint to the bank and I was advised by our Senior Trustee Officer to be more discreet in future. The previous occupants of my flat, Dick and Molly, had used much of their own belongings so when I moved in the bank replaced their heavy furniture but as my large living room was still somewhat bare I purchased two antique black lacquer cabinets and a matching ten panel screen, and this acquisition turned out to be an excellent investment. In June 1975 I was selected to attend an Intensive Financial Analysis Course conducted by Dr. J.L. Espy of Harvard and this provided me with a temporary moratorium on branch audits which was a welcome respite, and I made full use of the facilities in my new residence as well as enjoying as many summer evenings as I could on my boat, and I also spent several weekends in Macau in much the same way as I had visited Las Vegas when I was in California.

In July the time had come for me to undertake another branch audit and I was given the plum job of auditing our seven branches in Mauritius, much to the envy of my fellow audit officers. We were to be a three man team and once again I was to be Team Leader with the two Chartered Accountants who were contract officers of the bank. By this time both George and Vivian were well versed in bank procedures, we had undertaken several audits together, and this new audit was to be one of the most enjoyable in my career. The bank's presence in Mauritius was due to the acquisition of The Bank of Mauritius by the Mercantile Bank in 1916 and our subsequent purchase of Mercantile Bank in 1959, and the branches that we were about to audit in Mauritius were still operating in Mercantile's name.

The planning for the Mauritius audit was both complicated and unusual. As the seven branches were scattered all over the island we would not only have to rent a car for the duration of the audit but we would also have to stay in more than one hotel. There were no direct flights to Plaisance International Airport from Hong Kong, the CPA flight was via Perth, and I had no desire to go to Nairobi so we booked ourselves first class tickets on an Air India flight to Bombay on 19 July where we had a connecting Air India flight to Mauritius. Our General Manager Overseas Operations was an ex-Mercantile Bank man who had served in Mauritius and Ian was very helpful in briefing me on what to expect and how to organise the audit operation. "Do you like fishing?" he asked me before I left and when I said no he said that it should have been him and not me who was going to the island.

As we would have to move from branch to branch to complete the audit some element of secrecy would be lost but I decided that the audit date for each branch would be the day after our arrival, and that the three of us would separate and arrive unannounced at three different branches where we would each count the cash as soon as the bank was closed to the public. The next morning the three of us would be waiting at another three branches where we would each count the cash before the branches opened to the public. To achieve this I myself counted the cash on the first evening in the main Port Louis office in the north west, from where I rushed to the nearby Rose Hill branch to do the same thing, Vivian took Curepipe in the centre of the island and finally George went down to Mahébourg in the south east, and the following morning we each counted the cash separately in the remaining three branches. I had been told in Hong Kong that it would be impossible for the three of us to achieve this but no one knew that George's sister Caroline would be joining us from the UK and she acted as our unofficial driver dropping us off and collecting us from the different branches. I suspect that this was the first and the last time that there had been a simultaneous audit of all our Mauritius branches.

We had initially booked ourselves into a beachfront resort called the Trou Aux Biches Hotel and we occupied one of several circular bungalows with palm leaf roofs and these bungalows had three bedrooms each with its own kitchenette and verandah. There was direct access to a beautiful white sandy beach and there was a miniature golf course on the other side of the bungalows. The complex also had a casino and dancing every night and it was at Trou Aux Biches that I learned to dance the Sega, which is a traditional Mauritian dance that had evolved from Creole slaves. The movements of the Sega are very primitive with sensual dance steps, the songs were in French and the main accompaniment was the pulsating rhythm of the Ravanes which were hide drums, the shaking of the Maravanes which were a type of castanet containing dried nuts, and the striking of metal triangles. Once experienced, this dance is hard to forget, and the bottles of Mauritian rum which were on every table definitely helped us with our dancing, and there were plenty of girls to show us the steps. We stayed on at the Trou Aux Biches for as long as we could.

Our audit team in Mauritius was well balanced and we got on well together, which is a very important part of every audit. I relied on Vivian for his expert knowledge of accounting procedures and George, who spoke French with a pronounced Etonian accent, found all the best places for food and entertainment and he also organised all our travel and accommodation arrangements; I myself, as a veteran banker, was able to coordinate our activities without any difficulty. Wild boar and venison were standard dishes on all restaurant menus in Mauritius and George had located an Indian restaurant in Port Louis not far from the bank where we regularly ordered the venison curry for our lunches, which was well within our hotel Coffee Shop allowance. This necessitated a round of golf or an evening swim on our return to the hotel, before visiting the casino or joining the Sega girls. Auditing had never been so enjoyable! Eventually it was time to leave Mauritius and George had discovered that if we flew to Hong Kong on BA on a Saturday they would have to put us up overnight in a hotel in the Seychelles so I arranged for the audit to finish on Friday and we flew out to Mahé on 9 August.

Some days after returning to Hong Kong from Mauritius I was summoned to Group Finances and shown a letter from Internal Audit addressed to one of our non-banking subsidiary companies requesting confirmation of the balance of their account in Port Louis. "Did you authorise the despatch of this letter?" I was asked. I examined the letter, which had been signed by one of the CAs on my team, and I explained that it was simply a routine letter sent to a selection of the branch's customers asking them to confirm the balances of their accounts. The reply was firm and unequivocal. "The funds that you are asking us to confirm belong to the bank and not to one of its customers. Internal Audit is part of Head Office in the same way as Group Finances and you can't ask me to confirm funds which belong to the bank simply because they are in the name of a wholly owned subsidiary company. The registered address to which you sent this letter is just a brass plate in the Isle of Man, and that is why it has been sent to me. Surely you know the names of our subsidiary companies?"

I gave the matter some thought before I replied and so far as I can remember I explained that as our new auditors were not familiar with the names of all of our subsidiary companies future balance confirmation letters would be vetted by the Team Leader before despatch. I also pointed out that the fact that a chartered accountant had detected and selected the subsidiary company's account for verification would suggest that it might be more appropriate to keep the funds in an inter-branch account rather than in a current account, since current accounts were treated as customers' deposits. I had already learned some important accounting procedures from our CAs, and the nature of our audits was changing and the scope of our department was expanding. I had made my point and our audits would soon include our Main Office in Hong Kong which at that time was exempt from audit, although Head Office itself would continue to be self-regulated.

By November several new foreign staff officers had joined our department, a few of them being senior to me, and we also had a new Assistant Manager and I was not surprised when I was included in his team for an audit of Calcutta. My knowledge of the office was very helpful but as I was not Team Leader on this occasion there was no Audit of the Outside Office as such. However it was during my audit of the Cash department that I decided upon an unorthodox testing of the branch's alarm procedure. Routine testing of the tellers' alarms was standard practice but as everyone knew in advance that the alarms were about to be activated not much was achieved other than to know that the alarms were working properly, and this was always done at times when the bank was closed to the public. I therefore asked our Team Leader if he had any objection to my sounding the alarm without prior warning and Bill agreed to this without giving it a second thought, and I neglected to tell him that I intended to set off the alarm at a time when the bank was full of customers.

In order to set my plan in motion I entered the public area and joined a line of customers at one of the large payout tellers' counters. When I reached the head of the queue the *babu* recognised me immediately, and I switched on my pocket tape recorder. "Hello Banerjee" I said "this is a testing of our alarm system. Imagine that I have pointed a pistol at you and that you have just given me all the cash in your till. Now after I start walking away please press your alarm button and lie down on the floor, just like it says in your armed robbery instructions". Banerjee smiled and nodded his head in agreement and as soon as the alarm sounded I ran to the front door and out into the street and the bank's *jemedar* and his two armed guards simply remained stationary at their posts without making any attempt to close the doors, which was laid down in the emergency rules which I myself had compiled some six years earlier. When we discussed the incident later the *jemedar* tried to justify his inaction by stating that he had not closed the doors because he realised that it was a fake alarm, and I replied that if he had known that it was a practice that was even more reason for him to follow the rules. The branch manager agreed with me, and the *jemedar* remarked "It is good to be knowing that Tait *chotasahib* is not changing one little bit since leaving our office". We all laughed.

The Calcutta audit was scheduled to end on a Friday but as my work had been completed I asked our team leader if I could leave a day early in order to spend a long weekend in Bangkok before returning to Hong Kong, and Bill told me that he had no objection. I had booked a seat on an early morning SAS flight to Bangkok and I was already in the departure lounge when the SAS plane flew over Dum Dum airport without landing and this was a common occurrence for large planes when the early morning fog from the surrounding swamps made landing conditions hazardous. I was told that as the next flight to Bangkok was two days later I would be taken back to Calcutta and accommodated in an inferior hotel. This of course was of no use to me but since I had officially already left India I refused to leave the departure lounge and I was then given a boarding pass on a Bangladesh Biman flight to Dacca which would connect later with a Thai Airways flight to Bangkok.

There were no seat assignments on the Fokker Friendship turbo prop plane that was supposed to get me to Dacca but the check-in girl warned me that she had given me a boarding pass in spite of the fact that the plane was fully booked and that if I wanted to be sure of a seat then I should get onto the plane as soon as possible. There were three Japanese businessmen at the end of the line when I stepped onto the plane, but only two of them were allowed to board. Shortly before takeoff the pilot announced that as one of the engines was not working we would be flying at a lower altitude at a tilted angle of forty degrees and the air-conditioning would be switched off to conserve power. This and the aroma of the stale curry patties that we were served with our *nimbu panies* made the journey one of the most unpleasant trips I have known, but the worst was yet to come.

On arrival in Dacca I was refused entry to the airport building because I had no transit visa and I had no option but to sit on the tarmac while waiting for my connecting flight, and fortunately I had my hip flask with me. The heat was unbearable so I removed my shirt and used it as a pillow before I dozed off. Eventually a soldier prodded me with his bayonet and when I offered him a five dollar note he brought me a plate of food from his canteen and it was not until 11 pm that I checked into my Bangkok hotel. At midnight I had a chilli and ginger crab dinner in Bangkok's open air night market and my subsequent early morning and long awaited massage was well deserved.

During my sixteen months in Hong Kong I had completed seven branch audits, conducted two Special Investigations, and attended an intensive course in Lending, and whilst not specifically engaged in these activities I had taken an active part in the expansion of our department. My annual staff report had been submitted recently to the Staff Controller and I had every reason to believe that it was satisfactory. Anyway in December 1975 our Manager told me that I was to attend an interview with senior management at which the Staff Controller would be present, and he hinted that it could involve a new assignment but he declined to give me any other details.

When I had been posted to Los Angeles from Calcutta in 1969 this was the very last place that I had expected to go to and now, some six years later, I was once again to be given an unusual assignment that was totally unexpected. When I entered the Staff Controller's office I was given the usual résumé of my recent activities and I was then asked if I would like a temporary attachment to our London office, which would probably be for a period of about six months, at the same time remaining on the Internal Audit establishment in Hong Kong, and I immediately accepted the offer, as this would be the only time I would be in the UK apart from my training and holidays. I was told that the main reason for me staying on the Internal Audit establishment was to keep my UK non-resident status while in London, which was an important income tax consideration.

The reason for this unusual assignment was the final merging of our three separate banks in the City, Hong Kong Bank in Gracechurch Street, Mercantile Bank also in Gracechurch Street and British Bank of the Middle

The Obedient Banker

East in Abchurch Lane. All three branches were to be closed and the entire staff of the three banks were to be integrated into a single building at 99 Bishopsgate under the control of a new Manager, Europe who was then our Senior Manager, London, and my new boss. In order not to upset our Arab customers, BBME would retain its name and have a separate banking hall in the new premises, but the Mercantile Bank London branch would be totally absorbed into the Hong Kong bank - staff and customers alike - and it would thereafter cease to exist as an entity in the City. I was to be named as Acting Manager Mercantile Bank Ltd., and Relief Manager Hongkong Bank, and although I would continue to receive my salary in Hong Kong I would be paid appropriate housing and transport allowances while in London, and I would also be given an expense account to cover my entertainment costs.

I had met a Chilean girl in Hong Kong and we had been seeing a lot of each other until she had left for Los Angeles and the bank agreed that I could fly to London via LA to enable me to stay with my girl friend for a few days before assuming my duties in London. In fact I left Hong Kong on New Year's Eve and I was driven to Kai Tak airport directly from a party and I saw the New Year in for a second time in JAL's executive lounge in Tokyo's Narita International Airport while waiting for a connecting flight to LA. My girlfriend met me on arrival at LAX at 10 pm and I saw the New Year in for a third time at a large party to which we had both been invited. We had such a good time together in LA that Mariana agreed to join me later in London once I had settled in.

Although I was to be the last Manager of Mercantile Bank in London my office was on the mezzanine floor of the Hong Kong bank next door, and it was the same office that I had regularly visited with my schedules when I was a trainee officer in 1951. I took over my duties from the outgoing Mercantile manager who was later to be transferred to Dublin and Frank, who was also known as Fitz, explained that one of my unofficial duties was to take care of Mercantile's pensioners and he gave me a hand written register with their names and addresses and other personal details. Another of my new tasks was to read all the incoming and outgoing telegrams and registered mail of both banks, and I soon realised that I was being given many of the more trivial managerial duties in order to relieve the pressure on the other managers who were preparing for the move to Bishopsgate. This was understandable because they would have new responsibilities whereas I would be returning to Hong Kong, and this was the reason why

Jeremy Tait

the Senior Manager London had asked Head Office for an additional manager to help him over the transition period.

The Mercantile Bank was involved in a complicated law suit and Fitz gave me the file to read and told me that the parties involved had been invited to a meeting in our boardroom and that I should take the chair. When I entered the boardroom there were at least a dozen people there, most of them solicitors, and after about half an hour of legal wrangling I decided to interrupt. "This meeting was convened in an attempt to reach an out of court settlement" I said "and what I have so far heard convinces me that we are now further away from reaching an agreement than we were when the meeting started. The only thing you gentlemen have achieved is an increase in legal fees so we shall now have a half hour recess. When we reconvene if the lawyers concerned have not been able to reach an agreement together then the next time we shall all meet will be in court". Our lawyer was furious and he drew me to one side: "The City of London has a code of behaviour and you can't treat QCs as if they were Chinese coolies" he said, and I replied by telling him that he now only had twenty five minutes in which to reach an agreement with his colleagues, which I hoped he would be able to do.

When I had calmed down I went to see our Senior Manager to tell him what had occurred and he was expecting me. "Don't worry Jerry" he said "I know exactly what you have done. I have already had a string of lawyers complaining about your action and I have told them that you have my full support in this matter. Good luck to you, do what you have to do and let me know the result". I had worked with Norman when he was the Sub Accountant in Singapore and it was he who had given my ex-wife and myself our wedding reception. The episode with the London lawyers reminded me of my meeting with our unions in Calcutta in 1969 when I had given them a similar ultimatum and I was relieved when the lawyers announced that they had agreed an out of court settlement. Our own lawyer advised me that he would no longer be able to represent Mercantile Bank and Fitz later told me that this saved us the trouble of dispensing with his services. I had survived my first important managerial task.

Our London office had not changed very much over the years, we still had the Accountants in their glass cages and the banking hall was presided over by the Head Messenger who sat at an elevated desk with the lifts and staircase behind him. I was now a member of the Senior Luncheon Room which we shared with the Accountants and the wine was free whenever we had guests, which was virtually every day, and the hours were from

12 noon until 3 pm. We all sat at a magnificent mahogany table and our drinks were served to us by the steward Donavan whose livery had crested buttons. I was constantly being asked to bring new guests to our lunches and this I found a little difficult because I did not know many people in London. Sometimes I found these lunches to be too much of a good thing and I would walk down to the river at Tower Bridge with a sandwich or take a Central Line tube to Marble Arch and have lunch at the Playboy Club in Park Lane where I still had my Gold Card from California, and this would give me at least half an hour in the Casino before returning to the bank.

There was no lack of business entertainment in London and as all the resident Managers were married and most of them lived out of town they would frequently ask me to stand in for them. I remember on one occasion Norman gave me his invitation from an Arab bank to a Cocktail Party at Claridges and as I was helping myself to some caviar at the bar I heard a familiar voice with a Dutch accent "What zee hell are you doing here Jerry?" and there was my old friend Louis who had shared a junk with me in Hong Kong. Louis was now Manager of the Nederlandsche Handelsbank in London and it was very nice to be able to renew our friendship. On another occasion Norman asked me to deputise for him at a lunch with Antony Gibbs and I discovered the reason as soon as I entered their luncheon room, which was full of their senior management as well as a number of their directors. The bank had recently acquired a portion of Antony Gibbs' equity and Norman had correctly guessed that the reason for the invitation was to try to find out what the bank's future intentions were, although I don't suppose at that stage that Norman would have been any better placed to provide an answer than I was. I had been given several pink gins before we sat down, the wine flowed throughout the meal, and when the brandy was served with the coffee I think I told Gibbs that traditionally the bank tended to prefer majority rather than minority holdings because most of our subsidiary companies were wholly owned, but this they would already know from our balance sheet. In any event my reply seemed to satisfy them.

I was living in a family flat near Holland Park and I had recently purchased a second hand Toyota which I sometimes used in the evenings, but more often at weekends when I liked to get out into the country. My girlfriend Mariana had recently arrived from California and we visited all sorts of historic places such as Stratford-Upon-Avon, Stonehenge and Henley, and we also took in a number of West End shows. The Playboy

Club in London had recently changed hands and I now found myself a member of the International Sporting Club with reciprocal facilities in the Palm Beach Casino Club and Crockfords and I discovered that the Dining Room in the International Sporting Club provided one of the most elegant and reasonably priced candlelight dinners in the West End and it soon became one of my favourite venues, and this was reflected in my expense account.

One evening dinner that I particularly remember was the party we gave to mark the official end of the Mercantile bank in London and the majority of guests were retired officers of the bank. I told Fitz that as I did not know any of the Mercantile pensioners and they did not know me from Adam, he should be the host and not me but he insisted that as I was now the Mercantile's Manager I should fulfil this role. Fitz knew his colleagues, many of whom were Scots and most of whom had served in India at one time or another, and although wine was served with the meal Fitz told me to have a minimum of two bottles of Black Label whisky and one bottle of Courvoisier brandy placed on each table, and he helped me with the seating arrangements. When the main course was served a waiter came up to my table and asked one of the pensioners to extinguish his cigarette as smoking was not permitted in the dining hall until the coffee and liquors were served. "Git lost laddie" replied the pensioner "and bring us another bottle of whisky". By the time our guest speaker Malcolm Macdonald was introduced I had been obliged to order two more bottles of Black Label and Fitz later told me that he had put the bank's heaviest drinkers on my table. When I had finished off our table's bottle of brandy my companions told me that they could not have wished for a nicer chap to take care of them but I should make sure that there was no interruption in their pension payments when the new regime came into force. Most of our guests were twice my age but I left the party with a great respect for the men who had pioneered Mertcantile's activities in the sub-continent.

When the time came for relocation to our new London headquarters I had expected to return to Hong Kong but Norman told me that he wanted me to stay on in Bishopsgate as a relief manager until the bank had settled into its new premises and operations were running smoothly. In some ways it was a sad moment when we moved out of Gracechurch Street because it had served as our London office for a great many years and there were several traditions that would now be abandoned. Indeed many of our senior home staff took early retirement before the move and the atmosphere was then a mixture of excitement and sadness. At about 6 pm on my last day in the office we had all put the contents of our desks into cartons for delivery to Bishopsgate and I was going through some papers when the removal men entered my office and took away my desk and chair, so I had no option but to stuff the papers into my briefcase and turn out the light. I can honestly say therefore that I was probably the last bank officer to have worked in 9 Gracechurh Street, and when I walked out of the doors I felt a like a captain leaving a sinking ship. Our banking hall was subsequently converted into a Wetherspoon pub called the Cross Keys.

The innovative interior design of our new twenty six storey London headquarters was something that none of us had previously experienced and it took us a while to adapt to the new concepts and procedures that the building was designed for. Our office floors were open plan with movable partitions and as a manager I had a corner unit with windows facing in two directions. Each floor had several refreshment areas where staff and officers alike could help themselves to coffee or juices from dispensing machines and instead of individual secretaries we used a secretarial pool and instead of messengers there was a maze of pneumatic tubes that distributed incoming and outgoing mail and messages from intermediate platforms. Not only did these new innovations take some getting used to but we also had some initial teething problems so one of my main tasks during the first few weeks in Bishopsgate was to help resolve the difficulties that our departments were experiencing.

The bank building had a forecourt with parking facilities and this was specifically designed for BBME as it allowed our Arab customers to step out of their limousines and walk through a private entrance to conduct their business while their chauffeurs waited in a convenient lay-by. A very important focal point in Bishopsgate was the Senior Luncheon Room which was used by BBME's Head Office as well as by all our managers, assistant managers and heads of departments, and this was where we got to know each other. The luncheon room had a lounge bar and initially we would introduce ourselves and enjoy our drinks before going to a self service buffet and sitting down at individual tables with whoever we wished, and the whole operation was run by our old Gracechurch Street steward Donavan. I had no part in the planning of the Bishopsgate headquarters as this was handled by senior managers from each of our three banks who were named as Coordinators. Our coordinator Willy was later to be appointed Group Chairman, and the Mercantile's Coordinator Paul was contracted for the job shortly after his retirement, and as both of them were frequent users of the lunch room they were able to see for themselves how successful the room was in achieving integration of the three banks, at least at a senior level. I met a lot of new faces and made a number of friends there that I would meet again later on in my career.

It was not until July that Norman told me that my job in London was coming to an end and that he would shortly be advising Head Office that I would be available for relocation. My Chilean girlfriend Mariana had become my fiancée and we decided to get married in Hammersmith Registry Office on 2 July. This was not a hasty decision as we had known each other for over a year and although she was 14 years younger than me and had an entirely different background, we had many interests in common. In those days it was still necessary to obtain the approval of the bank before marrying anyone and when the approval came through Head Office asked me if I would like to take my accumulated leave before returning to Hong Kong to resume my duties with Internal Audit, and I was absolutely thrilled with this arrangement. Not only would the bank now pay for my wife's travel but we would also be able to use our Hong Kong allowance to fly to Los Angeles from London and to visit her family in Chile as part of our honeymoon.

We flew to Los Angeles on 25 July 1976 and this was to be our base until 6 October. We both had friends in LA and Mariana had some personal effects there to pack and ship to Hong Kong and we made several trips to the beaches in Santa Monica and Venice and we also spent some time in Palm Springs as well as driving up to the Yosemite National Park where we stayed in the Ahwahnee Hotel. We had arranged to visit Mariana's family in Santiago for a couple of weeks so on 15 September we flew to Chile stopping off in Lima en route, but we were unable to explore much of Peru due to an uprising that was taking place during our visit, although we did get to see an excellent folkloric floorshow in Lima's municipal theatre.

We stayed with my wife's mother Carolina and several of her family in their large house in the centre of Santiago, and I soon discovered that the family were supporters of the late Salvador Allende. Allende had committed suicide in his Presidential palace two years earlier when his government had collapsed as a result of a CIA sponsored coup d'état which enabled the military dictator General Augusto Pinochet to assume control as President of the Junta. Our arrival in Santiago coincided with the annual celebration of Chile's Independence Day and on 18 September I joined my wife's family and after watching a military parade we all went to a nearby *ramada* to enjoy the festivities. Our *ramada* was a partially open building with a thatched roof, underneath which was a huge dance floor surrounded by stalls selling food and drinks. What amazed me the most was that everyone was eating, drinking and smoking while they danced and most of the men had not even bothered to take off their hats, so I took my glass and cigarettes with me and joined in the fun.

The drinks were subsidised and every so often our glasses were topped up with jugs of pisco sour as we danced. Our dancing partners were whoever happened to be nearby and towards the end of the evening the girl I was dancing with was suddenly dragged away from the dance floor by several men and I instinctively followed them until they entered a room next to the toilets. I was then stopped by a Cababinero who told me that the room was a restricted area and that I should return to the dance floor, and as I walked away I could hear the girl's repeated screams from behind the closed door. Half an hour later the girl's body was removed in an ambulance and Mariana's brothers told me that she was a Peruvian without proper papers and that the men who had dragged her from the dance floor were members of Dina, the dreaded secret police, and they had all raped her repeatedly as a matter of routine before taking her into custody. Notwithstanding Mariana's family's antagonism to the Pinochet regime they were loyal citizens of Chile and it was natural for them to support their Independence Day celebrations.

The husband of one of Mariana's sisters however was an active member of MIR, which was the Movimiento de Izquierda Revolucionaria and he was under detention in the infamous Villa Grimaldi prison at Peñalolén on the outskirts of Santiago, and we all went to visit him while he was being detained in a wooden cell called a Corvi house. As we were entering the prison a Jesuit priest who was with us handed me a loaf of bread which he took from a basket of food and he asked me to bring the loaf into the prison as a gift for Enrique. I was immediately suspicious and I gave the bread back to him. When we entered the prison we were searched and a guard took the loaf of bread out of the priest's basket and broke it open, and inside the loaf was a steel bladed knife. The priest was led away, and we never saw him again, but perhaps he was not even a priest!

MIR had its origins in 1965 and it grew out of a students' union which supported Allende but when Pinochet's Junta cracked down on dissidents MIR emerged as a major insurgent group and no less than eighty thousand MIR supporters were incarcerated in Villa Grimaldi of who thirty thousand were tortured. Enrique himself was later reported to have escaped from Villa Grimaldi and to have blown himself up while attempting to throw a hand grenade into a police station. The truth is that after a prolonged session of torture which left him paralysed his prison guards drugged him and attached a timed explosive device to his body which was then placed on the pavement outside a police station until the device exploded. The ruins of Villa Grimaldi have now been partially rebuilt as a Park of Peace in memory of the thousands who had lost their lives or who went missing without trace as a result of the atrocities committed by the Pinochet regime. Enrique's wife Mirtha, who was a social welfare worker and Mariana's younger sister, was one of two hundred thousand Chileans who were exiled and she was given immigrant status in Norway on compassionate grounds, and we later visited her in Sandvika, Oslo.

When I arrived in Chile with my new wife I had no idea how involved I would become in the oppressive political background that existed there and I had never experienced such a large number of police and military personnel wherever we went. The arrogance of the police and the military in particular was amazing and if they met women with prams on the pavements, the women would push their prams onto the street in order to give the officials a clear passage, and if they decided to take a taxi or board a tram no payment was given or expected. Notwithstanding this I found Chile to be a lovely country and I was always treated with courtesy and respect wherever I went. One of my favourite places was the seaside resort of Viña del Mar and the seafood lunches there with white wine were fantastic. It was there that I discovered a delicacy which was the roe of sea urchins and this was served with bread and a wedge of lemon. I always ordered a bottle of vino blanco Carolina to go with my sea urchins because it had the same name as my new mother-in-law, but in actual fact it was an excellent wine anyway. In the Santiago restaurants we were invariably served with a variety of empanadas and as I have never been too fond of pastry I would generally have a Chilean vino tinto as an accompaniment. Towards the end of our holiday in Chile Mariana's brothers took a van into the country to collect a load of avocados and chirimoyas which they would bring back to Santiago and they invited me to join them. At first I was reluctant to accept the invitation because it would be a very basic "men only" expedition and we would be sleeping in the back of the van, but my wife told me that it would enable me to see a lot of the countryside and a different way of life, and when I agreed to go on the trip I was told to wear a pair of jeans and all I needed to bring was a blanket and a spare t-shirt. Before we arrived at the farm we were to spend the night in a public park and I was advised to put my wallet and my watch in a secret compartment which was underneath the floor in the back of the van and covered by a carpet. I was intrigued and I wondered what was going on, but I was not to be left in any doubt for much longer. As soon as we had parked the van under some trees we were surrounded by a group of gypsy girls and my brothers-in-law warned me that the girls were very skilful with their hands in more ways than one, which was why we had put our valuables in the secret compartment. They also told me that if I preferred not to join them in the back of the van then one of the girls could give me a massage in the front seat. It was time to open another bottle of Carolina!

We flew back to LA on 30 September for a final week and I had discovered that by taking a Pan Am Clipper flight to Hong Kong we had the option of breaking our journey for up to three days in Hawaii and this diversion rounded off what had been an unusual and exciting holiday.

When we arrived in Hong Kong on 11 October I found that the Internal Audit department had once again been enlarged by the inclusion of several more foreign staff officers and one of the main reasons was that our audit scope had now been extended to include our operations in Hong Kong. At this time we had a new Manager in Internal Audit and Tony, who was Irish and had a dry sense of humour, had previously worked with the Mercantile Bank as had several others of our new auditors. Although married men were sent on overseas audits it was more usual to deploy bachelors so for almost a year my audit work was confined to the Colony and within a week of my arrival I was engaged in an audit of Outward Bills in our Main Office.

In January 1977 I was given my third Special Investigation which was in our Current Accounts department and this was followed in February by an audit of our Inward Bills department. In April I was engaged in a complicated audit of Current Accounts which was a follow-up on my Special Investigation which extended into May, and an audit of Mongkok in June was then followed by yet another Special Investigation, this time in our Savings Bank department.

By September it was time for another audit of Calcutta and it was inevitable that I would be included in the audit team but I was allowed to take my wife with me, and we stayed in the Great Eastern Hotel on Old Court House Street where I paid a little bit extra for a large corner suite that had its own sitting room. A few days after we had checked in, the hotel Reception phoned and told me that there was a man named Salamudin in the lobby who wanted to see me and should they allow him to come up to our room. Salamudin had been my driver in Calcutta in 1969 and he had driven me to and from more cocktail parties than I cared to remember, so I told Reception to send him up. When Salamudin entered our room he was carrying a large bouquet of flowers and as he was presenting them to Mariana he suddenly withdrew his hand. "Wrong *memsahib*" he said, and he just stood there still holding his flowers. I explained to Salamudin that I had now remarried and after a little hesitation he apparently decided to accept the situation and he reluctantly handed the bouquet to Mariana. It was an awkward moment, so I reached into my pocket and gave Salamudin a fifty rupee note for old time's sake and he was smiling when he left the room. I had a lot of affection for Salamudin, and I would not have wanted him to think that he had wasted his money when he bought his flowers for someone who was thousands of miles away.

Our CA auditor George was with us on the Calcutta audit and he had arranged for us to watch a game of polo on the Maidan which was not exactly my cup of tea but it brought back memories of the Calcutta Transcendental Society. As George was a member of the Hong Kong Club this gave him reciprocity in the Bengal Club so it was there that we generally ate our lunches. I had not been a member of the Bengal Club when I had worked in Calcutta as it was then the preserve of the *burrasahib* and our audit team were about the only foreigners in the club. Apart from the framed hunting, shooting and fishing prints on the dining room walls the main thing I remember about our lunches at the Bengal Club was that as soon as we sat down for lunch the Indian businessmen at our surrounding tables stopped talking to each other in Bengali and switched into English. Parts of their conversation often drifted over to us, possibly intentionally, and one particular conversation still remains in my memory. "When are you off home, Sebastian?" "Has to be July, old chap. Cant miss Henley and Wimbledon, don't you know". Calcutta *burrasahibs* were still the same; only their faces had changed.

With the advent of computers Internal Audit had employed a couple of computer auditors who assisted us with our audits whenever necessary, but it soon became evident that this did not provide us with sufficient coverage so a separate computer auditing section was created within our department and the computer auditors then wrote their own programmes. We worked together on branch audits and whereas we would audit around the computer they audited through the computer and when our results were compared in order to produce a consolidated report there was often a remarkable similarity in our findings.

The Obedient Banker

Notwithstanding this, after completing an audit of our Automatic Payments Centre in Hong Kong in October I was told that I had been selected to attend a Computer Concepts and Auditing Course conducted by Lowe Bingham and Matthews Price Waterhouse and Co and after studying the course prospectus I told my manager that the course was designed for computer programmers and not for auditors and I doubted that I would be able to understand it. I was then told that even if I emerged at the bottom of the class I should still go on the course because I was bound to gain some benefit from it. I was still an obedient banker, and I had little option but to comply.

As I knew it would be, the course was horrific and way beyond me and it involved the use of COBOL which was a computer language that I did not understand but somehow or other I managed to survive until the conclusion of the course. I even tried to master the rudiments of COBOL each evening but as I had received a C grade at an earlier IBM computer aptitude test I knew that this was beyond my capabilities in view of the shortage of time. Fortunately each participant was asked to complete a course assessment and I had no hesitation in stating that I had been sent on the wrong course mistakenly and that I did not have any computer programming experience, and I was later complimented for having completed the course. I had however learned a very important lesson and on my future audits I always made sure that I would have the services of a computer auditor when required. In those days Windows were something you looked out of, and laptops were something else altogether!

I was still recovering from my computer auditing ordeal when I was asked to join an audit team that our Assistant Manager was taking to Osaka in November and Bill had also taken me with him on our first audit of Calcutta in 1975 as he knew that I had previously worked in both offices. When we arrived in Osaka it was the same office where I had worked in the mid 50s but all the officers including the manager were now Japanese. There were no vestiges of the earlier strike and although several of the staff remembered me there was no ill feeling. What I remember chiefly about this audit was the claustrophobic rooms in our hotel where the windows could not be opened and the central heating that could not be turned off, and also the exorbitant cost of a good Kobe beef steak. However, as I was not the Team Leader there was nothing much that I could do about these problems, and no audit of the outside office was included in our agenda. The pachinko parlours were still very much in evidence although the machines themselves had become more sophisticated and I soon realised that the pay out was electronically programmed and it made no difference how you manipulated the steel balls because the machine was no longer mechanical. Times had changed.

After we concluded the Osaka audit in December we took the bullet train to Nagoya to audit our office in that city and this was the only time I had been to Nagoya apart from the night I had spent there when driving down from Tokyo in 1954. The audit was uneventful and we arrived back in Hong Kong in time for Christmas.

I had already learned quite a lot about conventional accounting from our Chartered Accountants and I was supplementing this information by studying a number of books on internal auditing and I was also receiving monthly issues of the Internal Auditors magazine which enabled me to introduce new ideas into our audit programmes which were under constant revision. As a result of this research I was eventually elected as a member of the Institute of Internal Auditors and at about the same time the bank appointed me Senior Auditor. In January 1978 I was placed in charge of an audit team to go to Germany where we had branches in Hamburg and Frankfurt, but Germany was a country that I knew very little about and which I had never visited before. I was looking forward to this audit and after some time I would once again be in charge of the operation, so I was very careful to research as much as I could about our operations in Germany before we took off.

We were travelling in jeans and when the Pan Am plane on which we had arrived in Hamburg took off with all our luggage still on board I had no alternative but to delay our audit until our suitcases had been recovered. Next morning we used the airlines compensation payment to buy some new clothes at a local tailor's shop that was recommended by the hotel. The Plaza hotel, which was where we were staying, had recently opened a casino and it was while I was playing blackjack there the following evening that the man who was sitting next to me engaged me in conversation. "You speak excellent English for a native Hamburger" he said "where did you learn to speak it so fluently?" When I replied I told him that I was British and that I had been educated at a public school in Oxford and he was quick to respond. "I assumed that you were from Hamburg because you use the same tailor as I do and very few foreigners would know about his shop". He had recognised the unique style of the hand stitched lapels on my new jacket.

As can often happen on some audits the Hamburg branch manager was a friend of mine but I had learned not to let this influence me in any way, and this situation was always accepted without question. When our luggage finally arrived and the audit commenced I discovered that the branch's balance sheets were computerised and I was offered the alternative of a two day old computerised balance sheet or to wait four days for the next programmed balance sheet and I told the manager that neither alternative was acceptable and that I required a non-computerised balance sheet for the day on which we had counted the cash which was at the close of business the previous day. The branch had not produced a non-computerised balance sheet for several years and to do so now would be a laborious task because the balance of each account would have to be entered manually onto the balance sheet, but I was adamant and the staff worked late that evening in order to comply with my request.

The next day I asked the Manager why I had not yet been given the balance sheet and he told me that although it had been completed the total assets did not agree with the total liabilities and that his staff were still checking and re-checking the balances of each account in order to determine the reason for the discrepancy. I then asked Peter to give me the balance sheet as it was and I told him that it would be my job to discover the reason for the discrepancy, and when he wished me the best of luck I realised that there was a distinct feeling in the branch that I was being somewhat old fashioned in not accepting a computerised balance sheet, but my stubbornness would later be vindicated.

We used the irregular balance sheet to verify the balances of all the accounts which we audited and eventually by a process of elimination I had identified exactly where the discrepancy existed and it was in a mixture of Charges account and Interest and Discount Received account which were two of the most important sub-accounts in the Profit and Loss account section of the balance sheet. This was a very serious matter because it was a strong indication of possible fraud but further investigation was difficult because the accounts were computerised so I had little alternative but to ask our computer auditor to help me resolve the discrepancy. He then ran a series of tests and eventually identified a faulty programme which dated back to the time when the branch's Book accounts were first computerised. The programmer had introduced a shortcut into his programme whereby all the pfennig were eliminated from the individual Deutche Mark entries to the various accounts whose balances were included in the balance sheet.

In auditing parlance this is known as the salami process because it allows very small amounts which are almost unnoticeable to be sliced off and diverted and this is a favourite method adopted in many computer frauds. The negligible amounts can accumulate over a period of time into sizeable portions and an important part of such an operation is where the salami slices are deposited. If the programmer had been dishonest he would have diverted his pfennig into an account to which he had access such as a current account, but fortunately the man had been negligent rather than dishonest. Instead of simply eliminating the pfennig by diverting them to a profit and loss account his programme provided for the rounding off of each DEM entry so that DEM 49.51 became DEM 50 and DEM 49.49 became DEM 49, so the divergence was to some extent offset. However, each decimalised entry was unchanged in the individual accounts so the net difference in the suppressed pfennig had to exist somewhere and it was of course in the profit and loss accounts, surpluses going into Interest and Discount Received, and deficits ending up in Charges account, and as the amounts of these entries were negligible and as they were recorded as computer differences, they were disregarded. As P & L accounts are closed off periodically to establish the branch's overall profit or loss the totals of these salami entries would then cease to exist.

This complex situation was revealed because I had insisted on a conventional balance sheet with which I was familiar and which I understood, and as a result the computer programmer was replaced and I gave the incident a CDA (Corrected During Audit) classification in my report. I was later asked by the head of audit, when he was reviewing my audit report, that if I had used a computerised balance sheet where the total assets would have been the same as the totals liabilities, would we have discovered the discrepancy when we came to the routine examination of the P & L accounts. As I dislike hypothetical questions I replied by asking him if he would have questioned the existence of small computer differences and he smiled and said "Well Jerry, I guess we will never know the answer to this one".

One cannot visit Hamburg without seeing the Reeperbahn and although the district is best known for its street walkers and its sex shops, we saw several excellent floor shows in the numerous night clubs in the area. It was very cold in Hamburg with snow on the pavements and parts of Alster Lake were frozen but we still managed to do a fair amount of sightseeing in the city. When the Hamburg audit was completed we moved to Frankfurt where the bank had recently opened a branch in a modern building. The only difficulty that I had in Frankfurt was while auditing the Dealing Room and although I had a Dealing Procedure Manual I had no audit programme and the fact that operations were conducted in German did not help. To have abandoned my examination of the Dealing Room would have downgraded the entire audit so after having satisfied myself that the main provisions of the manual were being followed, such as a periodic surprise closing of exchange positions during dealing, I included a qualification in my report to the effect that the examination of the Dealing Room had been more of a survey rather than an in-depth analysis. I had learned this refinement from my Institute of Internal Auditors' guidelines for conducting audits.

It was while I was in Frankfurt that I was asked whether I could stand in for our External Auditors and conduct a Special Audit of the bank's advances in Germany, in addition to the loan audits that I had just completed. This was a central bank requirement that up to now had been performed by Peat Marwick GmbH, but in this instance the Bundesbank had agreed that I could undertake this task provided that my audit followed their laid down procedure. This procedure required that every single advance, including temporary overdrafts, be graded on a sliding scale A to E, the A grade being where the advance was fully secured and there was no element of risk, with the E grade indicating that the advance was an unsecured load with little or no chance of recovery, in which case it would either have to be fully provided for, or as a last resort written off.

I agreed to undertake the task, and when my audit team returned to Hong Kong in February I stayed on in Germany. I was given a senior English-speaking Loan officer from our staff to work with, and the two of us spent several days with our external auditors learning the new procedures. Peats were extremely helpful, considering that I was taking over their job, and the method I decided to adopt was to modify a proforma of the printed form they used for loan analysis and we then transposed the bank's name and Internal Audit Department onto the top of Peat's form and we added our names and titles with spaces for our signatures at the bottom. This was then superimposed onto computer print-outs of the balances of all the advances in both branches as at the date of the audit. Peats did not object to my crib and we had managed to produce an impressive document which I hoped would satisfy both the Bundesbank and our own Head Office.

The German regional officer and myself worked very hard together on the actual allocating of grades to each advance and I found the Intensive Finance course that I had attended in 1975 to be extremely useful in this operation. Each advance had a space for comments which we completed together and when the report was finished I had to admit that it was a far better representation than our own loan report which had only included those advances which we considered irregular or bad and doubtful. One of the advantages of the new system was that a summary of all the advances could be included in the report reflecting the exact percentage of the total of each grade in relation to the total advances and the Bundesbank took the view that if for example eighty percent of the advances were in the A category then this would indicate that the bank's loan portfolio was of a relatively high standard.

It was inevitable that when I reviewed my completed report with the Hamburg manager that he would object to a number of my gradings and I admitted that as it had been the first time that I had ever classified an entire loan portfolio I had possibly been somewhat overcautious and at his request I agreed to upgrade a number of my loan classifications. One of the last things we did on our overseas audits was to give the branch manager a summary of our expenses and when I had returned to Hamburg from Frankfurt I had booked myself into the InterContinental hotel which was a little more expensive than the Plaza, and this was reflected in their Coffee Shop prices which I had used as the basis for my meal expenses. Peter was not at all happy when I gave him my expense account but I reminded him that I had stayed on in Germany at his request in order to conduct the Special Audit on Advances and this had saved the bank a lot of money that they would otherwise have had to pay their external auditors. This did not deter Peter and he once again told me that he thought my claim was excessive and that I should resubmit it for a reduced amount.

In my opinion the claim was perfectly legitimate so I had little option but to tell Peter something that I was very reluctant to do. "I hesitate to tell you this Peter" I said "so it has to be off the record. Before I left Hong Kong the Staff Controller asked me to check out the Basket of Goods upon which your cost of living allowance is based, and when I compared the food prices last week in a supermarket I found that the figures in your Basket were a bit on the high side but I decided that as the margin of difference was not significant I would make no recommendation for any change in your cost of living allowance. If you really feel that my expense claim is excessive I might feel obliged to fall in line, in which case I would have to have another look at your Basket of Goods."

There was a long pause while Peter and I looked at each other and he gave me a very straightforward reply when he told me that he had inherited his Basket of Goods from his predecessor who was partial to caviar and smoked salmon and that he himself had not created any Basket of Goods as such, so it would probably be best if neither of us were to quibble over trivialities, and I had no hesitation in agreeing with him. In retrospect I was glad that I had told Peter off the record about the Staff Controller's instructions because I had strongly objected to them at the time but I had been told by the head of audit that they were to be implemented as a matter of routine for each country which produced a Basket of Goods. Obedient bankers should not allow their personal feelings to interfere with their instructions, particularly when they are internal auditors. However there are often more ways than one in resolving a problem, as was evidenced at the conclusion of the Hamburg audit, and I had been careful to adhere to the Institute of Internal Auditors Code of Ethics with which I was familiar. The moral here is best contained in an American saying "Never Fight City Hall".

My next audit in March was our Administration department in Hong Kong and this was a very diverse department that had never before been subject to audit. Two of us were allocated the Residences section and it would not be appropriate to comment on the irregularities that David and I discovered other than to say that most of our report was classified as SMO, meaning that circulation of the report was restricted to senior management only. In April I undertook a somewhat specialised one man audit of the Microfilm Library and in May I was placed in charge of an audit of our Savings and Time Deposits department.

A break from auditing came in June when I was selected to participate in a Kepner Tregoe course and this was the most interesting and useful course that I ever attended. The course is designed to improve a person's problem solving and decision making abilities and although the fundamentals are basically common sense the programmes when followed produce a style of organised and logical thinking. In this way priorities are established, probabilities are separated from possibilities, intuition is discouraged and emotion is eliminated. I was intrigued by this course and I have often used the material I was given for such mundane things as locating a lost item to an important decision such as buying a new house.

It was shortly after I had completed the Kepner Tregoe course that I was told to prepare for an audit of Bangkok and I was very pleased with this because although I had visited Bangkok on several occasions I had never worked in Thailand. We stayed in the InterContinental hotel in Bangkok mainly because it was in the Siam Centre where our Bangkok branch was also situated. We had ground floor chalets with verandahs overlooking the gardens and the swimming pool, and it was only a one minute walk to get to the bank from our chalets. At lunch time we would often take our meals at the hotel poolside and we would then change back into our suits in order to continue with our afternoon auditing. We generally used a back entrance of the bank and this gave me an idea for an audit of the outside office.

About half way through our audit I told our team to get up early the following morning because we were going to attempt to break into the bank before the staff arrived without setting off any alarms, and this turned out to be much easier than I had anticipated. We managed to prize open a ground floor window at the back of the bank and this led us through a kitchen and eventually into an area in the banking hall that was behind the counters. We knew exactly where the alarms were situated so we had no difficulty in avoiding them and as the door to the manager's office was unlocked I decided to sit at his desk and to await his arrival, and my team did the same thing by sitting at different officer's desks throughout the banking hall. As luck would have it the Manager had a coffee machine in his office so I poured myself a cup of his coffee and I could hardly wait to see the expression on his face when he entered his office.

I knew the branch manager fairly well, he had a sense of humour, and I would not have done what I did if the situation had been otherwise. When the bank staff arrived the whole thing was treated as a joke, the manager took us out for lunch, and we had a big laugh about it. However I did suggest to the manager that he put bars on his kitchen window and when this was done I wrote up the unprotected window as a CDA, but no mention of our unauthorised entry into the bank was included in the report. The correct procedure had been followed, and although the method we had used was unusual the result had been successful. More importantly the operation had relieved the monotony of the audit and it had shown the staff that auditors were also human beings.

It was in August after I had completed an audit of the Remittances department in Hong Kong that I was told that the Staff Controller wished to see me, and although I guessed that I might be given a new posting I was very surprised when Mike told me that I had been selected to open a new Internal Audit department in the United Arab Emirates and as such I would be seconded to The British Bank of the Middle East. I then conducted a final audit of Tsuen Wan in Hong Kong's New Territories and my wife and I flew out of Hong Kong on 27 September with round-the-world tickets. Our first stop was in Hawaii and after four weeks in LA we flew to Miami and the Bahamas and we also spent some time in Europe both in the UK and on the continent and after visiting Paris and Prague we flew to Madrid where we stayed with friends of my wife. When it was time for me to join BBME Mariana stayed on in Madrid for an extra month before joining me in Dubai.

CHAPTER NINE

DUBAI, HEAD OFFICE AND RETIREMENT

The British Bank of the Middle East, although part of the Hong Kong Bank Group, still retained its own name and it had no internal audit department, similar functions being exercised by an Inspection department in their London Head Office. Our Head Office in Hong Kong wanted BBME to adopt our audit procedures, and as a prelude to this BBME agreed to the establishment of an internal audit department which would be based in Dubai. BBME's Chief Inspector came to Hong Kong to familiarise himself with our audit procedures and apparently he was quite impressed with my February report on Advances in Germany and he had asked if I could be made available to undertake the opening and staffing of his new department, and this led to my appointment as Internal Auditor for the United Arab Emirates where we maintained twenty five branches in the seven Emirates. I was to report directly to the Chief Inspector in London, although administratively my establishment would be within the jurisdiction of the UAE Area Manager in Dubai.

In order to give Dubai sufficient time to prepare for my arrival and also to enable me to become familiar with BBME procedures I was initially sent to Muscat in the Sultanate of Oman where I arrived on 16 January 1979. I stayed in the beachside Gulf Hotel for two weeks and during this time I spent several days in each department in the Muttrah office on the Corniche and I also visited some historical sights including Nizwa Fort.

My wife joined me in Dubai shortly after my arrival and we were given a single story beachside villa in Jumeira but as it was not fully equipped we were allowed to buy new furniture and my wife was very happy with this. We were allocated an Indian cook boy but I told the area manager that I had already arranged with an employment agency in Hong Kong for a Filipina maid to join us and he agreed to this arrangement although it was a departure from normal procedure. This was the first of several concessions that Peter was to give me and it was an important beginning to the integration of the two banks that was to follow.

One of the first things to do was to get a car as I had already been allocated an Arab driver but a few days earlier Head Office had advised us to economise by not buying any more Mercedes cars so my driver and I selected a top of the range brand new Honda from the dealer's showroom and my new bank car was the envy of all the other senior officers because its air-conditioning was vastly superior to that of their old model Mercedes' and they would often borrow my car when driving up to Abu Dhabi through the desert, or when visiting nearby branches.

One aspect of Dubai which immediately appealed to me was our 36 hour week, which was Saturday to Thursday 8 am to 2 pm, with one hour less during Ramadan, and this meant that the afternoons were free and as the heat was oppressive it was normal to have a mid-afternoon siesta and to go swimming in the evenings after the sun had set.

My first long discussion with the area manager was concerning my new department and he asked me what sort of staff complement I anticipated, because he had received no specific details from his Head Office other than instructions from the Chief Inspector to provide me with such staff and facilities that I would need in order set up an effective Internal Audit department. Strangely enough I myself had received no indication of what size my new department would be and I was simply told to send the Chief Inspector weekly progress reports and these reports were to be copied to Internal Audit in Hong Kong.

Interviews with Peter were informal and relaxed, he always had his Arab Adviser with him and coffee and pastries were ceremoniously served on a silver tray before any of us started to talk. No matter how confidential the subject was the Arab Adviser was always present, and on some occasions the Dubai office manager was also included. On this occasion I told Peter that my department could extend to a dozen or so people and he immediately said that there was not sufficient space in the Dubai office for my department and I was therefore given a vacant portion of our Deira branch which was on the other side of Dubai Creek. I was then offered several local staff which I could select after meeting them and reading their personnel files, and although I did select two or three of them I told Peter that as my department would be highly specialised it would be necessary for me to advertise for suitable candidates and in the end I obtained most of my staff from a local employment agency, and once again Peter agreed to let me do this although it was not normal procedure. Initially I needed a good secretary and four auditors and when I found a suitable Indian stenographer with a university degree Peter was not only obliged to increase the salary of his own male Arab secretary but he also had to pay the agency's commission for my stenographer.

I had brought sets of audit programmes and questionnaires with me from Hong Kong and I had also accumulated a lot of material from the Institute of Internal Auditors so it was relatively easy for me to devise a simple test paper which all applicants had to complete and I was thus able to select the four most promising candidates as my new auditors, and it took me over a month of training before they were sufficiently proficient to start auditing. During this time I sent the Chief Inspector a document which I had entitled "Terms of Reference for BBME Internal Auditors – Duties and Responsibilities", and I had expected him to simply approve what I had compiled, and much of it was copied from my Institute of Internal Auditors Guidelines. I was therefore somewhat surprised when I received back my own Terms of Reference with a new heading "Terms of Reference for BBME Inspectors and Internal Auditors" and the rest of the document was exactly as I had composed it apart from a final clause that required Internal Auditors to conduct a follow up audit within six months of each inspection.

We had a Deputy Chief Inspector resident in Dubai and he had two foreign staff officers working with him as BBME inspectors and it then became apparent to me that London wanted them to continue their inspections in parallel with my audits, although I knew that it was Hong Kong's intention that Internal Audit was supposed to replace Inspection. I had no desire to simply check whether or not the Inspectors' recommendations had been implemented so I devised a system whereby I would wait a few months after receiving my copy of an inspection report and I would then conduct my own audit of the branch concerned using my own programmes and questionnaires, and my follow up of the inspection report was simply included as an addendum to my own report. Although I was complying with the Chief Inspector's instructions I was also in effect downgrading the inspection reports.

When I was ready to start auditing I told Peter that I had chosen his Stationery department to start with and when he expressed some surprise at my choice I told him that as it was to be our first audit I wanted it to be relatively simple, and he agreed with me. In fact this was not the entire reason because I had already noticed the poor quality of both the paper used in the bank's forms and ledgers as well as the print on the vouchers and letterheads and I had devised an entirely new audit programme for stationery that I wished to try out. One of my four auditors was a Sri Lankan who had adapted very rapidly to our procedures and I had appointed him as my senior auditor and his nickname was The Ferret for obvious reasons. Shortly after the audit had started the ferret told me that the name of the major supplier of stationery to the bank was the same name as one of our customers who had defaulted on a loan and this loan was now one of the bank's largest bad and doubtful debts. I told the ferret that I would now personally pursue this part of the investigation and that he should continue with the rest of the audit, and it did not take me long to realise that the contract for the supply of most of the bank's stationery had been given to the company specifically to enable it to start repaying its loan which the bank would otherwise have had to provide for.

I had already agreed with the area manager that whenever I discovered a serious irregularity I would discuss it with him and his Arab Adviser before taking any further action, and this is precisely what I then did. After the coffee and cakes were served Peter told me that he had no prior knowledge of this matter but his Arab Adviser admitted that he and the branch manager had made the arrangements and the branch manager was then asked to join in the discussion. Eventually an agreement was reached between us but I was adamant that the stationery contract should now be put out for tender and that it should not be awarded until the bank had received at least three independent quotations. This was part of our standing instructions, but I reminded the branch manager that the contract did not necessarily have to be awarded to the lowest bidder because the quality of the stationery was also an important consideration. Room had been left for the loan to be repaid provided there was no contravention of the bank's laid down procedures, and the recommendations that I was about to make in the stationery audit report would have to be followed.

The supply of stationery was not the only irregularity in the department because control over usage was lax and each department was given whatever supplies they indented for and the room where the stationery was kept was not locked and staff could enter and leave the room as and when they wished. I did not want to be too critical in my first audit report so I decided to select pencils in order to convey my message. I stated in my report that the number of pencils distributed by Stationery department in one month was sufficient for eight pencils per week for each member of the staff, and this meant that if each member of the staff had five children then each child could have received a new pencil each week leaving three pencils per week for use in the office. The point was taken, my humour had softened the impact, and new controls were immediately introduced.

It was during a subsequent audit of a suburban branch in Dubai that the ferret showed me a series of credit vouchers reflecting substantial cash deposits which had been made repeatedly to the branch manager's current account, and over a period of one month or so the total of these cash deposits was in excess of one million dirham. This was a most unusual discovery that had every indication of fraud but as the branch manager was a member of the Dubai ruling family, because he was a cousin of Sheikh Rashid, the matter was extremely delicate and I immediately phoned the area manager and told him that I needed to speak with him urgently. As usual the Arab Adviser was present and we all agreed that he and he alone should ask the branch manager what the large cash credits to his account represented, and within ten minutes we had the answer.

Each branch kept its overnight vault cash to a minimum because cash is a non income bearing asset. The main treasury was in Dubai and our armoured cash vans made regular runs between each branch to replenish temporary shortages and to remove surpluses. The branch we were auditing was constantly running out of cash and when the manager asked for a replenishment he was often told that he would have to wait for up to 24 hours before the next cash run, and sometimes the cash was needed on the same day. The manager maintained a current account in his name in Dubai as well as in his own branch and when his office needed more cash urgently he would take his own car to Dubai where he would draw sufficient cash out of his account which he would then deposit into his account with his own branch, and this cash was then used to satisfy the needs of his customers. I immediately checked his current account in Dubai and sure enough there were compensating debit entries for the exact amounts on the same dates.

"Thank God it's a false alarm" said the area manager. "Not so" I replied "the branch manager has contravened the laid down instructions for cash in transit and he has replenished the cash in his vaults by not declaring the cash movements to our insurance company. The premium we pay on our cash in transit insurance policy is determined by the amount of our declarations and the conditions of transit have to be adhered to. His failure to follow laid down procedure has jeopardised the entire arrangement". In many ways it was an advantage for the bank to have a branch manager who was a member of the ruling family but he had no banking experience and this made it easy for me to come up with a suitable recommendation. HH Rashid bin Saeed Al Maktoum's cousin would soon be attending a course on basic banking conducted by our training department. Everyone was happy with this solution including our new training officer who had just arrived from Hong Kong, and who said that he had never before had a member of a ruling family as a pupil.

By this time the area manager and myself had established a useful relationship and it was not long after I had arranged for the Sheikh's cousin to attend a training course that I was asked to undertake my first Special Investigation for BBME. The area manager told me that the entire stock of US dollar travellers cheques in Sharjah had disappeared and that the prime suspect was one of the branch's tellers. The Sharjah manager had investigated the matter but he was unsure of what to do and Peter asked me if I could take charge of the enquiry, and I told him that that was exactly what my job was all about.

When I arrived in Sharjah I discovered that there had been a large sale of several thousand dollars worth of American Express travellers cheques to an Arab customer and the head cashier had opened the vault and removed the reserve stock of travellers cheques which he had given to the teller to enable the teller to use part of the stock to make the sale. I asked the teller when he had last seen the bundle of unsold travellers cheques and he said that it had gone missing at about the same time that a portion of them were given to the customer over the counter. As the counter had no grille I realised that there was a distinct possibility that the customer had reached over the counter and picked up the stock of unsold travellers cheques at the time when the teller was recounting the travellers cheques that he had removed from the bundle. No one else had been close to the teller when the head cashier had given him the travellers cheques.

I then decided to put my Kepner Tregoe problem solving and decision making course to good use and I told the head cashier that I wished to re-create what had taken place, so I entered the teller's cubicle that was used for the transaction and I asked the teller to show me exactly where the stock of travellers cheques had been when he removed the cheques to be sold. He then pointed to a wooden drawer underneath the counter and said that he had taken the stock from the drawer before removing the cheques to be issued, and he also told me that he had replaced the unissued travellers cheques in the wooden drawer. If the man was telling me the truth and he had not placed the bundle on the counter, then the customer could not have taken them, so I immediately opened the wooden drawer and it was empty, as we expected. I then pulled out the entire drawer from its wooden frame and there was the bundle of unissued travellers cheques behind the back of the drawer, and this was obviously where they had fallen when the teller had replaced them.

Kepner Tregoe had worked. The probabilities had been identified and then eliminated until only the desk drawer and the teller himself remained. The deduction was logical, but it had only been achieved as a result of rationalisation. The teller was overjoyed, as was the head cashier, but they were both in for a big surprise. When I wrote up my report I recommended that both the head cashier and the teller be reprimanded, the head cashier for removing the entire reserve stock of travellers cheques from the vault, and the teller for accepting them, as this was in contravention of standing instructions. When the Sharjah manager told me that he thought my recommendations were on the harsh side I reminded him that if the travellers cheques had not been recovered no claim for any loss could be made to our insurance company because the teller's limit had been exceeded. In practice, if lost or stolen travellers cheques are reported to the issuers before any attempt is made to encash them the holder would normally be protected but in instances where the travellers cheques have no signatures on them, this is not always the case.

Shortly after I had recovered Sharjah's missing travellers cheques the area manager asked me if I would accept the position of the bank's Security Officer and after giving the matter some thought I could find no conflict of interests with my terms of reference and I accepted the position, and drew up suitable fire and burglary procedures for the bank to implement. It was about this time that we had a visit from a Chubbs salesman with a letter of introduction from London and the area manager asked me whether I was in favour of installing the laser resistant steel strong room and vault doors that he was promoting. The salesman advised us that the area manager in Lebanon had recently installed these doors in the bank's flagship office in Beirut but I advised Peter against it and we declined the offer.

Not much later the civil war in Lebanon took a turn for the worse and one of the foreign staff officers who I had worked with in Calcutta was evacuated from Beirut where he was involved in credit analysis, and he was temporarily attached to my department. With an extra officer I decided to audit Khor Fakkan where a recent inspection required a follow up. David and I took our wives with us on this occasion and although we initially booked into the Khor Fakkan Hilton we found this to be somewhat cramped so we moved into a cheaper but much more exciting resort complex called the Fujairah Beach hotel which was run by a Palestinian family and we had self catering facilities where we could cook our own fresh fish and have evening barbeques. David and Heather had been forced to leave Beirut in a hurry and David told me that the insurgents had tried several times to force open the bank's vault doors without success. These were the doors that I had rejected, and the insurgents in Beirut had finally detonated such a powerful explosion that an entire city block in Beirut including the Holliday Inn and our own flagship office were annihilated, and not one single item was recovered from our vaults. The bank had lost everything it owned there and all the contents of our customers' safe deposit boxes had been destroyed simply because of the powers of persuasion of a single Chubbs salesman. Sometimes people are unable to see the wood because of the trees.

There were some restrictions on our social life in Dubai, but they were not nearly as pronounced as those in Saudi Arabia. We had permits to purchase alcohol and although the drinks in the hotel bars were quite expensive, the prices in the liquor shops were very cheap. Women needed to be circumspect in their dress and we all had to be a little bit careful in our behaviour, particularly during Ramadan. A good friend of ours was the Food and Beverage manager in the Dubai Hilton and we would often join Alan and his Cuban girlfriend Lupe for dinners and shows together. On some Thursdays we would stay overnight in the Hilton in Al Ain which was an oasis township with date palms and mineral springs but the main attraction was the fifty percent discount that Alan obtained in all the Hilton establishments and I would reimburse him with our share of the expenses at the end of our outings.

It was when we were all together in a Dubai nightclub that we had a confrontation with two Arabs who insisted on dancing with Mariana and Lupe and when Alan and I intervened their bodyguards pushed us back against a wall and we then realised that we were dealing with members of the ruling family who were a law to themselves. I decided to show one of the bodyguards some documentation which identified Mariana as my wife, and Lupe and Mariana were released immediately because although single girls are fair game the Bedouins respect married women and they had assumed that Lupe and Alan were also married. When the Arabs left the nightclub we noticed that their car had the special licence plates used by Sheikh Rashid's family. An earlier contact with the ruling family had been much more enjoyable when we were invited to Zabeel Palace for an open air feast to celebrate Prince Mohammed's wedding, and it was a celebration long to be remembered with dancing and fireworks long into the following morning.

We took six weeks home leave twice while we were in Dubai and we were also allowed to take a week's local leave each year and on the first occasion we flew to Bahrain and on our second local leave we visited Jordan, and in both cases we stayed with friends. Our friends in Bahrain were Chris and Carmen from the Chartered Bank, who had originally introduced me to Mariana, and our friends in Jordan were Tony and Sarah, and Tony and I had undertaken several audits together when we were in Hong Kong.

I had already achieved what I considered to be a major audit breakthrough by obtaining an eighty percent positive customer verification of the Dubai branch deposits. Hong Kong Internal Audit followed a random selection process whereby ten percent or maybe even fifteen percent of the accounts would be selected at random for customer verification, but this was a numerical percentage of the actual number of the accounts. I had always insisted that an intelligent selection of accounts for verification created a better coverage and had a far greater chance of detecting anomalies than a glass jar full of ping pong balls, and by choosing accounts with large balances I could always achieve a far greater percentage value wise than that achieved by the random selection process. In other words, a random selection of ten percent of the accounts will generally cover about ten percent of the total value of the deposits, whereas I could easily achieve a coverage of fifty percent of the value of the deposits by an intelligent selection of only five percent of the accounts numerically.

When selecting my Dubai accounts for verification I discovered that a large number of them either belonged to or were controlled by the ruling family. When the confirmations were returned the signatures on many of them did not appear on our specimen signature cards and when I compared the signature cards with the account opening documentation I discovered that much of the documentation was both incomplete and irregular. In the cases of company accounts there were often no copies of the necessary board resolutions appointing authorised signatories, partner and sole proprietor forms were missing and in the cases of individual accounts powers of attorney and joint account mandates had not been completed. Virtually all of these discrepancies were in the accounts of the ruling family.

As usual I confronted the area manager with this situation and the Arab Adviser admitted that the only complete solution was to get Sheikh Rashid himself to personally sign the most important of the forms that I had prepared, and for his nominated delegates to sign the remainder. The ruler and his entourage were in Europe and they would not return to Dubai until Ramadan was finished, but the Arab Adviser said he would try to find a way to obtain the signatures when they returned, although this would be a difficult task and one that he would much prefer not to undertake.

The ruler of the smallest Emirate Ajman had recently lost all his deposits in his newly created central bank the Bank of Ajman when the European management of the bank had fled the country taking the bank's liquid assets with them, and a lack of proper account documentation had prevented the Sheikh from recovering most of his deposits. When Sheikh Rashid returned to Dubai our Arab Adviser reminded him of this situation and told him that the signing of the new documents would help to protect his deposits with BBME, and the ruler immediately signed everything he was given.

After my success with the deposit confirmations I decided to embark on a major audit of the Dubai branch which would involve virtually all their commercial activities and I would use my entire staff in this important project. We had only just started the audit when I received a telex from the Chief Inspector in London instructing me to go to Abu Dhabi to negotiate with Wang Laboratories for the supply and installation of a Wang Office Information System Word Processing unit in my department and I sent a telex reply stating that I was in the midst of a major audit and that I would be unable to undertake the mission until I had completed the audit. The Chief Inspector replied by telling me to abort my audit and to give the Word Processor project top priority.

Dr. Wang was a pioneer of information technology and his new OIS work station was not only top of its range at that time but its software was the forerunner of Microsoft Word, and it had just replaced an earlier 1200 WPS model. The new unit was very large and attached to the work station was a terminal which contained its own Zilog Z80 processor and the system used 5" floppy drives. After I had completed the purchase and delivery arrangements my stenographer attended a users' course in Abu

Dhabi which she passed with flying colours so she was given an additional job as computer operator and the area manager was once again obliged to increase his secretary's salary. The word processor had to be housed in its own temperature controlled room so my department was enlarged to accommodate our new acquisition. The bank had identical units in Hong Kong, London and New York and my word processor was the fourth to be installed and although we did not at that time communicate electronically with each other through our word processors I sent all my future audit reports in floppies via couriers simultaneously to London and Hong Kong for storage and distribution through their own units. Wang was not to last for very long because it was not IBM compatible but it was a huge enhancement to my department, and it soon became a showpiece for the bank.

I made it a point to make periodical visits to all the branches in the Emirates which came within my jurisdiction and after an audit of Ras al-Khaimah I sent my team back to Dubai and decided to conduct a one man audit of our smallest branch which was in a remote coastal area. To reach Hisn Dibba my driver followed an unmarked track through the desert and we had to rely on the Bedouin camel drivers we passed to point us in the right direction. What had intrigued me about Hisn Dibba was the huge annual profit of over one million dirhams that the branch had managed to achieve and as the only industry in the area was the local fish market I was looking forward to examining the branch's registers in order to discover how the profit had been obtained.

After I had counted the cash I examined the balance sheet which I soon analysed but it gave me no clue as to where the profit had come from, so I decided to work backwards from the dates that the amounts had been credited to profit and loss and I noticed that these amounts had been classified as exchange profits, but the branch had no import or export business, they held no foreign currency notes nor did they maintain any foreign currency accounts. When I finally came across the first set of matching entries I discovered that the profit had derived from the differences between the exchange rates used for simultaneous purchases and sales of blocks of sterling pounds and I also noticed that there was an abnormal divergence between the purchase and sale exchange rates and this had greatly enhanced the profit made on the transactions. I listed the various entries and asked the Arab manager to tell me how he had managed to achieve such a remarkable series of matching purchases and sales of foreign currency.

The Obedient Banker

The manager examined my list, and his reply confirmed what I was already beginning to suspect. "I have no idea what these transactions relate to" he told me "because the entries originated in Dubai and when they appeared in our inter branch account statement I responded to them in order to reconcile the account, and as the differences were profits in exchange they were passed to our profit and loss account". I thanked the manager for his explanation and as I left his office I noticed a herd of goats who were busy eating a pile of papers, so I walked over to them and to my surprise I noticed that the papers they were eating belonged to the bank and some of them were documents which could be considered to be of a confidential nature. In my subsequent audit report I wrote that I had no objection to the feeding of local goats with the bank's waste papers, but I was certain that both the goats and I would be happier if these papers were first passed through a paper shredding machine. This recommendation was widely quoted later with amusement as a one-off incident, but I told the area manager that all his branches should purchase paper shredding machines regardless of whether or not they had goats to feed. Hisn Dibba's exchange profit did not appear in my report, since I gave it a SMO classification.

The bank's branch at Hsin Dibba, with one of the goats who ate the bank's documents

There was no immediate need to discuss Hisn Dibba's exchange profit with the area manager because he probably knew more about it than I did, so when I arrived back in Dubai I asked my ferret to check the exchange profits of all our branches and he discovered several instances where Dubai had passed sterling exchange transactions through different branches in the same way as had been done in Hisn Dibba. When I had listed all the transactions it was time to confront the area manager, and he immediately summoned the Dubai branch manager and asked him to explain the position to me. "We have twenty five branches in the Emirates" David said "and the first million dirham of each branch's profit is tax free. As several branches do not make much of a profit we help them out by selling them sterling and then buying it back from them". Now the entire matter made sense to me, and I told Peter that I would need to study the terms of the tax exemption regulation and we agreed to reconvene the following morning.

There was no central bank in the Emirates at that time and the tax exemption regulations had been issued by the Controller of the Currency Board in Abu Dhabi, and there was nothing in the rules that specifically precluded the type of operation that David had introduced, but there was also the underlying intent to be considered. I therefore decided once again to use Kepner Tregoe to help me resolve the matter so I separated what had happened into a number of factual statements and each statement was given an acceptable or a non-acceptable classification. By a process of elimination only one statement emerged as non-acceptable and that was the divergence between the buying and the selling rates. The next morning I told Peter that I could live with the arrangement provided the spread in rates did not exceed ten percent, and this agreement between us marked a turning point because from then on I became part of the senior management team, and I was often consulted before new decisions were made and implemented.

By the end of 1979 I had completed over thirty audits and investigations and in January 1980 I was asked to audit The Middle East Finance Company in Dubai which was a wholly owned subsidiary of the bank specialising in hire purchase operations, which was a new area for me. It was also in January that BBME's head office in London was transferred to Hong Kong and this was the final stage of integrating the two banks. Several members of BBME's senior management in London retired including my boss the Chief Inspector, and the resident inspectors in Dubai, including the Deputy Chief Inspector, were transferred into my department. With the closing down of BBME's Inspection department Internal Audit in Dubai was now responsible for over ninety BBME branches in eight countries in the Middle East and once again I was under the direct control of my own Head Office in Hong Kong.

In February we had a period of consolidation and I undertook a complete re-writing of all our audit programmes and questionnaires which would be more suitable for the enlarged department, now that the inspectors had joined us. The Head of Audit in Hong Kong flew out to Dubai to familiarise himself with our operations and to generally supervise the consolidation and before he flew back to Hong Kong Doug advised me that I would shortly be receiving my appointment as Manager Internal Audit Middle East. It therefore came as a considerable shock when the Deputy Chief Inspector was appointed Manager and I was to be the Assistant Manager, with the other two Inspectors remaining as Internal Audit officers. Although all three inspectors were senior to me in terms of length of service I was not at all happy with the situation and it was obvious that politics were involved, and once again my role as an Obedient Banker was about to be fully tested. Two major audits were then conducted in Dubai with the ex-inspectors using our new audit programmes while I continued to remain in charge of the department as the new manager would not assume charge until I had relinquished my duties.

One of my favourite recreational pastimes was a private poker school that I had founded with a partner of Arthur Young and the Financial Director of Shell and we were often joined by oil riggers some of whom had more money than sense, and our dealer's choice no-limit rules would often lead to their downfall. Anyway, I was a good friend of the Arthur Young partner and when I told Philip that I was unhappy with my new job he asked me if I would be interested in applying for the position of Chief Examiner with the Inspection Division of the new Central Bank of the UAE which was about to replace the UAE Currency Board. When I expressed an interest Philip then gave me a letter of introduction to the Controller, whose name was Hammer and who he knew well, and Hammer was expected to be the new Governor of the Central Bank. Shortly after Philip had sent my CV to the Currency Board I was invited to attend an interview with Hammer in Abu Dhabi and there were several other Arab directors present. The meeting was very successful because I had already agreed in principal to the basic terms of the proposed renewable contract which were very attractive, and when I left the interview I was told that

I was now top of the list of applicants and that I would be advised of the final outcome within one month.

This suited me because I had already given my name to a firm of head hunters in London and a recruitment officer had flown out from the UK to interview me in my office and when she flew back to London she advised me that there were several Arab banks looking for expatriate directors to run their internal audit departments and that she should have no difficulty in offering me a suitable job. This in fact happened very quickly when I received several offers from the agency, the most exciting being from a leading bank in Jordan, but at this stage, and with the help of Kepner Tregoe, I had already made up my mind what to do. Firstly, I would not stay on in my department as Assistant Manager and secondly I would not accept any offer until I had first discussed my future face to face with my own Head Office in Hong Kong. Time was now of the essence, and as I had an accumulated leave entitlement under my previous terms of service with London it was agreed that I could now proceed on leave, but instead of going to either the States or the UK I flew straight to Hong Kong on 16 March where I asked for an interview with the bank's Chairman for personal reasons.

The Chairman was on leave at the time of my visit but the Deputy Chairman agreed to see me and I had worked with John in both Osaka and Calcutta, and he came straight to the point without any pleasantries. "I have no idea why you want to see me Jerry, but whatever the reason is it will have to be brief because I have a senior management meeting in exactly ten minutes time". I explained the situation to John and I ended up by telling him that I was unable to accept the position of Assistant Manager in a department that I had created and run for over a year and that I might decide to join the new UAE Central Bank as their Chief Examiner, although I also had some other options. John then told me that he would discuss this matter at his meeting with senior management which included the Staff Controller and that I would be advised of their decision within an hour. I was asked to take a seat in a waiting area where I was given a cup of coffee, and it was a long wait for me but eventually John's secretary told me that he was ready to see me.

"I can't give you a branch" John told me "but we would like you to come back to Hong Kong and take charge of our Economic Intelligence Unit, the Chief Economist will report directly to you and you will report directly to a new Deputy Chairman, as I am retiring shortly. It will be a promotion as well as a managerial position, with several other responsibilities and full details will be advised to you in your letter of appointment. If you accept this position we would expect you to complete the hand over of BBME's Internal Audit department to your successor before you assume your new duties". I thanked John for his offer and told him that I was very pleased to accept it. I did not tell him however that I had not relished the prospect of resigning with a reduced pension, although I think he knew me well enough to know this to be the case. I then flew to the U.K. to complete my leave and while there I received a letter from the Staff Controller advising me that the Board had approved my appointment as Manager Corporate Services in our Group Head Office effective from the date on which I relinquished control of BBME's Internal Audit Department in Dubai. I was still an Obedient Banker, but only just.

I returned to Dubai on 26 April, and my forthcoming appointment in Hong Kong made the hand over of my department to Peter much easier. I was preparing for my departure at the end of May when we received an urgent message from the General Manager International in Hong Kong, previously known as Overseas Operations, asking us to conduct an immediate audit of the bank's operations in the Yemen, where BBME's recent performance had been less than satisfactory. Apparently the Chairman himself had asked for the audit and the brief was to report on why the losses were increasing and what steps could be taken to remedy the situation. Peter was familiar with the situation in the Yemen and after we had discussed the problem together and I had studied the files, I came to a quick decision. I myself would conduct a final audit of the Yemen and the only help I needed would be a credit auditor from London to audit the advances.

North Yemen had become a republic in 1962 and when the British left Aden in 1967 it became South Yemen, and it was not until 1990 that the two countries were united. Entering the Yemen in 1980 was somewhat reminiscent of my visit to Saigon in 1975, but the squalor and congestion was far worse than anything that I had yet experienced, and the crowded markets and primitive living conditions throughout the country were in stark contrast to the orderly souks and well constructed houses in the UAE.

On 7 June, which was my forty-ninth birthday, I took an overnight Yemeni Airlines flight from Sharjah to Sana'a where BBME had a representative and I spent a couple of days in Roy's house, which was a typical multi-storey whitewashed Yemeni building made of mud and concrete with earthen floors. The bank's main branch was in Hodeidah and to get there we drove by jeep with an armed guard and we were constantly stopped and searched by local militia who served as regional police. It was an exciting journey and to make it more interesting Roy decided on a diversion in order to show me the mountain fortress village of Jibla which was an amazing experience. Roy was an Arabist and he was very helpful in giving me a clear insight into the difficulties in operating a bank in the Yemen, and apart from the rampant corruption that existed at all levels there was an emerging nationalism. I asked Roy what was being cultivated on the bright green terraces we were passing through and he told me that the crop was an evergreen shrub called qat which was similar to privet and the leaves when chewed create a gradual feeling of complacency. Qat is more of a sedative than a drug but as its use is a national pastime in the Yemen, it means that important jobs are best completed early in the day, and this was evidenced by the erratic behaviour of our driver when the jeep was approaching Hodeidah.

There were no acceptable hotels in Hodeidah so I stayed in the bank's compound with the manager and Gary drove us to and from the office each day. There was no nightlife to speak of in Hodeidah and the compound was exclusively used for entertainment and recreation and we ate all our meals there including our lunches. Gary was fortunate enough to have retained the services of an Indian cook boy who had been the mess boy in Aden and I can still remember the excellent curries that he produced. The compound had a tennis court and a swimming pool and most of the officers and their families spent their evenings together. There was a plentiful supply of liquor as the bank had acquired the residual supplies from Costains after they had completed construction of the airport's runways, a special liquor import licence having been granted to the construction workers.

The actual audit of the Hodeidah branch was relatively easy because the credit auditor flew in by himself directly from London and returned as soon as he had completed his report on the advances, and this left me free to concentrate on the profit and loss accounts. It soon became apparent to me that not only were the overheads and expenses excessive but they were escalating at an alarming rate at the same time as income was decreasing, and I could see no way whatever how the income could ever match the outgoings. The Charges account was unusually high and after I had analysed it I realised that the majority of payments were thinly disguised bribes described as procurement fees and commissions, but I accepted Gary's explanation that without them much of the branch's income could not have been generated. The underlying problem was the ever-increasing restrictions that the authorities were imposing upon foreign banks, not the least of which was the high level of statutory reserves that had to be kept with the Central Bank of Yemen. Previous inspection reports appeared to have either ignored or overlooked this situation, and I was convinced that no blame need be placed on the management who were working under extremely difficult conditions.

Having made up my mind that there was only one recommendation that I could possibly make which was to close the branch, I then had to make a recommendation as to how this could be achieved, so I decided to visit several local banks and government authorities and these included the recently established International Bank of Yemen and the Yemen Bank for Reconstruction and Development, both of which now had customers who had previously kept their accounts with BBME. These visits were very helpful and it was not long before I realised that the bank itself was unsaleable as an entity and that we would actually have to pay out money in order to transfer our assets and liabilities to a Yemeni bank, and the obvious recipient was YBRD. Hopefully the sale of the bank's properties might offset the cost of applying to the Central Bank of Yemen for the cancellation of our banking licence. I did not spend much time on my audit of the sub-branch at Ibb because it was primarily a deposit gathering branch in an agricultural area and it was operating at a profit. The manager of Ibb was popular with his customers and I not only congratulated Ed on his capable management but I also suggested in my report that there was no fundamental reason why the sub-branch should be closed if the bank wished to continue to retain a presence in the Yemen.

After my return to Dubai on 23 June I completed the hand over of my department and one of the last things I did was to press the button on our Wang Word Processor which released my audit report on Yemen which I knew would be highly controversial, and when I arrived in Hong Kong on 10 July I discovered that my report had arrived a couple of days before me and that it had created quite a sensation. After reading the report the Chairman had instructed International department to send a senior officer immediately to the Yemen to either confirm or to dispute my recommendations and on my first day in the office I was asked to discuss my report with the Assistant General Manager in International department who was in charge of the Middle East section, which included Yemen.

I had not met Derek before and after I had explained the reasoning behind my report he told me that he was flying to Yemen the following day and that he would let me know the result of his findings on his return. My reception in Group Head Office was cool because it is not everyday that an auditor recommends the closing of a branch and I detected a general feeling that I had overdone things in my report. The possibility of closing down in Yemen must have been known to senior management in Hong Kong in the same way as was the need to close in California, but in retrospect the reluctance to take such action can be attributed to the absence of any strong recommendation to do so. In the case of Yemen it was obvious that the transfer of BBME Head Office in London to Hong Kong had brought the matter to a head.

We did not have to wait very long before Derek returned from the Yemen and I was one of the first people he spoke to after his return. "I am not only supporting all your recommendations" Derek said to me "but I am also recommending that the sub-branch in Ibb should be closed as well as Hodeidah, and that the bank should withdraw entirely from the Republic of Yemen". He also told me, off the record, that never in his life had he been to such an inhospitable place. The word spread quickly and not only were people talking to me again but they were even buying me my pre-lunch pink gins in the Jackson Room. The Jackson Room, named after one of the bank's outstanding Chief Managers Sir Thomas Jackson, was a luncheon club for middle management and membership was by invitation only. Unlike the 7th Floor Mess which had a bar and informal seating, the Jackson Room was extremely formal and we all sat on upholstered chairs lining the walls of the lounge where drinks were served to us on silver trays. All conversation, which was mainly about bank procedures and golf at Fanling, was for general participation, and this continued until lunch was announced when we all sat down together at a long mahogany dining table laden with crested silver cutlery and crystal glasses, and the repartee continued throughout the meal. Several members enjoyed this, but I much preferred the informality of the 7th Floor Mess, where you could choose where to sit and with whom. The meals in the Jackson Room were not cheap, and this could be one of the reasons why the Number One Boy there wore a gold Rolex.

One of the pleasures of the 7th Floor Mess was the curry lunch that was served on Thursdays and the prawn and egg variety was my favourite. Bank curries were Malay style with numerous side dishes including sliced bananas, raisins, crushed peanuts, chutney, tomatoes, chopped onion and diced coconut all of which were added to the top of the curry, which itself was on a bed of rice. The papadums and Bombay Duck were eaten separately. Our undisputed curry king was called Ricky, and it was not

The Obedient Banker

unusual for a group of us to join Ricky with our heaped plates of curry which we referred to as our Kilimanjaros, because the last side dish to be added was the diced coconut which resembled the snow on the top of Africa's highest mountain. On one occasion I entered the Mess kitchens to see how the curries were made and I discovered that the secret of their success was that not only were all the herbs and spices individually ground instead of using pastes and powders, but also that the lightly cooked prawns and the hard boiled eggs were cooked separately and then added to the curry at the very last moment, thus ensuring that the prawns were crisp and the eggs were intact, both with their own flavour, and I have emulated this method of cooking in my own prawn and egg curries ever since.

The atmosphere and camaraderie in our Head Office had undergone a change and by 1980 the old family feeling, although still present, had been considerably diluted both by the merging of the three banks and by the recruitment of new specialists. The Group was undergoing an important transformation and we were no longer a colonial bank, regionalism having given way to multi-nationalism. The Staff Controller was now Controller Human Resources and instead of a dart board he had a committee who helped him to decide when and where postings would take place.

It was in many ways fortunate that the creation of my new Corporate Services department coincided with the move of our Head Office from 1 Queens Road Central to the Admiralty Centre and this move was necessary in order for our 1935 building at 1QRC to be demolished to make way for Norman Foster's revolutionary structure which would become our new headquarters. The decision to demolish a building that had become a symbol of the bank's solidarity for almost half a century was not taken lightly, and the destruction of the banking hall's famous mosaic ceiling, which was the second largest in the world after the Vatican, was sad but inevitable. The move however enabled a number of different entities to be relocated together for the first time and apart from the Economic Intelligence Unit I was given the Banking Services section, which produced the popular Country Profiles on each area where we operated, and to this were added the Head Office Library, a new Data Bank, the Editorial and Publications sections along with the Distribution centre as well as the Translation Unit. I was promised an assistant manager and when Hodeidah was closed the branch manager there was given the job as my assistant manager and Gary and I were never able to determine whether this transfer was intentional or a coincidence. Gary was a good administrator and he took charge of the Banking Services section under my overall supervision.

It took almost four months to fully integrate the five main entities into a fully operational department and by the end of 1980 we were writing and producing all the in-house publications, the Economic Reviews, the Group Directory and the International Surveys as well as composing articles and speeches for senior management. We hired two professional journalists and took on an Editorial Coordinator from the Hong Kong government and one of Peter's additional jobs was the creation of our Data Bank. One of our journalists was an American girl and I gave Dianne a difficult task when I asked her to write an important speech that the Chairman had been asked to deliver at a local function, and the topic was the very delicate subject of the bank's future relations with China.

We now referred to China as Mainland China instead of Communist China and this implied a tacit acceptance of China's claim over Taiwan, and we always referred to Hong Kong as a territory and never as a colony. After the Chairman had delivered Dianne's carefully prepared speech I was summoned to his office the following morning and unlike one of his predecessors Jake, who sent secret signals to his secretary, Mike sat on the edge of his huge desk when he spoke to me. "It's about the speech, Jerry" Mike said to me, and I immediately wondered what had gone wrong. "The sentence which says that I take a pragmatic approach to our future relationship with mainland China is absolutely fantastic. From now on I want pragmatism to feature prominently in the bank's future policy wherever China is concerned. Who was it who wrote the speech?" When I told the Chairman that Dianne was an American he was mildly surprised but he said that it gave his speech an international flavour.

By early 1981 the staff complement of Corporate Services had risen to thirty four of whom no less than fifteen of us were executive officers and we had emerged as a compact but important department of Group Head Office whose primary function was the creation, storage and distribution of a wide range of information.

It had taken a while to achieve this result because there was a degree of rivalry and competition in Head Office which had not existed before, but this was possibly inevitable considering the expansion that the bank was undergoing..

Corporate Services Economists and Librarians

Hong Kong had by now become very congested and there were long waiting lists for club memberships, the traffic was horrific and reliable domestic servants were hard to come by and to alleviate these problems my wife and I joined a holiday club on the outlying island of Lantau where we spent our weekends and we used the club's hydrofoil for transportation. A second blessing was when a vacancy occurred in a house on Middle Gap Road which had been divided into three flats and the ground floor flat in Highclere had a small private garden which was a luxury which we fully enjoyed, and which we used extensively for entertaining and evening barbeques.

Because of my wife's Chilean nationality several of our friends were from South America and many of them were in the diplomatic service including the Consul General for Argentina and his wife but these friendships would come to an abrupt end in April 1982 as a result of the Falklands conflict.

It was at this time that I felt the need for diversification and I joined the China Fleet Club in Wanchai which due to the demolition and rebuilding of parts of the R.N. Dockyard had recently moved into larger and more modern premises, and I regularly ate my lunches there in an environment that was far removed from the Admiralty Centre.

Jeremy Tait

Highclere, Jerry's last residence in Hong Kong

Sometimes I would have a quick sandwich lunch in my office and I would then climb up Ladder Street to explore the little Chinese shops and stalls in the alleyways which sold a multitude of junk, amongst which one could often find a genuine antique, and close by was Hollywood Road and Cat Street which specialised in stolen items. It was from this area that I gradually built up my collection of snuff boxes and other small metal boxes, along with similar ornaments, which are still treasured possessions of mine. Bargaining with the stall owners was a necessity. "Gui doh cheen?" I would ask, picking up a small engraved box used as an ink pad for Chinese chops. "Aye-yah" – (a meaningless expression used by the Cantonese when starting a conversation) – "Aye-yah, for you massah, tlenty dollaaar, special plice". Instead of offering the stall owner ten dollars, I would then pick up another box, which was the one that I really wanted, "Twenty dollar for two pieces" I would reply, and this strategy was invariably successful.

By this time I had become a member of the F.C.C. (Foreign Correspondents Club) and an associate member of the popular L.R.C. (Ladies Recreation Club), which was conveniently situated in the mid levels, and we would often spend our evenings in these clubs as well as the Hong Kong Cricket Club which had moved from the central area of Hong Kong to new premises with enhanced facilities in the same general area. The P.G. and Jimmy's Kitchen restaurants had now been replaced by The Eagle's Nest on the top floor of the Hong Kong Hilton and the revolving restaurant on the top of the Furama Hotel, and the Sunday buffet curry lunches with afternoon jazz sessions at the Excelsior hotel in Causeway Bay were extremely popular. Another "in" place for both lunches and dinners was The Godown which had wooden benches and long communal tables with bales of cargo hanging from the beamed ceiling. Even more informal eating was to be found in the night markets and we often frequented the food stalls which had sprung up in the open space in front of the Lantau and Outlying Islands ferry terminal.

The Peninsula Hotel with its afternoon teas and the Repulse Bay Hotel with its long bar now had formidable competition in the shape of new hotels which were shooting up all over Hong Kong and in particular in the Tsim Sha Tsui area of Kowloon, and groups of tourists were replacing American seamen as visitors going to new attractions such as Ocean Park. The Captain's Bar in the Mandarin Hotel however still catered to regulars who would stop off there for a quick one after leaving their Central District offices, Happy Hour was from 5 pm to 6 pm and at 6 pm sharp the "jackets only" dress code was enforced by using a motley collection of jackets that the steward would hand out to us, and invariably the sleeves of my jacket seldom reached much below my elbows. Upstairs the Chinnery Room was for gentlemen only where suits were worn at all times.

Persistent reclamation had resulted in an extension to Hong Kong's waterfront and although this narrowed the harbour it also provided additional space for new buildings facing the *praya*, and the rocks and earth used in the reclamation process were mainly taken from the mid-levels where new apartment blocks were also being constructed. However with the release of some Crown land in the Admiralty area due to demolition of much of the dockyard, a new narrow building known as the Connaught Centre had emerged as the colony's tallest building, and a unique aspect of this building was its round windows which were fitted with reflecting glass and this was why the building was often referred to as The Mousetrap or Hong Kong's Gruyere Cheese. The Chinese however gave the building their own Cantonese name and the name chosen was as ingenious as the nicknames given to us by the Compradore's staff. The Connaught Centre, because of its height, had an unrestricted view of the Wanchai red light district and this view was reflected in the numerous windows that overlooked Wanchai's bars and doss houses. I cannot remember the actual Cantonese nickname for the Connaught Centre, but I do remember that its literal translation was "The House of a Thousand Arseholes". Cantonese humour tended to be crude but clever.

Some things in Hong Kong did not change and Jardine's midday cannon was still fired at noon to signify the approaching *tiffin* break. Lawrence Kadoorie's Star Ferry, the vehicular ferries and the *wallah-wallahs* still provided transport across the harbour between Victoria island and the mainland but these were now supplemented by the cross harbour tunnel, and the double decker trams were now competing with a new underground rapid transit system, the M.T.R. Statue Square, which was the piece of land between the bank and the waterfront, although not built on was no longer used as a car park as it had been redesigned as an ornamental park although the bronze statue of Sir Thomas Jackson continued to contemplate the changing scene in front of him. The paws of Stephen and Stitt, the two bronze lions on either side of the bank's Des Voeux Road entrance, were even smoother than they had been when I arrived in Hong Kong, and this was because of the thousands of passers by who had stroked them in the hope that some of the bank's wealth would pass to them. Stephen and Stitt had been the names of two successful managers of the bank and the Hong Kong lions had been sculptured by a Shanghai craftsman named Wagstaffe, and they were larger replicas of the lions that still guard the bank's original building on the Bund in Shanghai. When facing the bank, Stephen is on the left hand side of the entrance, his expression is more severe than Stitt's, and his backside still has bullet marks which date back to the street fighting which took place when Japan occupied Hong Kong in December 1941.

Jerry in a hand tailored safari suit with Stitt in 1975

The landscaped gardens with its trees and open areas in Statue Square made it a popular meeting place and it often became very crowded especially during lunch time and on public holidays. At dawn hundreds of Chinese would assemble in Statue Square to perform *tai chi* and on Sundays the square was taken over by Philippine maids who took advantage of their weekly day off work to meet each other in the square, and they invariably brought their picnic lunches with them.

For many years Lane Crawford had been the major department store in Hong Kong but now not only did they have to contend with the Wing On, Sincere, Welcome and Dragon Seed department stores, but also with the huge mainland Chinese emporiums which sold everything from furniture to provisions, not to mention clothes and jewellery. Hong Kong had already started to prepare for the transfer of sovereignty which would take place in 1997.

Seniority in the bank according to length of service as an officer had long since been replaced by the appointment system but job titles did not always reflect the seniority of each incumbent because pay levels for each job varied. This was partially corrected by an assessment system whereby each job title was graded with upper and lower limits of pay and this grading was introduced at the time I was putting my new department together. Foreign staff officers were now called International officers and I found that my salary was at the upper end of my grade, and in addition to this a new retirement scheme was introduced. Under the existing scheme we were due for retirement either at the age of fifty five or after thirty years service, whichever came first, and in my case the date for retirement was May 1981. The new terms of service raised the age of retirement to fifty five regardless of years of service, and although I was given the option of either staying with the old terms of service or adopting the new terms, I chose the latter because of the increased pension that would become available to me, and because I had joined the foreign staff at the age of twenty I now had a possible four more years of service left to me.

An example of the regulated system under which we now worked was the 56 page Executive Director's Memorandum which was the authority for the creation of Corporate Services department and which served as my terms of reference. By the end of 1981 I had achieved most of the aims included in the Memorandum although an important clause requiring closer collaboration and cooperation with Marine Midland Bank, in which we then held a 51% equity, had yet to be implemented. As one of the main functions of my department was communication I therefore drew

Jeremy Tait

the attention of the Deputy Chairman to this matter at one of our regular weekly progress meetings and Roy told me that he would bring it up at his next senior management meeting. In the old days such matters as this were decided on the Fanling golf course, but not any more.

A week or so later Roy told me that it had been agreed that I should fly to New York to meet with Marine Midland's management and directors, and that I should be prepared to make an hour long presentation to them explaining the role of my department and by answering any questions they might have to the best of my ability. The arrangements for my visit were handled by our New York manager who had been the bank's manager in Singapore at the time of my 1975 audit of his office, and Angus had booked me a suite in the Waldorf Astoria Hotel on Park Avenue. My first full day in New York was spent with my own bank but on the second day I was taken on a conducted tour of each of Marine Midland's departments after which I gave their senior management including all department heads a half hour presentation on the role of Corporate Services and I allowed another half hour for questions as I was a somewhat nervous speaker.

Staying at the Waldorf Astoria can be a rewarding experience and on my second evening I was exhausted so I ordered a prime rib dinner to be served in my room which was just within my meal allowance and as soon as the waiter had wheeled in the trolley and left the room I opened a bottle of burgundy from the case I had purchased from the liquor store I had spotted below my window. The following evening I visited the famous Oyster Bar in Grand Central Station which was less than a block away from the hotel, and I had a bottle of Chablis with a dozen Blue Point oysters on the half shell and a second bottle with the cracked steamed crab, and there was still enough money left from my expense account allowance to enjoy a Knickerbocker Special sundae and a Harvey Wallbanger. This was downtown Manhattan at its best, and my internal audit training was being put to good use.

The next day it was time to fly up to Buffalo to meet with Marine Midland's directors and my lunch in their board room reminded me of a somewhat similar lunch that I had enjoyed with Antony Gibbs' directors in London in 1976. I had already made the same presentation in Buffalo that I had delivered in New York so at the luncheon Marine Midland's Chairman asked me if I had ever seen Niagara Falls and when I told Ed that I had never been there he arranged for the Vice President of his Public Relations department to take me there the following day. Pamela was a very attractive lady and she was a charming companion who was eager to find out as much as she could from me about Hong Kong, and I knew that most of what I told her would be relayed to Marine Midland's senior management upon our return to Buffalo.

Someone must have appreciated my presentations in the States because it was shortly after I had returned to Hong Kong that the Deputy Chairman told me that I was to fly to the U.K. and repeat my performance at a Group Seminar in London, only this time it was to be an audio-visual presentation. It was a rushed job to prepare this but with the help of our Methods Research department I created some flow charts showing the lines of communication and distribution for our various publications and activities and these were projected onto a screen by means of slides during my speech, as well as being handed out later in leaflet form. A condensed version of my speech with photographs of my department and our staff was subsequently reproduced in the bank's magazine Group News.

On the face of it my department seemed to have everything going for it but three developments were about to occur that would have a major impact on Corporate Services. The first development was the appointment of a General Manager Planning, and Bernard came to us from Henley Research and for an outside specialist to assume such an important job from scratch was not an easy task. Until now my Economic Intelligence Unit had produced material for general circulation as well as completing specific assignments for Group Finances but with the advent of a new Planning department the economists were now being regularly used by Bernard which was understandable, and when I discussed this with our Chief Economist, Vincent told me that he was happy with the arrangement. Both Bernard and Vincent were to progress upwards in the bank but to begin with Bernard did not have an easy time because he was unfamiliar with our procedures. He used to visit my office regularly and on one occasion he pointed to my desk top coffee maker and said "What do you have to do to get one of those?" and I replied "First you go to Lane Crawford to buy it, and then you go to Asia Provisions to buy the coffee. But don't try to claim the cost on your expense account because we are all supposed to have our coffees in the new coffee lounges in Admiralty Centre".

The second development was that the Deputy Chairman was spending more and more of his time on Norman Foster's new building which was now his responsibility, so Roy told me that from now on I would be reporting directly to the Assistant General Manager Technical Services instead of to him, and I then found myself to be in a totally different environment. Although John was an expert in his field my department did not fit easily into his sphere of activities, which were computer oriented.

The final development was the bank's decision to make a bid to take over the Royal Bank of Scotland, as we were attempting to enlarge our presence in Europe, and specifically in the U.K. The two General Managers who were mainly involved in this attempt were Bernard and Willie, the latter was at that time General Manager International, and as he was a Scot he was sent to the U.K. to coordinate the bid. As we had no Mergers and Acquisitions department as such it was Corporate Services who were used to collate most of the material used in the bid, and the fact that our offer was turned down by the U.K. Monopolies and Mergers Commission was no fault of ours, but we had gained a lot of experience which would help us in our later acquisition of Midland Bank Limited, which enabled us to move our Head Office to London and to change our name to HSBC, although this took place after my retirement.

When our offer for RBS was finally rejected a vacuum was created in my department because International department were expanding and my economists were mainly working for Planning department, and I was told in September 1982 that the EIU was to be transferred to Planning department, and the rest of my department would be absorbed by International. My salary at this stage was effectively frozen and when I was offered the opportunity of taking early retirement I accepted the offer immediately, as did a number of my contemporaries who had agreed to the new extended terms of service. I had already served for almost one and a half years more than I had expected and the circumstances under which I had been appointed as Manager Corporate Services were unusual, so when the Controller Human Resources explained the position to me I was quite happy with the early retirement terms that Bob offered me. I had known Bob since we were trainee officers sharing digs together in New Beckenham.

As my grandmother used to say, you can't make an omelette without breaking eggs and when I handed over the various sections of my department they were all in good working order which is more than could be said of some of them when I acquired them. A case in point was the old fashioned Library which we had taken over and my new Head Librarian had disposed of most of the ancient books and acquired new material which was used solely for reference purposes in conjunction with the Data Bank and we had in fact converted a Lending Library into a modern Reference Library. By the end of September the handover was complete and the Obedient

Banker became an Obedient Pensioner on 1 November 1982. Despite its short life Corporate Services had achieved everything set out in its terms of reference, and it had undoubtedly made an important contribution to the bank's future development.

SEQUEL

The saga of the Obedient Banker has now come to an end but some readers who have followed his exploits over a period of roughly thirty years may be interested in discovering what happened to the Obedient Pensioner during the ensuing 27 years, and this sequel will fill the gap.

Prior to retirement my wife Mariana and I had decided to move to North Carolina on the east coast of the U.S. below the snow belt but above the mosquito belt where I would operate a small drive-in market garden outlet as a one-man holding company. My entire savings and my bank pension would be ploughed into the project which would never make a profit due to depreciation and overheads, thus ensuring a tax-free environment where I could potter around with my African violets, and hang up a closed sign whenever I wanted. We had already applied for U.S. permanent immigration visas to make this dream a reality but as our visas had not been granted at the time of my retirement the bank had agreed to keep the cartons containing all our personal belongings in storage in an air-conditioned godown in Hong Kong, as part of my early retirement package, until such time as we had purchased and moved into our new property. My wife then flew to the States and I came to Spain where I stayed in a three bedroom beachfront apartment that I had previously purchased in Benalmadena Costa as a holiday home.

These arrangements were intended to be temporary pending the granting of our U.S. residence visas, so it came as a complete surprise when my wife commenced divorce proceedings against me from her sister's residence in Chicago. After the divorce was final I decided that there was no point in retiring in the U.S.A., as originally intended, so I allowed my U.S. entry visa to lapse and I started to search for a new permanent home in Spain. In 1984 I bought a large house adjoining the Church Square in the centre of Marbella's Old Town which was over 500 years old and which had at one time served as a monastery.

Much as I loved my new home, it was impossible for me to manage it by myself so I looked around for a live-in housekeeper, and when Norma Pascua Artajos accepted the position, my entire life changed.

Jeremy with his wife Norma in Marbella, after retirement

Norma was a qualified midwife who had worked for the Philippine government for five years before coming to Spain to join her sister in Marbella. After she moved into the house a strong relationship soon developed between us, we were married in Gibraltar in 1986 and Norma then acquired Spanish citizenship.

In October 1987 we had a son William Philip who received his elementary education at the Swans School and his primary education at Aloha College, both in Marbella. After a short course in Art and Design at the London College of Communication William transferred to the University of Wales Newport in 2007 where he is presently on his final year of a three year BA (Hons) degree course in Documentary Film and Television at their School of Art and Design in Caerleon Campus. In 2005 we sold our house in the Old Town, where we had lived for over twenty years, not only because it was too large for us but also because it was becoming too difficult and costly to maintain, and we then moved into a smaller and more modern townhouse in an Urbanisation on Marbella's Golden Mile. We continue to keep in touch with HSBC and we regularly attend the Chairman's annual October Cocktail Party in London for Retired International Staff.